Early praise for *The Unknown Internment*:

"An intelligent and important study of a neglected subject."

—John Morton Blum, Yale University

"[Un*Civil Liberties*] adds fascinating new pieces to the puzzle of American wartime concentration camps. It is tragic history told by survivors in poignant anecdotes."

—John Christgau, author of *"Enemies": World War II Alien Internment*

"By utilizing interviews and widely-scattered records, Fox has brought to life the completely neglected [relocation] of an entire national group during World War II. Those of us who have written histories of Italians in America have dealt with this episode, but only in a sketchy way. Bravissimo!"

—Andrew Rolle, Occidental College

"A first-rate work of research in oral history that recaptures the poignant emotions of a people whose experience would have been forgotten had it not been for the sensitive scholarship of Stephen Fox."

—John Patrick Diggins, University of California, Irvine

Stephen Fox

*Un*Civil Liberties

Italian Americans Under Siege during World War II

UnCivil Liberties:
Italian Americans Under Siege during World War II

ISBN: 1-58112-754-5

Universal Publishers/uPUBLISH.com
USA • 2000

www.upublish.com/books/fox.htm

SERIES EDITOR'S NOTE

T*HE UNKNOWN INTERNMENT* [the original title of this work] powerfully demonstrates oral history's ability to challenge common assumptions. Scholars have taken for granted that the federal government, when it moved to relocate and confine thousands of Japanese Americans during World War II, took no action against German and Italian Americans. Yet through his interviews and then through archival research, Stephen Fox has discovered the existence of a government program to relocate Italian Americans in California—a program briefly implemented, quickly rescinded, and largely forgotten. In no way did government actions against Italian Americans compare in magnitude with the Japanese [relocation]s, but both resulted from the same wartime hysteria. The painful, long-suppressed memories that Fox has elicited in these interviews serve as a reminder of the fragility of the civil liberties of all people in a time of national crisis and the need for greater resolve against appeals to nativist impulses.

Historians since Herodotus have interviewed eyewitnesses to great events, but twentieth-century technology provides the opportunity for more widespread and systematic collection of oral history. First on wax cylinders, then with wire-recorders, reel-to-reel and cassette tape recorders, and video cameras, modern interviewers have captured an enormous quantity of reminiscences, from presidents to pioneers, literati to laborers.

Oral history may well be the twentieth century's substitute for the written memoir. In exchange for the immediacy of diaries or correspondence, the retrospective interview offers a dialogue between the participant and the informed interviewer. Having prepared sufficient preliminary research, interviewers can direct the discussion into areas long since "forgotten," or no longer considered of consequence. "I haven't thought about that in years," is a common response, uttered just before an interviewee commences with a surprisingly detailed description of some past incident. The quality of the interview, its candidness and depth, generally will depend as much upon the interviewer as the interviewee, and the confidence and rapport between the two adds a special dimension to the spoken memoir.

Interviewers represent a variety of disciplines, and work either as part of a collective effort or an individual enterprise. Regardless of their different interests or the variety of their subjects, all interviewers share a common imperative: to collect memories while they are still available.

Most oral historians feel an additional responsibility to make their interviews accessible for use beyond their own research needs. Still, important collections of vital, vibrant interviews lie scattered in archives throughout every state, undiscovered or underutilized.

Twayne's Oral History Series seeks to identify those resources and to publish selections of the best materials. The series lets people speak for themselves, from their own unique perspectives on people, places, and events. But to be more than a babble of voices, each volume will organize its interviews around particular situations and events and tie them together with interpretive essays that place individuals into the larger historical context. The styles and format of individual volumes will vary with the material from which they are drawn, demonstrating again the diversity of oral history and its methodology.

Whenever oral historians gather in conference they enjoy retelling experiences about unusual individuals they met, unexpected information they elicited, and unforgettable reminiscences that would otherwise have never been recorded. The result invariably reminds listeners of others who deserve to be interviewed, provides them with models of interviewing techniques, and inspires them to make their own contribution to the field. I trust that the oral historians in this series, as interviewers, editors, and interpreters, will have a similar effect upon their readers.

—Donald A. Ritchie, Series Editor *Senate Historical Office*

Any strictly rational approach to history distorts it as much as a road map distorts reality. The most sophisticated theories of why what happens suffer from a flat-earth syndrome; missing are the dimensions of fear, centuries of hate gathering in poisoned pools, the darkness of bigotry, ignorance, despair. The irrational, by definition, eludes the reasoned unraveling of causal connections, slips through the mesh of logic, and locks men into its own version of the truth.

—Ernst Pawel, *The Nightmare of Reason: A Life of Franz Kafka*

CONTENTS

FOREWORD TO THE REVISED EDITION

THIS EDITION INCORPORATES minor factual and editing changes, but the most significant alteration is the title. Inadvertently, the previous title, *The Unknown Internment* and some of the original content—clarified throughout this version—contributed to the confusion between "relocation" and "internment." The new title, of course, Un*Civil Liberties*, plays with words and ideas that give the story its meaning in the largest sense. Although the revised edition includes a reorganized chapter on individual internment and exclusion, the book remains primarily the untold story of the *relocation* of several thousand West Coast Italian Americans for a brief period at the outset of World War II. Since 1990, the original publication date, I have looked more thoroughly at internment and exclusion, and I report those findings in *America's Invisible Gulag* (New York, 2000).

President Bill Clinton signed the "Wartime Violations of Italian American Civil Liberties Act" (PL 106-451) on November 7, 2000. It gave the Justice Department a year to account for the government's internment, exclusion, and other harassment of Italian Americans, which it did. But the report is far from complete. In all likelihood, we will never know the exact number of relocated Italian Americans; legally, the Justice Department did not have to count them. The best evidence is that the relocation order of February 1942 affected eight to ten thousand enemy aliens—Italians, Germans, and Japanese. The number of individual citizens and aliens of Italian ancestry whom the army *excluded* is hardly more precise. On the West Coast, according to a wartime report, exclusion orders were issued to eighty-eight naturalized Italians and an unknown number of aliens, as well as to some of the sixty-nine East Coast exclusions and some of the sixteen exclusions within the Southern Defense Command. (The government's 2001 report, which it admits is incomplete and does not incorporate available scholarship, lists only fifty-nine Italian Americans as either excluded or arraigned before individual exclusion boards.) As for individually *interned* Italians, the Immigration and Naturalization Service says that it detained 3,278, including voluntary internees and those deported to the United States from Latin America. The Justice Department reports having interned 418 of them for varying lengths of time.

—McKinleyville, California, June 2002

FOREWORD

MARTINI BATTISTESSA. Giuseppe Mecheli. Stefano Terranova. Giovanni Sanguenetti. During five days in mid-February 1942, these elderly Italian men in the San Francisco Bay Area took their own lives. Along the north coast, near Eureka, the ocean simultaneously gave up the bodies of two Germans, Max Pohland and George Heckel. Their despair had matched that of the Italians. Why?

SOME YEARS AGO an older student in my World War II class, who had lived in the area in 1942, asked if I knew that the government had forced Italian and German aliens to move out of the waterfront areas of Arcata and Eureka, California, during the war. "No," I said incredulously, "only that the West Coast Japanese had been relocated." But it occurred to me that if I, a professional historian, did not know about the other removal, probably few others did either.

A quick trip to the library proved my student correct: Italian and German enemy aliens had been relocated in 1942, but with the exception of the aliens and their families, no one I spoke to in the next few years had heard of the policy. A letter to the editor of the *San Francisco Chronicle* in the spring of 1988, from a woman who condemned the treatment of the Japanese in 1942 and supported their compensation, typified this void. "German Americans were not interned [or] restricted in any way," she wrote. "No one suggested similar treatment [to that of the Japanese] for the German Americans because they were Caucasian." I checked on books about the home front. One said simply, "Those [Italians and Germans] affected [by relocation or internment] found physical movement and employment opportunities limited." Another writer wrote that the Italian Americans were the objects of a "mild loyalty scare." And the Justice Department in 1942 described the restrictions as "irritating" but not too "confining."[1]

Why was it done? West Coast Italians and Germans faced nothing like the racial animosity borne by the Japanese, and Italy and Germany posed no realistic military threat to that coast. Did the government seriously believe that moving European enemy aliens a few blocks from the waterfront would lessen the danger to strategic areas and defense installations? Were they relocated because some Italians still professed a love for their homeland, spoke only Italian, read only Italian newspapers, listened to Italian short-wave broadcasts, had never become American citizens, or bragged that "Mussolini made the trains run on time"? Yes, in part. For a brief time, such indiscretions were taken seriously in California, where many people distrusted the Italians and Germans as much as they did the Japanese. But more fundamentally, officials panicked, and when they came to their senses they reached the practical conclusion that they could not possibly finish what they had started without doing irreparable harm to the war effort.

Before the American naval victory at Midway in June 1942, authorities in California and Washington, D.C., were under intense pressure to do something to prevent alien sabotage and espionage. These demands came from every level of officialdom and every corner of California. Contrary to opinion today, Italian and German aliens and their families were viewed as genuine threats to American security, a fact that soon moved politicians and the military to relocate them away from designated strategic locations along the West Coast. Later, the military came very close to relocating the European aliens on the East Coast as well. Additionally, several hundred Italians and Germans—including American citizens—found themselves either interned in guarded army camps in the interior of the country or excluded from all U.S. coastlines at least 150 miles. Policy-makers had been stampeded by a combination of bad news from the war front and the public's—as well as their own—worst instincts. At the White House, the war and electoral politics took priority over humanistic concerns. But to be fair, with their army and navy on the run across the Pacific, those in Washington acted instinctively rather than reasonably.

Some authorities panicked more than others. In the War Department, which eventually wrested control of the alien program from an unenthusiastic Justice Department, a contest of wills developed between the men around Secretary of War Henry L. Stimson and army officers in California whose primary responsibility, as they saw it, was to defend the Pacific Coast. Once convinced that going beyond alien relocation would be a disaster, it took Stimson's men three additional months to bring the reluctant soldiers around. If they interned hundreds of thousands—perhaps millions—of Italians and Germans, it would tax the army's over-extended logistical network, threaten the country's defense industries, and lower civilian morale to a dangerous level. Why only the Japanese were relocated is one of the most important questions answered in this book. There is compelling evidence that when the size of the Italian and German populations nationwide were reckoned, the Japanese aliens by default became the only available scapegoats for a policy that originally the public demanded—and the government intended—be applied to *all* enemy aliens.

While this bureaucratic debate raged, the relocation of the Italians and Germans began—unrecorded and little noticed outside the affected communities—two months *before* the well-known roundup of all Japanese Americans began. Relocation broke up families, interrupted education, forced bread winners to find new employment and new homes (in many cases families had to maintain two residences), resulted in individual internment for petty violations, lowered the aliens' self esteem, and, in general, heightened their anxiety about what lay ahead.

In marked contrast to the government's meticulous and voluminous record keeping in the case of internees and the relocated Japanese, the archives are eerily silent about the experiences of Italian and German aliens during the four to eight months they were kept away from their homes and jobs. While the decision to relocate the Italians and Germans is recorded in cold, impersonal detail, the documents report nothing about the effects of the policy on its victims. Apparently, the authorities hoped no one was looking. From government records we learn only that on February 15 and 24, 1942, for reasons of "military necessity," approximately ten thousand enemy aliens were prohibited residence and work in, or travel to, specified restricted zones along the coast. That on June 27, 1942, the government, realizing that what it had done in February was a mistake, permitted Italian and German aliens to return to their homes and jobs in the restricted zones. And that finally, on Columbus Day, October 12, 1942, as the Americans readied their fateful plunge into the Mediterranean and the country honored its most famous Genoese citizen, Italian aliens were removed from the enemy alien category.

Government documents do not even reveal that the aliens actually moved. Were they told where to go, and by whom? Did they return home when the restrictions were lifted or months later? Was any effort made to let them know they could return? How did they make it economically? Did the government accept any financial responsibility? What *was* the human cost of panic? And what about the cost to the nation's self image?

It seemed clear that to answer such questions I would have to ask the victims: "What did you do?" "What did relocation mean to your life, to your family, to your future?" "What did you *feel?*" Surprisingly, their attitudes were not uniformly negative. For those who had sons in the armed forces, those who were interned, those whose family responsibilities increased as a result of the relocation, or those who lost property, the experience was difficult and has left a legacy of bitterness. But they endured—most of them. For others, it was a matter of adjusting to a new way of life, or a better life. Most—crying and laughing at the same time—accepted their fate as the consequence of a war that threatened their adopted homeland. But they understood—some admitted: "It was necessary."

Still, nearly all thought it was silly—"crazy"—for anyone to believe that they were saboteurs or spies, or that moving only the aliens and not naturalized Italians and Germans across the street—as regulations in some cities required—could possibly deflect the destructive intent of dedicated Fascists or Nazis. As one non-Italian explained: if the Italians really wanted to raise hell, the best way to do it would be for them to become citizens and thereby gain access to the waterfront. Apparently, the government believed that people who had lived peaceably and productively for twenty or thirty years, raised their children, educated them, and sent them off to places like Pearl Harbor and Wake Island would be deterred from sabotage by their oath to a piece of one 150-year-old parchment. It was, as they say, "the times."

"We're the 'aliens' now," one Italian told his son in 1942, "but the Russians will be next." What happened to the Italians and Germans in 1942 was part of the dress rehearsal for the McCarthy purges of the 1950s, precisely because in this case the aliens were targeted not for racial but for ideological reasons. In the fifties the FBI and the House Committee on Un-American Activities (HUAC) found it easier to compile lists of aliens, and the army, similarly, to build concentration camps for domestic enemies because it had all been done before—in 1942. At what cost to the democratic spirit, this obsession with national security?

What gives this story poignancy and irony, and elevates it beyond locale is its theme: betrayal. But it is not simply about aliens who might betray their adopted country or nativists who betrayed the aliens' trust. It is also that native-born Americans betrayed themselves and their professed values. They turned their backs on perhaps the most central of their country's democratic faiths: faith in the idea of America itself. It is one of the ironies of World War II that the patriots who championed the country's entry into the war had so little confidence in the promise of the America, which they were prepared to defend with American blood in every corner of the globe. Not so, however, the editors of *Colliers* magazine, who refused to go along with the wildly popular Fifth Column fantasy, and instead lectured their panicky countrymen and women that "our Italians" were not about to "carve up our government and hand it to Mussolini on a spaghetti-with-meatballs platter."[2] It is time to retire the notion of a Fifth Column in the United States during World War II. None of the anxiety widely reported in the popular and academic presses and gobbled up by gullible government officials and the citizenry was justified by any reality. The imagined legions of dedicated domestic enemies of democracy simply did not exist.

THE STORY OF the wartime relocation and internment of civilians on the West Coast, which to date (1988) has focused entirely on the Japanese, cannot be completed without adding to it the trials faced by the Italians and Germans. But it should not be thought that what happened to Italians and Germans on the West Coast was comparable to what happened to the Japanese; relocated Italian and German aliens and their families knew no Manzanar, no Heart Mountain, no Tule Lake, and no so-called fire sales. Certainly, nothing in the pages that follow is intended in any way to brush aside the severity and cruelty of what the Japanese faced. But this work is frankly revisionist in its analysis of the rationale behind relocation, and in *principle* there was no difference in policy. Were the authorities more principled, for example, because they relocated the Italians and Germans a few blocks or a few miles instead of putting all of them in camps? Or, to put it another way, did the authorities adhere more rigorously to the rights of Italians and Germans whom they relocated because of their nationality than they did to the rights of the Japanese who were relocated because of theirs? Were the authorities acting on principle when they stopped short of putting Italians and Germans in relocation camps simply because they discovered there were more of them than there were Japanese? What if the situation had been reversed? What if there had been millions of Japanese scattered throughout the country and only a few thousand Italians and Germans clustered in California, and they were put away instead? Could it then be argued that the Italians and Germans were treated differently, in principle? In compensating the Japanese financially, have Americans resorted to principle? To conscience? Or to political expediency? What price can be put on one's dignity and pride? Were the psyches of loyal Italians and Germans seared any less than those of the Japanese by the label "enemy alien"?

If history provides any lesson in this case, it is that patriotism must have something to do with faith in the principles of the Declaration of Independence and the Bill of Rights—principles that native Americans expected the aliens to learn, and yes, to die for in 1942. This story shows again—and the repetition seems necessary—that it is possible for a nation like the United States, proud of its traditions of democracy, individual liberty, and fair play, to come near to losing its soul in a time of crisis, even during a "good war." This, of course, does not mean that the virtues of the United States go unappreciated among its critics. But Americans must always be conscious of the gap between history and myth, ever vigilant in defense of liberty while continuing to build on and to strengthen the foundations of freedom. It also means that Americans, as they have in the past, will continue to face difficult choices in moments of crisis when the temptation to run with the mob will doubtless be overpowering. There, it seems to me, is a role for history, to serve as a national conscience, to give us pause, not during the heady days of summer, sunshine patriotism, but during the cold, dark winter of national crises.

THERE ARE THREE principal sources for the information in this book: government documents, newspapers, and interviews with the Italians or their surviving family members, from Humboldt Bay in northern California to Monterey Bay in mid state. I tape-recorded each interview, then obtained an approval from subjects for a final edited draft. Two years after our conversation, one man chose to rewrite those portions of his interview that appear here. Alfredo Ciopolato, whom I could not visit personally, answered my questions in a detailed letter. I asked each person a few standard questions having to do with their background and experience, but for the most part our conversations were free-flowing rather than structured so that the interviewees could relax and express themselves spontaneously and candidly. Researchers can find the tape-recorded interviews on deposit at the Bancroft Library on the campus of the University of California, Berkeley.

I began this project intending to document the experiences of the Italians *and* Germans, but limitations of time and money forced me to choose between them. Moreover, for reasons that are not entirely clear, though most likely having to do with the strong sense of community among California's Italians, they proved easier to locate than the Germans. I do not believe that interviews with Germans—were they possible—would alter my conclusions appreciably. I have provided documentary evidence and newspaper reports about the Germans—particularly the political refugees—as a basis for comparing their experiences with those of the Italians. I believe that what happened to these Italians and their families, varied as they are, accurately mirror those of the 10,000 persons relocated. Nothing in official records or newspapers suggests otherwise.

The documents come largely from the microfilmed collection of government files gathered from scattered locations after 1981 by the U.S. Commission on the Wartime Relocation and Internment of Civilians, and from congressional hearings and reports.

There was a fourth source: luck. I got the name of my first interviewee from our department secretary, whose mother happened to be Italian. Interviewees, in turn, added other names. I scanned newspaper obituaries and contacted surviving relatives of deceased relocatees. One phone call to a man of Irish descent in Monterey, whose name came from another Monterey man, whose name I got in Arcata from a friend who knew someone at the Monterey County Board of Education, opened some doors there. I learned the names of other potential interviewees after the campus student newspaper did a story on one of our maintenance men, who happened to be an Italian American from Monterey. And so it went. But for every door that opened, three were politely shut. People said they did not want to see me because, "That thing happened a long time ago. Let sleeping dogs lie." But the curious historian doesn't let sleeping dogs lie. So I dedicate this book to those who opened their doors, and I hope that readers will share vicariously the warmth of feeling and wealth of experience that I discovered in that community.

ACKNOWLEDGMENTS

MY THANKS TO the Humboldt Foundation, whose financial assistance permitted me to transcribe some of the interviews. Erich Schimps shepherded me through our library's labyrinthine document section. Sherry Gordon of the interlibrary loan office tracked down all the sources that could not be found locally. The staffs of the Pittsburg and Monterey Public Libraries, the California State Library, the California State Archives, and the Doe and Bancroft libraries on the campus at the University of California, Berkeley provided professional assistance.

Dee McBroome typed scores of letters and handled the details of obtaining permissions from the interviewees. Jackie Mottaz transcribed the interviews, shortening the project by months, perhaps years. Several of the people I interviewed, as well as friends, provided valuable leads and encouragement: Santo Alioto, John Anderson, Alessandro Baccari, Jr., Frank Buccellato, Stephanie Cincotta, Peter Coniglio, Joe Dolan, Anita Maiorana Ferrante, Mario Flores, Murl Harpham, Lee Hawkins, Lawrence Lazio, Mr. and Mrs. Tom Lazio, Al Massei, Bill McClendon, Peter McNair, Judy Satterlee, Vitina Spadaro, and Fr. Gabriel Zavattaro. John Hennessy, Sam Oliner, Rod Sievers, and Roy Sundstrom read the entire manuscript at a time when it was least convenient for them, and I am grateful for their suggested improvements. John Gimbel, a true scholar-teacher, inspired and encouraged by example.

Each of my sons showed interest in the project in different ways, Kevin by asking from time to time, "How's the book coming, Dad?" and by giving invaluable computer assistance. Chris, a bit more practical, approached it this way: "How much money will you make?" Francoise knows how important her support has been throughout, not the least being that she took a leave from her job to assist me on a research trip after I had a serious accident. This book simply would not be without her encouragement when my energy flagged, her patience and confidence in the absence of my own, and her sound editorial advice.

ONE

"One does not melt souls"
Italian American Assimilation

If present-day America does not seem to present the picture of a happily integrated humanity that she might, blame the hasty and mechanical concept of the melting pot. A day will come when the American people will fuse together spiritually and culturally, and isolated groups of Italians, Germans, and Irish within the commonwealth will be only a memory. But this will be, not because these groups have repudiated their origins, but because they have felt the supreme moral beauty of a new nationality whose aim is to guide the world toward a life without hatred and without egoism. On that day—and not before—the last barrier between Mayflower Americans and Ellis Island Americans will have gone down.
—Carlo Sforza, *The Real Italians,* 1942[3]

THE LOCOMOTIVE ENGINEER probably never saw the object that lay ahead of him on the tracks that cold February night. Nor would he have known why it was there. The next morning's newspaper gave only a brief, impersonal account of the incident: sixty-five-year-old Martini Battistessa, an Italian alien, could not understand why he should give up his locksmith and saw-filing business of twenty years. Unable to complete his naturalization before being declared an enemy alien by his adopted country and expelled from his home, he went to a bar and offered a friend fifty dollars to shoot him in the head. The friend laughed and Battistessa left. A short time later he threw himself in front of the southbound passenger train as it passed through Richmond, California.[4]

When authorities told Giuseppe Mecheli that he could not live in his Vallejo home after February 24, the fifty-seven-year-old fisherman cut his throat with a butcher knife. And before sixty-five-year-old Stefano Terranova leaped to his death from a building, having refused to leave his home as ordered by the Justice Department, he left a note that read in part: "I believe myself to be good, but find myself deceived. I don't know why.... It is my fault for blaming others. My brain is no good."

Near Stockton, Giovanni Sanguenetti, sixty-two, unable to live with the stigma of being called an enemy alien, hanged himself.[5]

Probably few readers of the morning newspaper around San Francisco Bay paid much attention to the two or three lines reporting these last desperate acts, dwarfed as they were, literally and figuratively, by the news from global war fronts. The Japanese were overwhelming the western Pacific, adding Bataan to the American pantheon of bloodied shrines. Closer to home, a Japanese submarine would, in a few days, boldly lob a few shells near Santa Barbara, inflicting minor damage. But the aliens' deaths, incidental as they might have seemed in the rush of world events in 1942, were important pieces in a larger mosaic of human tragedy, a tragedy for the country as well as the aliens, a tragedy that could have been avoided.

WHEN FISHERMAN PIETRO ("Pete") Maiorana left the island of Marettimo off the coast of Sicily for the United States in 1920, he had never heard of Benito Mussolini or of Fascism. It would have been inconceivable to him that the same ship that would carry his family to the United States in 1934 would shortly thereafter transport America's first handful of Italian "volunteers" back across the Atlantic to fight Il Duce's aggressive war in Ethiopia. Nor could he have imagined that only seven years after the fall of Ethiopia, his native land and his adopted country would be at war with each other. Nor that his wife Giuseppa and thousands of other Italian emigrants who had left Italy seeking a better life for themselves and their families would suddenly be considered enemies of the country they had come to love.

As unlikely as this possibility might have seemed to Italian Americans in 1920, it did not to millions of native-born Americans twenty years later. With each advance of Nazism across Europe in the 1930s, Americans in and out of government became convinced that the greatest threat to American security would come from within. They believed that Hitler's successful aggression was attributable in part to his supporters inside countries like Austria and Czechoslovakia, who had paved the way for the Nazi legions with campaigns of propaganda, sabotage, and espionage. The man exercising near-dictatorial power over aliens of enemy nationalities after Pearl Harbor, Lieutenant General John L. DeWitt, who headed the Fourth Army and Western Defense Command in San Francisco, believed that Fifth Columnists lurked along the West Coast, waiting to strike on orders from Rome or Berlin.

WHAT WAS THERE about the conduct of Italians in the United States during the first half of the twentieth century that made them candidates

for relocation, internment, exclusion—and suicide? Italians
United States for the same reasons that other European im
come: a combination of depressing social, economic, and p
tions at home. But Italy's standard of living, particularly in u..
was among the lowest in Europe. Over 80 percent of Italians dependeu
on agriculture for their livelihoods. Many of their homes were one-room,
earthen-floored hovels with no windows or chimneys, which they often
shared with domestic animals. Their furnishings were simple; perhaps a
bed, a chair, a bench, a wooden chest for their meager possessions. They
ate mostly potatoes and corn. Italians were, as one historian describes
them, "a peasant–proletariat," driven out of Italy by the squeeze of economic necessity. They had endured periodic famines, high taxation, and
widespread unemployment. Land ownership was restricted; in overpopu-
lated provinces the soil belonged to the nobility, who put little of their
profits back into the soil. Rain fell heavily during the wrong seasons
(usually autumn and winter), carrying the precious topsoil downstream.
Tenants were leaseholders or landless agricultural workers, who paid high
rents and turned over a large portion of their crops to landlords. Sons and
daughters of such peasants had little reason to be optimistic about the
future. There was in Italy during the late 19th and early 20th centuries, a
"psychology of scarcity." In 1913, one person in fifty left the country.[6]

Indeed, before the Great War almost one quarter of Italy's people had
left. Most Italian immigrants to the United States arrived between 1880
and 1924. Five hundred thousand came in 1901 alone. Nine years later
the U.S. federal census showed that 1,343,000 Italians had arrived; the
next decade brought another 1,109,524.[7]

Preliminary census tabulations provided to Congress in 1942 by the
Alien Registration Division in the Justice Department detailed the boom
in Italian emigration to California from 1900 to 1924. Before 1899, only
3,610 Italian aliens lived in California, but after that, and before the new
immigration law of 1924 cut the flow of immigrants to a trickle, 36,910
took up residence in the Golden State. Only 6,452 were added between
1925 and 1942.[8]

Eighty percent of Italian emigrants before the First World War were
males. It is not difficult to understand why. Young men were drawn by
the adventure of travel and life in a new land, by the urgent need for labor in the United States, and by the promise of higher wages. They fled
military conscription, parental authority, and rural immobility. As for
women, conditions abroad were unknown and the necessary financial resources were hard to come by. But, after the war, a growing familiarity
with life overseas gleaned from relatives' letters, the firsthand accounts of
those who returned either permanently or to visit, and the desire to be

reunited with loved ones gave a new impetus to female emigration. Now whole families migrated together. By 1942, there were 1.2 Italian males for each Italian female in California, the closest ratio of women to men on the West Coast among identifiable ethnic groups.[9]

The Italians were the last great immigrant group to arrive in the United States before the Second World War, and the least assimilated numerically. By the early 1920s, the first generation Italian immigrants averaged only seventeen years residence as compared with thirty-four for the English, fifty-one for the Irish, and thirty-eight for the Germans. Nearly three quarters of the Germans living in the United States in 1920 had been naturalized, two-thirds of the English, but only twenty-eight percent of the Italians.[10]

By 1940, 100,911 foreign-born Italians (about half of them naturalized) lived in California. This compares to 71,727 foreign-born Germans and 33,569 alien Japanese. More Italian aliens (21,519) clustered around San Francisco Bay than anywhere else in the state. (There were 7,641 in Los Angeles County.) Added to San Francisco's 12,183 alien Italians in 1942 were 9,336 in the other Bay Area counties of San Mateo, Marin, Alameda, and Contra Costa. According to the Justice Department, Italian aliens in California at the outbreak of the war numbered 51,923, just over half the foreign-born population of the state. There were also 19,422 German aliens.[11]

The Italian American communities surrounding Humboldt Bay (540 aliens), San Francisco Bay (24,089 aliens), and Monterey Bay (1,057 aliens) derived, for the most part, from two areas of Italy: in and around the city of Lucca in the northern province of Tuscany, and the island of Sicily. Tuscany had been the intellectual center of Italian life since the 13th century, including, as it does, the cities of Florence and Pisa. It was a rich agricultural area but boasted little industrial development. Nonfishing Italians in San Francisco and around Humboldt Bay proudly called themselves "Tuscani." Along San Francisco and Monterey's fishing wharves, a majority of the Italians were from Sicily. In San Francisco—and probably Monterey as well—this meant the Italians were a community within a community, virtually untouched by the outside world except for the requirements of business.[12]

Thanks to a study of San Francisco's Italians in 1935 by sociologist Paul Radin, we know something about life in Lucca at the turn of the century. Based on two interviews conducted by Radin, it is not difficult to imagine why some that had the opportunity to leave did so:

Life in Lucca, Province of Tuscany, Italy

Mr. M. was born in 1880 in Lucca, Province of Tuscany, Italy, and about 5 miles from Pisa. There is a sufficient amount of comparatively level ground around Lucca to support enough farmers, engaged in raising grain and produce, to take care of a large industrial population.

Mr. M. says that at the time he was there, there were a great number of textile mills engaged in the manufacture of cotton thread, woolen goods and sacks (tow) but the principal industry was the manufacture of olive oil. The oil from the crushed olives, aided by the spray of very hot water, flows into a series of glass-lined cement tanks where it is graded and then pumped out.

The olive pits are dried and form the principal fuel used by the people. While some are given away, most of them are sold for a lire a sack.

The average wage paid at the plants at that time was about four lire per day, the day being from ten to twelve hours.

Mrs. M., who was raised in the country a short distance from Lucca, says that there was absolutely no heat in their schools, although they had quite severe winters. The heating problem was solved by having each child carry a terra cotta utensil, similar to a flower–pot with handles, filled with coals of dried olive pits. The pits were ignited at home and after the fire had settled down into embers, more pits were added and a layer of ashes placed over all. The pots were then carried to school and placed on the floor between their legs, and the heat thrown out during the day was sufficient to keep them comfortable....

Although Mr. M's father was a farmer, he (Mr. M.) preferred to make his living by selling. He bought and sold and traded foods and produce. When he worked at a place to the east of Lucca, up in the hills, he would start at three o'clock in the morning and would walk until eleven that evening to reach the particular place where he could do his most effective trading.

His average load, carried on his back, would be about 50 kilos—which is about 110 pounds. Generally he carried tomato paste into the hills to be exchanged for dried mushrooms which were readily salable in town. On his trips to the south he carried butter and eggs....

Mr. M. came to New York in 1904.... Through letters from his family in Italy he is told that the people are very heavily taxed. The small towns especially seem to feel the pinch. He says that all industry is fully under the control of Mussolini and that production is regulated. If, for instance, during a given period an excess is produced, production in that line ceases. Wages, however, continue.

On the other hand, during illness the sick one must be taken care of by relatives, as he says there will be no aid extended as long as a relative is believed to have any money to contribute.[13]

Anonymous,
San Francisco

I was born in the city of Lucca in the province of Tuscany, Italy. My boyhood home was a large house used by several families and fronted on a square court set back from the street. The court had a stone fountain with a tank like a horse-trough in the center. This is where we got our water for cooking and washing. The water came in through a terra cotta pipe, from where I never knew.

Our cooking was done over a charcoal stove, sometimes out of doors in good weather.

We had no plumbing, the slops being emptied into the gutter, and other waste carried to the street where it was picked up by a donkey cart.

Our food was mainly macaroni, polenta (corn meal mush) vegetables, some fish—rarely meat; olive oil and wine.

I did not have much time for play for from as early a time as I can remember, I had to take care of my brother who was two years younger than myself. When I was six years old we often made excursions together around the district, picking up anything we could find that we thought worthwhile bringing home. My mother encouraged us in this and we would get vegetables and pieces of charcoal which could be used at home. We often had to fight to hold what we had, as older boys would try to take it away from us, and if we went into another district too far from home, we were almost sure to get into a fight and be robbed of everything we had found.

I did not go to school as I had to help my mother with the family which kept increasing, though one brother and two sisters died before we left Italy.

My father, who had no regular job, did not stay home very much, but probably did the best he could to keep his family.

We were very poor and often the neighbors who were little better off than we, helped us. My father often spoke of going to America where his brother had gone some time before. When I was fourteen, my uncle Frank, who had a ranch on Sherman Island [Sacramento River delta] sent us money to come to California.[14]

Did Italian immigrants assimilate? Historians and sociologists do not agree but most believe not. If assimilation means the casting away of all vestiges of old-world culture and the speedy adoption of American citizenship, the answer is no, Italian immigrants did not assimilate readily. But if it means the integration of the immigrants into the American economy and the education of second generation Italians in American values, while retaining respect for Italian tradition and culture, then the answer is yes. Historian Andrew Rolle argues the affirmative based on his study of Italians in the West, where a freer social and economic atmosphere gave them equal access with the native-born to wealth and power. Sociologist Paul Campisi, who studied the Italians in a middle-sized Illinois city in 1942, found their history in America to be one of continuous isolation, in which the emigrants sought comfort and prestige in "affectionate ties" to Italy. John Diggins believes they were "unwelcome strangers" torn between two worlds who retreated into ethnic enclaves to fend off the wave of "One-Hundred Percent Americanism" sweeping the country in 1919 and 1920. They felt betrayed by Wilson's rejection at Versailles of Italian control of Fiume and by the discriminatory immigration laws of the 1920s. Italian American journalist Max Ascoli writes that when war broke out in 1941 a large section of the Italian American population was still not thoroughly absorbed into American society. Many still had strong attachments to their native towns and were unified into a national block by the hostility of other Americans who called all of them "wops."

The problem of assimilation was also generational. The Italian government encouraged parents overseas to teach their children the Italian language as a way of tying the family closer to the Old World. But the young, not inclined to accept parental authority at any time or place, viewed old-world customs as a barrier to their assimilation.[15]

AS THE GOVERNMENT contemplated the status of enemy aliens in the immediate aftermath of Pearl Harbor, it was troubled—like many citizens—by the fact that so many remained unnaturalized. To those outside the immigrant communities, whether a newcomer took out American citizenship was the most tangible means of judging allegiance. Yet some had lived in the United States for up to forty years. That the immigrants evidently preferred to remain aliens persuaded officials in the Justice and War Departments that they were under the ideological spell of their respective Fascist and Nazi homelands.

The same officials also believed that the maintenance of dual citizenship—holding American and foreign citizenship concurrently—made for a prima facie case of disloyalty. Although the officials directed their concern about dual citizenship primarily at the Japanese, both Italy and Germany insisted on adherence to the principle even more tenaciously than Japan. In both Italy and Germany, the bond of race and blood was a central ideological tenet. Membership in the German *Volk* was not a matter of choice; it was predetermined. Nazi propagandists also defined as German "those of German descent and German blood who live abroad." Italian law strictly applied the principle of citizenship by descent. A child, no matter where it lived, was Italian if either parent was Italian.[16] On the final page of instructions issued with passports during 1926 and 1927, the Italian government reminded emigrants that space and time placed no limit on their loyalty to the homeland:

What it Means to be Italian

The immigrant should never abandon his feeling of the value of being an Italian....

Keep alive, at all times, the use of your mother tongue and the practice of your own institutions; bring up your children in a love for your Fatherland and teach them the language, history and geography of Italy. And even if you assume the nationality of the country in which you have settled, never deny and never forget the sublime moral inheritance of your ancestors and transmit to your descendants the sacred flame of the love of the distant Fatherland. Thus will you ever remain a true son of that world-extensive and strong Italy.

Long Live Italy, Forever[17]

Such pressure suggests one reason why so many Italian aliens might have hesitated to become American citizens; more of them than the Germans remained unnaturalized when war broke out in December 1941. Of the foreign-born living in the United States at that time, 42.5 percent of the Italians and 25.4 percent of the Germans had not obtained American citizenship. The differential in California was even greater: slightly more than half of the Italians and 27 percent of the Germans.[18] Did the majority of Italian–born in California remain unnaturalized because of their ties to Italy? Were the aliens contemptuous of American democracy? Were they waiting for the right moment to strike a mortal blow at the United States as some officials and citizens feared? Or were they too busy supporting and nurturing growing families to find time to meet naturalization requirements? Were they sufficiently educated to pass the tests? Was it essential for them to become citizens to get along on a day-to-day basis in America or to feel "American?" Did they think of themselves as Italian first and American second?

In Paul Campisi's Illinois town, illiterate immigrants lived in a close, familial Italian American community on which they depended for information. Their understanding of the war in 1942 was vague and nebulous; perhaps England was to blame, they thought, although they did not even know where England was. Their understanding of Fascism went no deeper than their knowledge that it was the government of Italy and Mussolini was its president. They had no idea what a dictator was. To most Italians, Fascism was "an ideologically meaningless term." What Italians wanted for themselves and from Americans was prestige, respect, and recognition. Campisi found no reason to question their loyalty to the American government. But there was every reason to question the wisdom of stigmatizing them as enemies, which he feared would lead to greater isolation and withdrawal, precisely the characteristics that had initially made them suspect.[19]

The interviews that follow show that an immigrant's decision to become American was pragmatic and spiritual: its necessity in daily life, the time available to prepare for the examination, their educational background, the war, their isolation from native-born Americans, and the extent to which they felt "American" rather than "Italian."

Howard Williams (pseudonym),
Eureka, California

I had very close friends in the Italian community. I've always thought that one of the reasons that they weren't more harsh on the Italians was because we had an Italian resistance going in Italy, and that put them in a little different light than the Germans and the Japanese. Also, a lot of the Italians in this area used to joke openly about "Ol' Il Duce," particularly the kids. They seemed to reject totalitarianism. I've often wondered why some of them failed to get citizenship.

What did people think about what was happening?

Just like the Japanese relocation, I think people were in favor of it. I'm sure the Italian community wasn't too thrilled with it, but I don't remember people other than Italians getting too upset. Of course, everybody was so darn gung-ho in high school, and patriotism was just going like crazy in 1942 because we were in the "big one." I had three older brothers already in the service, and all three of them were in combat by that time in the South Pacific. So, yeah, there was little or no sentiment favoring anyone who was not a citizen of the country. And even Dan [Banducci]—he'd been here for years and years. A lot of us used to feel like, well, he should have been a citizen by now. I never could figure why they lived here that long, and they seemed to enjoy living here. But somehow or another they wanted to maintain their

*identity with the mother country. And my God, to be an American citi-
zen in 1942, everybody should be an American citizen.*

Steve Antongiovanni,
Eureka

*When the war broke out, I was almost nine years old. I was born here,
so I was a citizen. My sister was a citizen because she came here on my
father's passport, and my dad had become a citizen in order to be able
to bring my mother and sister over. He came in 1921. He had left my
mother and sister, who was a month old at the time. When he got over
here his intent was to accumulate some money and then send for his
family. A year or so after, while he was trying to get the money together, he found out that he had to have been here five years, and be a
citizen, before he could bring them over. So all together, he had to wait
about seven years.*

*He became a citizen in Bakersfield. By then, times were even worse.
We're looking at 1928, '29, and those years were real bad as far as any
type of employment at all. Then in 1930 he was able to call his family
over, but there was absolutely no work for any immigrants. Of course,
there was a lot of bootlegging, and he did that with some of his relatives, but he still couldn't seem to accumulate enough money. So in 1930
he borrowed and sent for his family.*

*In 1930, there was no immediate need for my mother to become a
citizen. But when the war broke out, she felt that there could be problems; if she didn't become a citizen, the family could be separated again.
There was a chance that the family could be expatriated back to Italy, or
separated, or treated like the Japanese. A lot of Italians were worried
about that, and so they immediately wanted to become citizens. 'Course
they understood that we were closer to Japan; if anything, we'd be attacked by Japan, not Italy.*

*The other risk was what if they [Italy] lost the war? Now they had
become American citizens and traitors. I remember them discussing this.
But they decided, "We're here and that's the way to go." There was no
hope at that time of ever going back to Italy. Times were too hard. They
had to build a house, raise a family, and get the passage. From California to Italy in 1939, '40, '41, it was ten, fifteen days just to get
there. So she became a citizen in 1942.*

Did your mother have to go through any waiting period for her citizenship?

No, there wasn't any that I recall. I remember she used to sit by the hour and try to learn. She was a good student at school. She helped me through math clear up to Algebra. So she had a good basic education, but there was always difficulty with the pronunciation because the Italians had colonized so much over here. There were a lot of Italians around here, and they had their own functions in lodges and so forth. Learning English was not a priority. I knew kids my age that were born in San Francisco, and when they'd come up to visit relatives in Scotia they spoke with broken accents just like they'd come off the boats from Europe. And they were born here!

There were big masses of 'em going for citizenship. I used to help my mother with questions; she was real interested in that. And she passed it with flying colors. But they asked her why she hadn't learned English yet. She said she was in the house all the time and there were Italians all around.

Dominic Banducci,
Eureka

My grandfather, who I had a lot of respect for, was a great guy. He used to take the immigrants in at the Buon Gusto [hotel] and help them until they could get jobs. He fed them and made sure they saved their money so that later on they could send for their wives, although some of them never did. But he would help them out, make sure they got beds and clothes, and even when the wife would come, put them up at the Buon Gusto for a period of time to get them readjusted. A lot of these people had to move out of the hotel, too. They were appreciative of being in this country; many of them came from a lot of poverty. They couldn't really understand what was happening to them.

They had a phrase—"L'ho trovota l'America," which translated loosely means, "I have found America." It's beautiful. We'll put up with it. What we've got here is a lot better than what we left. Let's just keep our mouths shut and it'll work out. Everybody will realize that we're not opponents of the United States. It'll take some time, and it will all be realized in this beautiful country where we're all free. Let's just take it and be quiet. That was the attitude. I'm sure a lot of these people suffered more the way they had to come from the old country, steerage and whatever. There was nothing they were going to do to jeopardize their ability to live in this country. Everybody was just proud to be a part of America; it would all work out. Later on my father became a citizen.

My grandmother had two sons in the service, and because of that it became a lot easier for her to become a citizen. Of course they couldn't understand why they had to learn about the American government and learn how to speak English. One of my father's favorite jokes was, when the judge asked him what flew over the capitol, he said, "pigeons." There was no real call for citizenship in those days. A lot of the reason for citizenship today is benefits that people get. Those were not available in those days, or there wasn't a great concern about them—particularly social security, or getting an FHA loan. Being a permanent alien meant only a slight difference in one's life.

Gino Casagrande,
Eureka

When did your father come to this country?

He was a young man. He was born in 1885 and was in his twenties when he came. Then he sent for my mother and she came a couple of years later. They were married in San Francisco. He worked when he first came here. I'm not quite sure, but he had a job at the quarry up Warren Creek. I don't know how long he stayed there, but later he came down to Eureka and went to work for the Roma Bakery up on California Street. After a short time he and his brother had a chance to buy this bakery here which was called the Italo-American Bakery. They bought it, changed the name to the Humboldt Bakery, and ran it until 1944 when he sold out to Fluhrer's Bakery, the same Fluhrer's as today.

I think it was in the early thirties when he was going to night school. He finally got his citizenship papers. My mother became a citizen after the war. They had to learn the preamble [to the Constitution] and stuff like that.

Why didn't she become a citizen when your father did?

I don't know if you can understand it or not, or anyone else for that matter. Here's an immigrant, who can't speak the language. She's a housewife; she worked in the bakery along with the rest of the bakers; she took care of the apartments; she took care of the three kids. Why is she going to think about getting citizenship papers? I don't think people understand that. They can't. The only thing she was worried about was taking care of her family. She wasn't worried about being a citizen. Not that she had anything against the country, but she never thought about it. That's all. She was a housewife spending eighteen hours a day working, and maybe six hours sleeping. You have to understand the foreigner to understand her way of life. My dad, of course, was in business, and it was an advantage for him to be a citizen of his adopted country. In fact, he got into politics pretty heavily at times.

Jennie Maffia,
Eureka

I think my mother said she was about nineteen when she came over. And, of course, she had no schooling. She was the baby of the family; there were eight of them. Everybody else could read and write, but when it was her time to go to school she had to stay home and take care of her grandmother, who was a little senile, while the rest worked out in the olive fields. Her brothers came over here, Angelo and Charley Batini. One had the garbage company for many, many years. The other one had a pig farm and then a winery out at Ryan's Slough. Naturally, my mother wanted to come. It was probably a heck of a lot better living than she had over there. So they sent for her, and I think she said it was a hundred dollars to come over on the ship.

One thing that I've thought about is that my mother never mentioned Ellis Island. None of the old timers that came over did. All I remember her saying was that "they herded me, and slapped a sign on me like a salami, and shipped me to Eureka." God, can you imagine? They must have been scared to death the way they herded you through. Can you imagine how frightened my mother must have been? She was nineteen years old; seasick the whole time; didn't know anybody. I don't see how they found their way to get on a train. I have a hard time being able to read signs at the airports now!

Mother was from Lucca. We've been back there—very beautiful. Her name was Amelia Batini. She met my dad here and married him. They set up a tavern down on Second Street in Eureka, and then the war came along with all the hullabaloo about the aliens and so forth. Neither one of them were citizens, and my dad couldn't read or write. They never became citizens. As the years went by it became more difficult, and the fact that they couldn't read or write really deterred them. You had to go to classes, and that'd really be something if they handed you a book and you're holding it upside down!

In those days, her brother, Angelo Batini, had quite a bit of pull in town. If my mother had pushed, it wouldn't have been any problem to get her papers. It wasn't like it is now, where you have to take an examination. You knew the right people. The papers were just presented to you, probably for a nominal fee. I guess when you're grown up you're rather ashamed of the fact that you can't read or write. I know my mother and father were always very embarrassed by it. I know when I wanted to get my driver's license I just had a terrible time. Well, fortunately my boss knew a guy so that my folks didn't have to go. He witnessed their cross, or whatever. This is one reason that they never got their papers. And they worked. In those days, you had to work. There wasn't time to take off for school.

Ugo Giuntini,
Arcata, California

Dad never became a citizen. He came in 1913, and we followed in 1921, when I was ten. You see, the reason he wasn't interested in becoming a citizen is that when he came, in those days, the Italians just stayed in their own little group. The people that they knew, that's all they needed. He came to Korbel he made a home for us there where he was working in the mill; and the only people he knew were Italian. He could understand English, but he couldn't answer back. My mother really worked hard to get her citizenship papers; many an hour when I was going to high school and college I'd spend with her. She was so scared when she went for her hearing. In those days it was all in open court.

I worked with her and gave her the third degree on the same questions: "What are the three departments of our government?" and so on. She knew the answers backwards and forwards. And then, because we thought perhaps we ought to get somebody else—you know, when you try to teach your wife to drive? Good idea to get somebody else. So, a friend of ours, Mr. Zampatti, an attorney in Eureka, said, "I'll help, too." So he did and eventually she went to get her papers.

People just flocked there; they were there when I got mine, too. Nowadays it's much simpler. The first question the examiner asked her was, "What's your name?" She just froze! And the more questions he asked, the worse she got. Finally the examiner turned to the judge and suggested that perhaps she'd better be put off until the next hearing in six months. This judge was a good man. He was the same one that was on the bench when I got mine. Anyway, Mr. Zampatti took us off to one side, calmed her down and said, "I'm going to talk to the judge." He went back in and told the judge that he was satisfied that my mother knew the material, but that she had panicked with all those people there.

Mr. Zampatti suggested to the judge that if possible, could he see his way to squeeze mother in somewhere at the end and give her another chance. The judge said, "Well, of course you know that we have so many of them to get through first. Tell her to stick around. We'll get her in here." So, when everyone else finished, they called her back in. The judge put her at ease with a few jokes, and by God, then she started answering the questions—bing, bing, bing—like that. And of course, I was happy. You should have seen that attorney—"I told you so!" They got so far and the examiner says, "That's enough, that's enough. Recommend." Pandemonium broke loose. She was so happy. Eventually, she learned to speak English pretty well.

I got a letter from Mussolini when I was eighteen. His government suggested that it was time for me to serve my hitch in the Italian army. Well, I had just got my first papers, so I said to them, "See this? Talk to Uncle Sam." I went through the same thing as my mother, but I got my papers during the time I was at Humboldt State College [in Arcata], taking a course in American Government, so I knew all I needed. They tried to stump me, but they couldn't. Came my twenty-first birthday. I was supposed to get my final papers, so I got a date to appear—ten o'clock. I was third in line; there was a bunch of us, and the place was packed. And the audience would giggle when people made errors. The first person was asked, "Who's president of the United States?"

"Roosevelt."

"OK, admitted." That's all.

To the second person: "What are the three branches of government?"

"Executive, legislative judiciary."

"Admitted." That's all.

I was ready; it looked so easy. But do you know I was there for about thirty minutes? One question after another, but I didn't miss. Finally the examiner said, "What did you do for preparation?"

"Nothing. I took a course in American Government up at Humboldt."

The examiner says to the judge, a little embarrassed, "Your honor, if you look at that pile of papers there, you'll see that I already examined this man." I had been given a pre-examination. "I was satisfied in examining him yesterday and his papers are OK. He passed yesterday." People smiled 'cause I had a lot of friends there. I was really afraid that it was just a matter of time until he caught me as soon as I don't know one, that'll be it. He was bound and determined that he was going to trip me up.

Anita Maiorana Ferrante,
Monterey, California

My dad went back to Italy to marry my mom in 1928 and came back alone to Monterey to fish so that he could make enough money to bring his family back to America. It took him six years to accumulate the fare. I had been born, but I didn't know who my father was, and he had never seen me. Finally, in 1934, he came over and gathered his family and we arrived in San Francisco, August of 1934.

A lot of the Italian fishermen from Monterey come from an island called Marettimo. It's a group of three islands off the coast of Sicily. That's where I was born. We came on the S.S. Rex, across the sea, and then by train across the United States to San Francisco. We stayed with my aunt, and then made our home in Monterey. And we've been here ever since.

My mother became a citizen after relocation when they got back from Salinas and realized what had happened. She wanted to be an American citizen so desperately because they never wanted this to happen again. There was a woman who had a school on Pacific Street, and she would take these housewives, or anyone that wanted to become a citizen, and teach them what they had to know. And religiously, with their babies, and their work and their problems, they went to this school so that they could graduate with their little certificate and go take their test and become a citizen. That was a great day for them. My mother hadn't become a citizen because she had children; she needed to be at home. There was no need. My father was a citizen; she was very comfortable.

After [relocation] happened, all of a sudden there was a realization: "We've got to get this done. I want to be a citizen. I want to be with my family." She would have been the only alien, and it was very important. So she went to school. All the Italian ladies went to school. The Italian fishermen went to school. And they studied very hard, passed their tests, and looked forward to the moment they would be called to the court- house to be sworn in as American citizens.

John Molinari,
San Francisco, California

You were a member of the "Citizens Committee to Aid Italians Loyal to the United States"?

Yes. It was organized as a non-profit corporation titled, "Italians Loyal to the United States." It was not a "citizens committee" in the sense of a general, citywide committee, but it was composed of people of Italian descent. The reason for the creation of the committee was that the [Italian] community was rampant with rumors that after the evacuation of the Japanese by the military authorities in this area, the people of Italian extraction would be next. And so the committee was formed to forestall any such activity. The committee met from time to time to attempt to persuade the Italian population that the rumors were unfounded. But, in any event, as happens during wartime, there was considerable apprehension that this might happen to people of Italian descent. The committee did have meetings with Earl Warren, the attorney general of the state of California, who had taken a position [favoring] the evacuation of the Japanese. He assured us that to his knowledge there was no such action [re the Italians] contemplated. We then asked for a meeting with General DeWitt, commanding general of—I believe—the Fourth Army at that time, and who was the general who would issue the order for evacuation.

We would have supported all aliens as well as citizens because the aliens—so many of them never got around to getting citizenship—had been here for thirty, forty, fifty years. Joe DiMaggio's father, for example, had never applied for citizenship; he was a fisherman. He eventually passed, but it took him a long time. Mostly the fishermen were people who had not gotten around to getting citizenship, and there were a lot of them. They were busy, or they were afraid of the examination, or whatever. I remember in my law practice I was speaking more Italian during the course of the day than I did English. I had clients who couldn't read or write, even in Italian, let alone English. They'd never gone to school in Italy. You see Italy was a new nation if you really analyze it. A lot of these people came here at the turn of the century, and Italy was unified in, what was it, 1870? So the public school system had never taken hold.

Anita Pera,
Eureka

I was born in this house and grew up in this neighborhood. There were Italians living across the street; there were Italians living in the back of us; there were about ten blocks here that were really all Italian. You heard the Italian language all the time, and all of the kids spoke Italian. My generation, most of us, knew a little bit of Italian that we could get by on.

My grandfather came over in 1910, and my grandmother and her daughter and son came over in 1928. My other grandfather on the Pecchia side went back and forth. He'd come over and make a little money, and then he'd go back. His last time here was just prior to 1914. My father came over in 1920. He met two brothers who were already here, and he never left this area.

At one time, my grandfather brought my grandmother over and they lived in Chicago. She thought that there were no Catholic churches there; she couldn't speak English. She lived in an Italian neighborhood, but she couldn't understand the priest. He was an Irish priest, I guess. So anyway, as a result, she packed up her two children—she was pregnant with her third—and went back to Italy and never returned to this country. All but two of her children came back, though. My father was naturalized before World War II, I think around 1935. My aunt Bruna, who lives next door, and my mother became citizens at the same time, in 1943.

I remember my mother studying the Constitution; I can still see her. She'd put up her ironing board right there [points]. *We had one of those hanging single light bulbs in the middle of the room, and she'd be there studying that Constitution till eleven or twelve at night. Her teacher was Cecile Clark, who hated the Italians and the Irish. She hated anything; she thought she was a pure-blooded American. There was this little Italian lady, who has since passed away. Her name was Mrs. Frediani. She was from Busano, Italy, so everybody called her "Busana." And she was a neat old lady; she had a quip for everything. One day Cecile Clark was going on and on about all these people who were sitting there going through this citizenship thing, and how they were nothing but migrants—immigrants. Really putting them down. So Busana raised her hand and said, "What nationality are you?"*

"I'm English."

"Well, I thought the only native Americans were the Indians!"

Why didn't your mother become a citizen earlier?

Don't forget, she still had this basic love for Italy, and a lot of these people hated to give up their Italian citizenship. I think that was the foremost thing on their minds. Secondly, she had never needed it before the war. And you know, when she became a citizen she became a regis-tered voter. She voted in every election until the day she died. Even that last year when she was sick, she went down and voted in 1981. She said, "Go get me my absentee ballot and I'll vote this year too."

Don Raffaelli,
Eureka

My mom has a favorite story from that time. When she would cross Fourth Street—which was the restriction line for aliens—and go down to the wharf to buy fish, some of the Italians who were not allowed to cross Fourth would caution her, and tell her she shouldn't go across. But she'd just wave her naturalization papers and go on her way. She took a lot of pride in that. Many of the Italian immigrants in those days wanted to live in the United States, but they were reluctant to give up their Italian citizenship. Of course, that changed rapidly when the re-strictions came.

Mother took some abuse from other Italians because she was natu-ralized and gave up her Italian citizenship before World War II. I don't recall it being real severe, but I remember the discussions and her feel-ings were hurt. She was no longer one of them, excluded from the group because she was no longer "fit."

The Italians in Eureka were not bad off economically; generally speaking the men had jobs. The Depression, though, was a different story. A lot of them were bootleggers during Prohibition, pure and sim-ple.[20] In fact, one gentleman I recently went to see, who's ninety-three, ran a place called the Mission in Eureka. It was a soda fountain down-stairs and a whorehouse upstairs. He was shut down in the days when Edmund G. Brown, Sr. was attorney general of the state. He came in and took over the police department for a couple of months. Cleaned up the town and left. The Mission was on the northeast corner of Third and E. There's a parking lot there now, opposite Ten Window Williams.

Anyway, they were bootleggers. Hey, they didn't make any bones about it; they knew how to survive. Those that were active during the late teens and early twenties, when Prohibition was in effect did quite well. I remember hearing stories about them greasing the palms [of officials], making sure that the revenuers didn't come in and break up the stills. There was hard liquor; there were spirits; and there was wine, of course. Wine was always available. It was sinful to have Prohibition, Un-Christian [laughs]. *Later on, the bootleggers became legitimate and functioned as brokers. One was Spadoni, the old man. I guess it's his grandson who runs Spadoni's Market on Fourth Street. I think one of the Toninis, old man Tonini, who was Agnese Tonini's husband, was also a broker. First they would get the orders for grapes from each family, usually about a ton per family, which made, in a good year, about a 180 gallons, in a bad year about a 150 gallons. Then they'd go to the Napa Valley and order the amount of grapes necessary to make the Italian—the hard, heavy—burgundy. One or two carloads would be shipped up by rail. When the broker delivered, he would also usually loan a press for crushing the grapes. All the neighborhood men would go around crushing everyone's grapes. Just like making sausage and salami, they'd all pitch in and help each other. Then, after all the grapes had fermented, they'd do the same thing all over again. I remember one year the crusher broke and even the kids had to help stomp the grapes. You don't get as much wine that way as with the new–fangled electrical contraptions, but that was the custom every fall.*

The men had to get a permit, though, from the alcohol, tobacco, and firearms agency. You were allowed so much for home use and had to have a piece of paper. They were very proper about it. I don't think in the eighteen or nineteen years that we made wine that anybody ever came by to check to see if we had a stamp. But they all got their stamps anyway and kept them above their cantinas.

Ratzi Trezza,
Pittsburg, California

My mother was fourteen when she came from the old country. She never got her citizenship papers because she had all those little kids. She wouldn't go to school, but she'd go to the store and make the owner understand her, some way or another. She died in 1980 and never became a citizen. She was eighty-seven when she died, and she always said, "If they give it [citizenship] to me I'll take it, but I ain't gonna go through all that." She was afraid because she could see what her sister was going through, and she didn't want to go in front of the judge. They should have given papers to all those people. They were over here, right? Most of them were old. Here my mother had all those kids, never was in trouble. Give them the papers. She ain't going back to Italy. I don't know what they thought they were going to do.

My dad became a citizen, though. At first he didn't have time, being a fisherman, and having fourteen mouths to feed. He fished for about fifty years without being a citizen, but they told him that if he wanted to go to Alaska to fish in the rivers there he'd have to be an American citizen. So he started going to school, and he got his papers. When he came over here, sometime around 1889, he couldn't speak any English, but he learned to speak it as good as you or me.

Fr. Gabriel Zavattaro,
San Francisco

I was born in Italy in 1909, and I remained in Italy until I was fifteen years old. By that time, I expressed my desire to join the religious life with the Salesians, and I was studying in a junior seminary.

At that time I met the Provincial [of the Salesians] from the United States who wished to open schools. The Provincial is the superior of the Salesian religious of the area. He was looking for young boys willing to come to the United States and follow their studies in our country, learn the language, get a degree, and eventually teach in the schools. So I was one of about five or six who came then to the United States.

We first studied in New Rochelle, New York, and were there for two years, then in Goshen, New York. By that time, we were practically through with college studies. In 1927, the United States was divided into two Salesian provinces, with headquarters at New Rochelle and San Francisco. I was assigned to the western province, and arrived in California in 1927 and taught at Watsonville—St. Francis in Watsonville—for three years. Then I went back to Italy for four years for theological studies. After I was ordained priest, I came back to California.

When you went back to Italy, you knew you would return to the United States?

Oh, yes. I belonged to the western province of the United States. Even when I went back to Italy, I went there as a student from the western province. I thought about becoming a citizen. At first, as a student, I could not become a citizen because I was under a special permit. But when I came back, I came as an ordained minister. This was within the [immigration] quota, and I immediately applied.

In the meantime, I was transferred from Richmond, California, to Don Bosco College, in Newton, New Jersey. I had received a master's degree from the University of California at Berkeley, in Latin, and I was sent to Don Bosco to teach Latin to college students. I remained there two years, and in 1940, I came back again to Richmond since I was made Superior of the junior seminary at Richmond, which was called then, Salesian House of Studies. And so I happened to be there in 1941.

Meanwhile, I had reapplied to become a citizen, because in all my moving around there were difficulties in getting the necessary documents. I tried to get my citizenship in Newton, but I had only the testimony of one witness from California; they required two. So it didn't go through. I came back to California and had to wait another year. By that time the war broke out, and even though I had sworn my allegiance at the time of my application, passed the exam and everything, I still did not have my documents as a citizen.

The fishermen found it very, very hard. They had worked here all their lives, sometimes for about twenty-five or thirty years. They were not citizens for the simple reason that when they came to the states they had come from southern Italy, especially from Sicily. They did not know how to read or write. So they could not become citizens. They would have had to go to school, but that was out of the question for them; they just lived here with their families. They could send their children to school until they were well educated, and that's what most of the Italians here did. They were very poor, they worked very hard, but they went out of their way in giving their children a good education. But they were not citizens. And so they were considered as enemy aliens. And of course they felt it was unjust because they had been loyal, and done nothing else but work all their lives. And their children were Americans, and they were fighting with the Americans. It was a sad situation.

Vitina Spadaro,
Monterey

My father came to this country as a young boy in 1919, then went back to Italy and married my mother. I was born in Italy. In 1936, when I was about six years old, my father sent for my mother and me to join him here in this country. We did, and I became an American citizen because of my father being a citizen. But my mother was an alien. She spoke very little English because coming to live here in Monterey, there were a lot of Italians nearby, and they spoke a lot of Italian. Even at home, our language was Italian.

My father, my mother, and I were born in Marettimo, Sicily. As a young boy my father dreamed of coming to America like everyone else. It was the land of prosperity, the land of all our dreams come true. Coming from a small island, there wasn't much hope to get ahead there.

My father became an American citizen because he thought that was the thing to do. My mother had not because of the language barrier. But when we moved to Salinas, she realized that it was important that she learn the language and the Constitution, which at that time was very difficult for her. All of a sudden, she realized that she was considered an alien, so she wanted to be a part of this country; she wanted to be an American citizen like my father and me, and she did.

I remember going to Palermo and going through the examination to see if we were healthy before we entered the country. We came with other immigrants, friends of the family. It was easier that way because of the language; we didn't understand a word of English. After we landed in New York, we boarded a train for California. I don't know what happened with other people, but we were on this train for four days and nights, and I was hungry. But we didn't know how to ask for food. I kept looking and hoping that somebody would do something. Finally I told my mother, and she was telling other people with hand motions that I was hungry. It worked because right away somebody brought us sandwiches, apples, and milk. It was difficult.

Alex Frediani,
Eureka

In 1942, mother had to get her second [citizenship] papers. She actually should have had her papers before. But she was raising a family, and my dad worked seven days a week. I don't even remember the Depression because he worked all the time. And she would have had to come on the ferry at night, I guess, to go over to school. So my dad held school for her at home; he taught her. Then once we left Samoa [across Humboldt Bay from Eureka], and were here, that was the first thing she had to do. My dad insisted, "Now, let's get a decent teacher." She went to school in the afternoon.

I went with her to the old courthouse [for naturalization] to make sure that she went in from Fifth Street, that she didn't go in from the "wrong" side, you know, because of the line [restricting aliens]. We were worried about her, too, because she'd had surgery for a tumor. I

*was in the courthouse because of a civics class in high school. They'd
take the people that were going up for citizenship into the courtroom in
front of a Superior Court judge. The examiner would question these
people: "OK, Fine." And the judge would give his stamp of approval in
open court. I felt resentment, not so much on account of my mother, she
could handle it. She would get her papers because my dad had coaxed
her and coached her. But the examiner asked one lady there what kind of
government they had in the old country. And I think she wanted to say,
"monarchy," but it came out, "anarchy." Everybody laughed and she
got a little flustered. So the examiner says, "Do you have any children
in the service?" She said she had lost a son. I don't remember if it was
at Pearl Harbor or Wake Island, but he'd been one of the first draftees
in 1940. He got killed, and she got all shook up. Well, they turned her
down, even though the examiner said, "OK." But the judge told her to
go back to school and come back in six months. I thought, "Oh, this
guy's bad." But what was I gonna say? I saw another guy go up who
had been a bootlegger, and he got them [papers] because he had an
Italian attorney speaking on his behalf.*

*Then I went into the service, and after I got out this particular judge
was running for re-election. I had just turned twenty-one and could
vote. There was a place called Classic's Billiards, kind of a soda foun-
tain/pool hall on 4th Street. Dan Banducci owned it. I'll never forget
this judge coming in there soliciting votes, and I got to tell him off. But
I thought, "What if he wins?" Fortunately the guy was defeated; I felt
good about that.*

IF THE APPROPRIATE measure of assimilation was whether the aliens
learned English and spoke it with their children, became citizens and
moved out of ethnic ghettos, then the foregoing interviews suggest that
the Italians of California were not assimilated before the war. They first
thought of themselves as Italian, then American. And considering the
effort put forward by some of the aliens to become citizens, it is not easy
to accept the claims of others that their parents were just "too busy" to
do it.

If, on the other hand, assimilation is judged by the key economic positions occupied by aliens—fishermen, shopkeepers, hostelers, craftsmen,
vintners, farmers, laborers—or that they did not plan to return to Italy—
that living in America made them "American"—then some of California's immigrant Italians were assimilated by 1942. The truth is that each
of the aliens met one or more of the criteria of both assimilation and
nonassimilation. They had been under considerable pressure to adopt the
basic elements of American culture, and some of them did so, while pre-

serving at the same time their native culture. The Italian aliens believed they were Americans, but Americans who had deliberately retained some of their old-world traditions.

But was it reasonable to assume that unnaturalized Italians represented a threat to American security? Were the prewar activities of Italian and German Americans provocative enough to prompt the government to prepare a portfolio of restrictions—including relocation, internment, and exclusion—in case of war?

TWO

"There is dynamite on our shores"
Fascism and the Italian Community

*To say that Germany and other nations want war is madness. What
the DEFEATED nations like Italy are looking for...[is] to find a place
in the sun WITHOUT WAGING WAR.*
—*L'Italia*, San Francisco

FASCIST AND NAZI attempts in the 1920s and 1930s to enlist the Italian and German American communities in their causes through the foreign-language media—a key to the possibility of Fifth Column subversion—alarmed many Americans. Following Hitler's humiliation of France in June 1940, this fear took on near-hysterical proportions.

Italian Americans had flirted with Fascism, a romance with roots in post-World War I Italian nationalism that evolved through three stages: passing interest, partial acceptance and participation, and withdrawal and repudiation. That it was never more than a flirtation was due largely to the Italian Americans' quiet absorption of democratic values before the 1920s. Most had bettered their lives since leaving Italy, and it helped, too, that the United States had been associated with Italy during World War I.[21]

The change to partial acceptance of Fascism came in the mid-twenties, after the full effect of immigration restriction and its underlying xenophobia was felt. Fascism now gave Italian Americans an ethnic identity, and many of them turned to this refuge to recover their battered self-esteem. As the Italian American journalist Max Ascoli put it, there was no reason to be surprised at Mussolini's appeal; he was the "wop" on the front page. An Italian fisherman at Hunter's Point near San Francisco told an interviewer in 1935 that he would like to return to Italy to see Mussolini: "Everyone wants to meet Mussolini. He's a great man."[22]

The rapprochement between the Catholic Church and Italy in 1929 also disposed Italian Americans to look more favorably on Mussolini.

To follow up this successful initiative, the Italian government used Italian organizations in the United States as propaganda conduits during the 1930s: the Italian embassy and its network of consulates, the Dante Alighieri Society (intended to promote Italy's cultural heritage), the Fasci Abroad, the Sons of Italy (over 300,000 members in the 1920s), chambers of commerce, and the Italian-language media. Italian consulates distributed Fascist textbooks and worked closely with "educational agents" who were sent from Italy to serve as curricular aides for teachers of Italian descent in special after-hours Italian American schools. There may have been as many as five or six such schools in San Francisco and thirty others across the state. The California assembly's Un-American Activities Committee heard testimony from San Francisco's chief of police that students who received such schooling in Fugazi Hall in the North Beach section of the city wore the uniform of the Balilla, the Italian Fascist youth club.[23]

John Molinari

There were Italians who had been vocal in support of Italy, people on the Italian radio, for example, who extolled Mussolini and the virtues of his accomplishments. Some of the most vocal...aliens were actually deported or at least placed in camps. I think the Italians at that time were sent to a camp in Montana—Ft. Missoula.

We had an Italian school in North Beach, which I attended as a boy. It was community supported, but the books and teachers were subsidized by the Italian government. All of us had to go whether we liked it or not; our parents wanted us to learn Italian. I could only speak the Genoese dialects. I did not know the official Italian language, which of course is the Florentine dialect. So our parents wanted us to go to Italian school, and we went there five days a week, from four to six P.M., after American school. When I attended, which was in the 1920s, there was no [Italian] government propaganda at all. We had innocuous textbooks, but very fine teachers. And whatever Italian I know to this day, I learned there. The school was not for propaganda. As far as I could tell, the monarchy was never interested in propagandizing its people in foreign countries. They were interested in preserving the language and the heritage. But I have no recollection of any of the teachers giving us any propaganda about what Italy was going to do militarily and so forth. They praised all of [Italy's] cultural attributes, and they had a right to do that.

*When Mussolini came to power, I was aware that school was begin-
ning to become an agency for propaganda. The students would march in
the Columbus Day parade, and they wore the Balilla uniform. It was a
uniform similar to that worn by Mussolini's youth organization known
as the Balilla. Balilla was a young Italian boy of Genoese descent who,
according to history, threw a rock at a French general when Napoleon
occupied Genoa, starting a riot that resulted in the expulsion of the
French. Balilla was always considered a patriot, particularly for the
youth. And so Mussolini had this youth organization, which had a special kind of uniform with—I think it was a black shirt, much like the
others. I can remember these young students marching in the parade.
Whether they did it voluntarily or they were told to do it, I don't know.*

*There was a feeling in the community that the school was being
used to acquaint the students with Mussolini and his attributes. While I
had no relationship with the school, it was generally known that the
teachers who had been sent over were naturally sympathetic to their
own government. Of course, the school closed down when the war broke
out and Italy became an enemy of ours, and the school as such has never
been resumed. There are Italian schools in the community, but they're
operated by separate agencies that have no connection with the Italian
government.*

Did government officials ever tell you that they suspected these schools
of teaching Fascism?

*No. When I spoke to officials, I was unaware that they were concerned
about Italy ever being an enemy of ours until war was declared. That
took everybody by surprise, although I'm sure our government was concerned that Mussolini had gone to war on Hitler's side.*

*There was a segment...in the community that was vocally anti-
Mussolini. They just didn't like him. Some believed in democracy; some
may have been socialists. Who knows? And I'm sure that these people
were naming names of people who had praised Mussolini.*

*Some of them that I knew, for example, were veterans of World War 1
in Italy. They were our allies; they came here as young immigrants.
They couldn't join the American Legion, so they formed an organization
called the Italian Legion. From what I hear, some of them may have
gotten up at their meetings and extolled Mussolini. The result was that
most of them were taken on that first sweep, even those who had kept
their mouths shut. That organization really had no relationship with
Mussolini, except that they had served in World War 1 under the king.
They were our allies; they helped us win the war. But here again it*

shows you how things get distorted. When you think back to those days, everybody was scared. The authorities were scared. Everybody was act-ing with an abundance of caution.

During the war, I had an office in the North Beach district. At that time the area was practically 100 percent Italian. The FBI agents, whom I got to know fairly well, would use me as a contact. They'd come in: "Do you know So-and-So? Is he all right? Is he a danger?" Things like that, involving individuals. There were two agents from back east, two lawyers, who decided that I was at least somebody in the commu-nity who knew a lot of people, and apparently had checked on my back-ground and loyalty.

One day, one of the Italians that was a client of mine came in and said, "The FBI's been down to see me." He was president of a social group called the Balilla Social Club, named after the group I told you about. My father was a charter member. It had been formed in 1918 as just a group of Genoese Italians who had picnics, dances, and dinners. I used to go to the picnics as a boy, and it was just a nice social gather-ing. Well, being named Balilla, and this organization in Italy being named Balilla, the FBI got all excited. And so this guy, this client of mine, was afraid he was going to be deported or something. So I said, "When the FBI agent comes back, tell him to come up and see me." It turned out the agent was one of two men that I had known, both non-Genoese lawyers from the East Coast. I think they were either Neapoli-tan or from southern Italy. So they probably wouldn't have heard of Balilla until this thing came along. I explained to them that Balilla was formed before Mussolini ever came on the scene. We were the first. We had the name before he adopted it. I told them the story about Balilla, what a patriot he was and so on, and that was the end of that story. But it just shows you. They were doing their job.

There was an Un-American Activities Committee in Sacramento, and a few people in our community were summoned before it. Here again, people had reported to the committee that So-and-So was not loyal be-cause he had said some nice things about Mussolini. Even before that committee got curious, there were some people in the community that were really maligned because of some Italian connection. You have to remember that at the time I grew up most of the first generation Italians whose parents were born in Italy had a strong affinity for Italy. My father had served three years of compulsory military service in the Ital-ian army under the king. And he was always proud of his service. So the first generation of Italians was kind of a bridge generation, and they'd heard all these wonderful things about Italy. Some of them may have said, "I think Mussolini's doing a good job. He got the trains running on time." I think everybody in the community soured on him when the Ethiopian thing came along. But before that, I think there was the feeling that maybe this fellow was doing something for the country. Of course, the biggest mistake he made was to align himself with Hitler. Until that time I think you could generally say that the Italians thought he was doing a good job for Italy. I think he did a lot of things internally that were good for the country. So people would only hear about those things, and they weren't too concerned about his political alignments with other nations, but they were aware of those alignments.

The Italians were smarting a bit in that they thought they got a bad deal after World War I under the Versailles Treaty. And they thought that Italy didn't get what it deserved as one of the victors. So Mussolini sold that concept. Italians here said, "We think he's right. Look, we lost all of these people and we didn't get anything but Trieste or something." So you could see that that feeling was there, that there was some belief that the Italian cause had some merit. Some of these people may have spoken favorably about Mussolini, and I could hear, I remember some of them saying, "He's telling Great Britain off. Nobody else did before him. But he's telling them off. The king didn't do it, but he's doing it." Anything that would put Italy in a better light among nations they supported.

Apparently Mayor Angelo Rossi was accused of being a Fascist?

I remember that occasion because I was active in politics. That was the most ridiculous thing, because Angelo Rossi was already a first- or second-generation Italian, born in the mother lode area [Sierra gold rush country]. *He came down to San Francisco, couldn't speak a word of Italian, had never been to Italy, was from an area where there was an Italian community, but not as vocal about things Italian as they were here. The only thing Italian about him was his name, really. To my recollection, he never took part in Italian community affairs. He was appointed a supervisor because he was a downtown businessman, and when Mayor* [James] *Rolph was elected governor, Rossi was appointed by the Board of Supervisors as mayor. He had taken a trip to Italy when he was mayor, and they published a picture of him in* Time *or one of the literary digests, I forget, with his hand outstretched. And they made a lot out of it, that he was un-American. It turned out that he was on this liner going to Italy and he was pointing at the Statue of Liberty. But the way the picture was taken, he had his hand so that it looked like a Fascist salute. He was maligned for awhile, but some of these things were political. Some people just didn't like anyone else, and began to exploit the situation.*

Ettore Patrizi was the editor of L'Italia, *one of those earlier newspapers. He was pretty vocal in favor of Mussolini. And, of course, he was asked to leave. Here again, he was an Italophile and probably believed that Mussolini was a great man. My generation all read the American dailies, but my folks, of course, subscribed to* L'Italia. *They liked it, and a lot of Italians in the outlying areas were subscribers. I'm sure there was some propaganda in those papers, at least until the Ethiopian campaign. Again, I remember Italians who thought, "Well, England didn't give us what we wanted as far as colonies are concerned, so we have the right to go out and get one." Mussolini was trying to convert Libya to an agricultural country, and he was sitting on all that oil and never knew it. His whole orientation was agriculture; it never crossed his mind, apparently, that Italy could be the industrial nation that it is today. I remember that his theory was that it was a burgeoning population that Italy had, and you needed places to send them to. Colonies, that was his theory.*

I remember going to Italy during Mussolini's time. I was a college student, and my father took the family back for a trip, his first after thirty years. I remember the trains running on time, the black shirts, and a lot of rigid controls. Black-shirted militiamen would accompany the ticket collector on the train. You had to show your ticket to get out of the station, not just to get in. I personally was not bothered. I was a tourist.

Mussolini was one of the great public speakers of our time. The crowds loved him. As a matter of fact, some of his speeches have been incorporated in books containing the outstanding speeches of all time. He had a facility of immediately getting control of a crowd. And they'd listen to him, and, of course, he told them what they wanted to hear. I remember one of his speeches. He took it right out of Shakespeare's "Mark Antony." He said, "Friends, brothers, listen to me." Those were his first three words. He called me a brother. If you study him from the aspect of a speaker who wants to communicate a message, and at the same time get people to listen, I guess he was good at it. And so people would praise him here for his speeches. "Look at that guy. He's telling England off."

ITALY'S INFORMAL APPROACH to its American cousins, first put forward by cultural societies and consulates, was soon eclipsed by the more blatant propaganda controlled by the Ministry of Popular Culture. Because Italian Americans wanted to believe in Mussolini and his regime, the new program enjoyed some success until 1935. Then, several events heralded the period of withdrawal: the visit of Piero Parini, Director General of the Italian Fasci Abroad, which galvanized anti-Fascists in the United States; the House of Representatives Un-American Activities Committee (HUAC) investigation of the Fascist threat; and disgust among non-Italians in the United States with Italy's invasion of Ethiopia. But for many Italian Americans the Ethiopian War was cathartic, and they reacted positively for the same reason they liked Mussolini: they were tired of humiliation. Parish priests blessed the steel rings that Mussolini exchanged for gold wedding bands sent to him by Italian Americans to help the war effort.[24]

Benito Vanni,
Daly City, California

My dad came over two or three times, the last time in 1928. I was born in '29. He lived in North Beach. His name was Ermete Vanni. He was born in Cardozo in the Provincia de Lucca in 1899. He was a member of the Regimento Alpini, which is the equivalent of the Green Berets here in the United States. Those were the Italian Alp climbers. They packed guns, everything, up the cliffs of the Alps. He was decorated. When he came over here he belonged to the Ex-Combattenti (World War I veterans), a lodge for all those who had served in the military in Italy. He was pro-Fascist, 150 percent! He loved Mussolini; he loved Mussolini very much.

In 1939, Mussolini was asking for gold, for people to send their gold rings over to Italy, and in return, he sent back a steel band. Naturally, after wearing a "steel" ring for a while, your finger'd turn green. [laughs]

They had their Columbus Day parades too. Dad dressed up in his Italian uniform with the sash. The uniforms were kind of tan, tan or beige. And they had those high boots where your pants tucked in, and the Italian march step. North Beach had a lot of Italians that belonged to the Ex-Combattenti, all ex-military people. He was also an officer in the Figlii d'Italia, the Sons of Italy. I remember seeing one of his membership cards.

He didn't get his citizenship papers until after he got out of the concentration camp. It was just that his heritage was Italian; he was an old fashioned dago, let's put it that way. He figured Mussolini had no choice but to be hooked up with Hitler. Germany and Italy were next door to each other, so it was easier to be hooked up with them than with America, 'cause, hey, Hitler, he'd run all over 'em; he'd kill 'em all. But he was all for Italy; he wasn't really for Hitler and the German army. When he came over here, he was 100 percent Italian and American second. He was happy to be here, but he was still an Italian at heart.

WALK THROUGH ANY Italian community in the country, one contemporary observer proposed. You will see Mussolini's picture everywhere. You will hear that Fascism made Italy great. You will learn that most Italian Americans of local or national importance have to be pro-Fascist.[25] Thus, the California legislature's Joint Fact-Finding Committee, looking into so-called un-American activities in the state, described Fascist activities in San Francisco as "intense."[26]

Albert Mangiapane,
Monterey

What did you think about Mussolini before the war?

Before the war, he straightened up a lot of things. There were too many gangs and dope, like the United States today. After Mussolini, everybody could sleep with his door open. To me he was all right. He tried to help all Italians to have jobs and a better life. You talk to any Italian. He will tell you that Mussolini was a good man. But when he went to war, he ruined everything.

Jennie Maffia

How did your parents feel about Italy?

They were very angry at Mussolini and the castor oil treatment and all that stuff. The castor oil treatment—didn't you hear about that? If they interrogated you, and you wouldn't talk, they dosed you with castor oil. The feeling here ran against Mussolini. This was their country now. They found it a heck of a lot better here than in Italy. Yet, when my husband and I have been in Europe and visited family and friends in Italy, they say that Mussolini did a lot of bad things, which he did, but he also did a lot of good things for the country. Italy's always been known for going wrong, for God's sake. I always joke about this.

Dominic Banducci

There was a lot of furor about Mussolini. Some of the Italians expressed favoritism toward him, how he did a great job for Italy by keeping the railroads running on time, and that he wasn't such a bad guy for the country. Then the rest of them said, "Keep your mouth shut or we're all going to find ourselves in a concentration camp." They worried about my aunt's house—where the families gathered—being bugged, or somebody being a plant from the FBI or the government. Someone said, "sta setto! (Shut up!) If you keep talking about Mussolini we're all going to find ourselves in jail." You know how quiet Italian wives are? Gee, they used to get mad, and they said, "If you mention this word again you can never come here at night again to have coffee or anything else. I don't want you in the house if you're going to mention Mussolini's name."

Gino Massagli,
Eureka

In 1936 or '37, when Mussolini was really in power, and he was going into Ethiopia, they sent a lot of propaganda films over here. I remember the old Rialto Theater. We used to go; all the guys used to go. I think I was a young Fascist there for awhile.

I was a very militant kid, very much so. The stirring martial music, the bands, and the old Fascist songs really got to me. I can still hum a few of them. While I was waiting to get in touch with a couple of buddies of mine, we were harassing the draft board. We knew we were going to get drafted. They said it'd be another month or so, so I went down to the longshoreman's hall. I'd just quit my job with my dad, but no one called me for work down at the hall, so I went down in the cargo hold of a ship anyway. While I worked, I sang an old, Italian victory song from Ethiopia. And here comes this nice, young, strapping, clean-cut fellow, first time I ever saw the man. He worked right alongside me. Finally he said, "Gino, you know you shouldn't sing those kind of songs. You know our countries are at war." How in the hell he recognized that song God only knows. I said, "Oh hell, I'm just doing it in time with moving the lumber." That was all; I never saw him again. I think it was an FBI check on me. He must have been trained to recognize that song somewhere. He knew it immediately. I didn't do it anymore. Once our country was attacked, there was no more Fascist in me.

Don Rafaelli

What did your parents say about Mussolini?

Well, they made the typical jokes about the trains running on time, which they still do. And after being subjected to American transportation systems, you'll appreciate the European ones. But Mussolini was one of the reasons that my dad got out of there. He did not appreciate the Fascist style of government. Both of my parents' families had people living away from Italy. My mother came to the United States and her brother emigrated to Argentina to escape the Fascists.

My mother has never said much of anything one way or the other, except that Mussolini "wasn't good for Italy." Her family had a disastrous experience as a result of Mussolini's alliance with Hitler: the Germans shot her brother-in-law in a reprisal execution.

My dad definitely spoke out against him. I think that's one of the reasons why he tried to assimilate so readily into the American community. They both had really severed their ties. If they felt anything positive, it was that Mussolini had stabilized certain things.

The negative thing about Mussolini was that he was building a military state. His philosophy was not to my parents' liking; it was contrary to basic Catholic teaching. His marching and his invasion of Ethiopia didn't sit well with my dad. Obviously, my uncle on my mother's side, who emigrated to Argentina, wanted no part of it either.

CLEARLY, THERE WAS an Italian American flirtation with Fascism, or more accurately, with Mussolini. But when Il Duce bound Italy militarily to Hitler by way of the "Pact of Steel" in May 1939, Italian Americans' attitudes toward Mussolini changed to repudiation virtually overnight. Most students of the Italians in America agree that despite the subversive intent of the Mussolini government against the United States, the community as a whole had given up on Fascism prior to 1940 when it became clear that Italian diplomacy was on a collision course with the United States. The immigrants had always approved of whatever regime or party happened to be in power in Italy, but put to the test after December 7, 1941, Italian American Fascism proved to be more sentiment than substance.

The Fascists among Italian Americans were never more than an "impotent minority" according to one authority. Following Pearl Harbor, *L'Italia*, published in San Francisco by Ettore Patrizi, and admittedly pro-Fascist, urged tolerance and understanding of the city's alien population and, in lieu of its usual commentary on the personalities of Mussolini and Hitler, devoted its war coverage to the Pacific. The father of federal judge Alfonso J. Zirpoli resigned from the Italian consulate in San Francisco in 1939 when he saw war coming. Between June 10, 1940, when Italy declared war on France, and December 7, 1941, Italian American sentiment hung suspended between the hope that the United States would stay out of the war and fear that they would have to fight their own families. First-generation Italians were not ready psychologically for the war, according to Paul Campisi's research in Illinois. Their first reactions were of anger, amazement, and shock at Pearl Harbor, then sorrow and pain: it was "impossible"; there was "no reason for it"; it had not happened.[27]

Alfonso Zirpoli,
San Francisco

Throughout the war, the Italians demonstrated tremendous allegiance to the United States. My father had been the secretary and acting Italian consul for over thirty-four years. In early 1939, he resigned; he saw the war coming. He anticipated that we would join the Allies against the Axis. The people in San Francisco, as far as Mussolini was concerned—well, this was quite an Italian community. You have to understand that, particularly during this period, the people in San Francisco thought that Il Duce was pretty good, that he was doing a lot of good work in Italy. So did the Hearst press. They ran article after article in the newspapers about Mussolini and the great work he was doing. The Pathé News flashed photos of Governor [Paul V.] McNutt of Illinois: "The American equivalent of the dictator, Mussolini, who's running an efficient state government!" Of course, when Mussolini joined up with Hitler, everything changed. The Italians were very unhappy, and throughout the war they contributed to the Red Cross and purchased savings bonds. They put on tremendous campaigns for such purposes.

My father had a cousin who was the official photographer for the House of Savoy and Mussolini. When he took photographs of them, he would send my father a copy. My mother had quite a collection of photos of the king and Mussolini and Hitler and all these people. When Pearl Harbor came she put them all in the stove and burned them. They would have been quite a treasure today. But she burned them all.

That's the way things were. Those were the reactions. As far as the war effort was concerned, I doubt if any group contributed to a greater degree than the Italians of this community. You have to bear in mind that the Italians, particularly in San Francisco and northern Califor-

nia, were really pioneers; they came over here as early as 1847. They built up quite a community of second-generation Italians, particularly in the mother lode country and in San Francisco. Take the year 1920. If you walked up Columbus Avenue, you'd hear Italian spoken. Rarely would you hear anyone speak English. I remember being behind two men who were arguing, and finally one of 'em turned to his friend and said, "You goddamna righta!" So that was the English. It eventually came out.

Lily Boemker,
McKinleyville, California

When I came home from school, where we were taught the events that were going on in Italy, I would try to explain to my father about Mussolini, what he was doing. Our views were so different, though. My dad, he was a true Italian. We would go 'round and 'round about Mussolini: he "did a lot of good," and so forth. That's all he could see, what Mussolini did. We wouldn't argue, but we had misunderstandings. It got so that when I'd walk in from school I'd say to my dad, "Viva Italia!" You know how Mussolini would say, "Viva Italia!"? Oh, dad would hit the ceiling. He spoke from the heart, though. He was quite a fella. And my mother—she studied that Constitution. She could give you every page, just like that. She itemized everything; she was so proud.

How did your father react to that?

He just overlooked it. He said, "If you want to do it, you go ahead."

Did he react when Italy declared war on the United States?

Oh, yes. At first, he felt the Americans deserved it. But then as time went on he could see the wrong that was coming out of it. He was a very kind man, a good man.

Marino Sichi,
Arcata

I remember my dad had one or two records of Mussolini making speeches. He kept them; he was for Italy, and, let's face it, the Italians were for Mussolini until he got mixed up with Hitler. We wanted no part of that. That's why the Italian army just deserted and laid down their arms by the thousands. That was my impression at the time, at least. The Italian people were proud of what Mussolini was doing for their nation. He was bringing them out of poverty; he had the trains running on time; he was modernizing the farms. For the first time in their lives the peasants had some tractors to work with, machinery. And they had something to eat besides a piece of bread and a slice of goat cheese. But dad took those records out in the back yard and smashed 'em into a million pieces and buried them. Now they'd be collectors' items.

Steve Antongiovanni

Most of the reactions about Mussolini from over the backyard fence were that he didn't have too much choice. In the First World War Italy was allied with England, and when it came to dividing the pie, Italy didn't get anything that was promised her. I remember the men saying that this time they had to go the other way because they certainly didn't get anything last time. And aside from any dividing of the spoils, Hitler would have marched right in and taken over Italy like he did the others. Mussolini was not looked at as a bad person because he did a lot of good things for the Italian population.

Families don't want to see their kids go to war no matter which side they're on. But as far as them wanting to defend Italy, there was none of that. The feeling here was that it was pretty dumb to tackle a nation of this size.

Joseph Maniscalco,
San Francisco

My father had great admiration for Mussolini. He idolized him, and that was one of the reasons why he became so irate when there was a war with Italy. We tried everything to dissuade him from saying nasty things about the government and becoming so emotional. He knew that we were citizens and he was not. There was a lot of personal hurt in that. And yet, as much as he respected Mussolini and Italy, he never wanted to go back to Italy, and he never did. We wanted him to go many times, to go and see his ancestors over there; he couldn't have cared less about Italy. They came over here when they were so young that they couldn't make any connection outside of maybe an older aunt, an older

*uncle, a relative who probably had died anyway. They had no corre-
spondence because my father and mother didn't know how to write.
Their relatives who were there didn't know how to write either. So how
could they possibly communicate? We children were too young to know
who they were in Sciacca, Sicily. So there was a complete severance of
any relationships.*

Was your father disappointed, angry when Italy declared war on the
United States? Did he blame Mussolini?

*He blamed Hitler. He listened to the news intently. And when television
came along, he watched that. He became a self-educated man. He was
able to rationalize that all these things were not personally against
Mussolini, because Mussolini had done an awful lot for the Italian people. He did a tremendous amount of reorganization of the country and
unification of the language; there were so many dialects. And there were
also numerous things he did for the economy of the country. It was unfortunate; he just got involved with the wrong man. When [my father]
saw that the Italian people were very deeply offended by Mussolini's
actions and his ignominious death, he began to realize that Mussolini
did make a big mistake, and felt very pro-American, even more pro-
American than before. He loved America; he loved the country; he loved
the area. To him, Italy was North Beach. It was, to him, his own
world. He had so many friends and relatives.*

HOW REALISTIC WAS the threat of a Fascist Fifth Column in the
United States and how seriously was it taken? Italian propaganda broadcasts directed at New York's and Boston's Italian neighborhoods, the
Italian American press, the HUAC investigation, and the efforts of the
Mussolini government to establish Fascist organizations in the United
States in the 1920s aroused some suspicion. And an article in *Harper's*
magazine by Marcus Duffield in November 1929, alleging that Mussolini could turn Italian Americans into soldiers and saboteurs overnight,
sparked an investigation by Secretary of State Henry L. Stimson, But he
told Congress that much of the article was mistaken.[28]

One of the principle concerns of anti-Fascists was the popularity of
the foreign-language media; not the German American press, which for
the most part steered clear of Germany's politics, but Italian American
journalists whose "politically impassioned newspapers" were an important source of ethnic solidarity. The Italians took to Fascist propaganda,
according to historian John Diggins, with "ravenous gusto." It did not
occur to non-Italians that, for a largely unassimilated and illiterate immi-

grant audience, Italian radio broadcasts were a major source of information, if nothing else.[29]

Even before December 1941, the existence of a Japanese media had frightened Californians. But if the number of foreign-language publications is the standard by which to measure the danger posed by aliens in general, the Italian and German threat far outdistanced that of the Japanese. Of more than one thousand such publications in the United States in 1937, only nineteen were Japanese-run (eighteen other immigrant groups published more newspapers and magazines than the Japanese), and the two most prolific publishers were the Germans (197) and the Italians (135).[30]

Anti-Fascist sources claimed that in 1940 all but a few of the German-language dailies and weeklies (178) gave favorable treatment to the Nazis, and that 80 percent of the 120 Italian-language periodicals were pro-Fascist. *Fortune* magazine, however, listed only about a dozen German papers as being pro-Nazi in 1940. Another survey taken in 1942 estimated that at least one-fifth of the German-language press still displayed a divided loyalty and attempted to skirt war issues. The most strident of the anti-Nazi papers was *Neue Volks Zeitung*, published in New York City primarily for educated workingmen, among whom it was estimated there were about 10,000 readers. The paper repeatedly identified its prime suspects as "Nazis who hide behind citizenship" and those who claim diplomatic immunity. Most editors of the Italian American press believed that Italians could be for Italian Fascism (meaning Italy) and American democracy at the same time.[31]

Because the pro-Mussolini slant of the Italian American press during the Ethiopian crisis raised some doubt about the loyalty of Italian Americans, *Fortune* magazine urged that friendly Italians and Germans—handicapped by the superior financial resources of the totalitarian governments—be set up with their own radio stations and newspapers. The alternative, warned *Fortune*, was the likely alienation of the loyalty of millions of immigrants and "good citizens": "There is dynamite on our shores and we should explode it in the right direction." Carmelo Zito, the anti-Fascist editor of *Il Corriere Del Popolo*, told the California Un-American Activities Committee in 1942 that radio broadcasts heard in California were still tinged with Fascism: "It's not the fault of the Italian people of California if they go around saying 'Roberto will win the war.' What do I mean by this Roberto? Why, just take it apart: Ro for Rome, ber for Berlin, and to for Tokyo."[32]

President Franklin Roosevelt worried about what he called "seditious and subversive" newspapers, although he also had in mind publishers like Detroit's radio priest Father Charles Coughlin, R. R. McCormick

(Chicago *Tribune*), and Eleanor "Cissy" Patterson (Washington *Times-Herald*). Secretary of the Interior Harold Ickes, who thought Attorney General Francis Biddle a "dilettante" when it came to subversion, began a campaign in the fall of 1940 to create an anti-Fascist propaganda agency or newspaper, or both, to counter the effects on Italian Americans of the pro-Fascist papers. He was aided by a number of luminaries: Assistant Secretary of War, John J. McCloy, Jr., who wanted to get into the war against the Germans personally; Carlo Sforza, the most prominent anti-Fascist refugee in the United States; Roosevelt's assistant, "Tommy" Corcoran; by the attorney general; and Californians Ernest Cuneo, Divo Gentili, and banker A.P. Giannini. Most of this came to naught, but FDR did promise to send Fiorello LaGuardia to North Africa in 1942 to "soften up" Italy with a propaganda barrage and then allow him to cross the Mediterranean with the invasion forces. LaGuardia lobbied the president heavily to get into combat, but Roosevelt told him he was "too old and too fat" to do the kind of flying he had done in World War I. The president, according to Ickes, also wanted to make Sforza the "Provisional Chief of State of Italy in North Africa."[33]

Contemporary estimates of membership in pro- and anti-Fascist organizations in the United States are suspect; each side's figures buttressed its ideological point of view. For example, the anti-Fascist *Fortune* reported in 1940 that Mussolini could muster twenty-five thousand Fascists in the United States in case of war, many of them naturalized citizens, plus 100,000 "fellow travelers." The magazine further asserted that the overwhelming majority of the five million Americans of Italian ancestry were more or less sympathetic to Fascism and Italian American Fascists were numerically stronger and better organized than the Nazis. The magazine estimated anti-Fascist forces at 100,000. Carlo Sforza, one of the best known anti-Fascists in the United States, told President Roosevelt—obviously hoping to spur the president into action—that Italian Americans were predominantly pro-Fascist. But Carmelo Zito told NBC news in June 1940 that in California 75 percent of Italian Americans were anti-Fascist, 15 percent had no interest, and only 10 percent remained steadfastly pro-Fascist despite Mussolini's alliance with Hitler. Another analysis of the potential threat posed by Fascist sympathizers in the United States appeared in *Foreign Affairs* in 1937. Italian Fascist organizations were not an immediate threat to American security, the writer opined, but they exercised a much stronger influence than the Nazis: "The solidarity of the Italian groups in large American cities and their resistance to the melting pot process undoubtedly provide a favorable field for Fascist propaganda." James H. Rowe, Jr., an assistant to Attorney General Francis Biddle in 1942, believed that unnaturalized aliens had in some measure retained their devotion to the fatherland and were the most obvious targets of enemy propaganda. Most of those who had investigated right-wing movements in the United States before World War II agreed with Rowe.[34]

WHAT ABOUT THE American Nazis? Nationally, estimates of peak membership in the German American Bund range between twenty thousand and twenty-five thousand, with steady growth in the 1930s. In California, there were locals in Los Angeles, Oakland, Petaluma, San Diego, San Francisco, the San Gabriel Valley, and Santa Barbara. The Bund appealed to the least assimilated Germans: two-thirds of its members were aliens and the remainder naturalized citizens. An alleged Communist party spokesman by the name of Bert Leesh told the state Un-American Activities Committee that an exhaustive report by the CIO central council concerning the employment of known Bundists in defense plants in San Diego had been ignored. There were other reports that San Diego was a hub of Bundist activity. A contemporary study estimated that there were 118 Bundists in Los Angeles in 1934, and about 100 in San Francisco. More recently, another historian characterizes the pro-German element as a loud, lunatic fringe of Germans in America.[35]

A boisterous and crazy minority, maybe; but the anti-Fascists and anti-Nazis were so successful in branding a majority of Italian and German Americans as disloyal that the government did not feel it could sit idly by as the war clouds gathered. Congress, fearful that alien propagandists were undermining democracy, passed an alien registration act in the spring of 1940, which FDR signed into law in June. Three million aliens would be re-registered and fingerprinted before the end of the year.[36]

But if Italian Americans stood accused of harboring pro-Fascist sentiments, what is to be said of the American government, which accepted the rise of Fascism in Italy for several years with an air of nonchalance? Official American policy toward Mussolini and Fascism in the 1920s was friendly and hopeful. Throughout the 1920s and up to the Ethiopian war, Republican and Democratic administrations shared four assumptions about Mussolini: he was bringing economic and social progress to his people; he was a dictator but popular; he might moderate Hitler's behavior; and therefore, he was good for Italy and the United States.[37]

In fact, most non-Italian American citizens initially admired Mussolini. He was that rare breed of politician, a charismatic leader with a program. To middle-class property owners in the United States he was a savior of capitalism in a world struggling against communist revolution. His contempt for the League of Nations drew the applause of those who rejected Wilsonian idealism. Former progressive reformers and Protestant fundamentalists approved of his attacks on materialism and his anti-clericalism. And Mussolini's brand of Fascism appealed as well to those in the United States whose disillusionment with democracy was nearly total in the 1920s and 30s. In the rush of events after June 1940, it was conveniently forgotten that the Fascist disease "had been a national phenomenon rather than an ethnic importation."[38]

Of no small concern to President Roosevelt and his political advisors, however, was their sense that Italian electoral districts, particularly in New York, were "wild" about Mussolini. After FDR's June 1940 "dagger in the back speech" condemning Mussolini's declaration of war on France, Italian American voters in New York, San Francisco, Philadelphia and elsewhere tilted toward Wendell Willkie's candidacy. Harold Ickes was very much taken with Carlo Sforza's view that Willkie was an "unconscious Fascist" and that something needed to be done to stop Italian Americans from gravitating toward the Republicans. Sforza tried to warn Roosevelt that, despite anything the president might have heard, Italian Americans were pro-Fascist and anti-FDR.[39]

American attitudes toward the people of Italy mellowed in 1940 when it appeared that Italians did not share their government's infatuation with Nazi Germany. John Diggins believes that by 1940 almost all Americans were prepared to accept Italians—if not Italian Americans—as allies in the struggle against Fascism. But native-born Americans were not sympathetic to political refugees from Fascist countries. A poll conducted by *Fortune* in July 1938—the same year that the United States sponsored a refugee conference in Evian, France—revealed that more than two-thirds of Americans preferred to keep the refugees out of the country altogether. Only 18 percent would tolerate unrestricted refugee immigration, and 5 percent wanted to encourage them to come but under stricter immigration quotas. The rest had no opinion. In the lingering Depression, Americans were worried about their jobs but also the threat of a Fifth Column.[40]

Events in Europe leading up to the collapse of the West in June 1940 predisposed Americans to believe in a Fifth Column. But historian Bradley Smith, who has exhaustively studied this threat to the western democracies, comes to a number of startling conclusions about its reality. In the Low Countries in 1940, "the [F]ifth [C]olumn reports were virtually all fantasies," he says. Furthermore, in Britain there was "no trace of evidence" in 1940 of an organized German Fifth Column of aliens, refugees, or anyone else. And in the United States in the summer of 1940, there was no German Fifth Column or any danger of an imminent attack on the Western Hemisphere.[41]

The selling of the Fifth Column idea in the United States got a substantial boost from William ("Wild Bill") Donovan (soon to head the newly created Office of Strategic Services) and Edgar Mowrer, a journalist posted to London and later associated with the OSS. Together the two men produced a series of syndicated articles that were later published as a pamphlet, "Fifth Column Lessons for America." The German colony of several million in the United States, Donovan and Mowrer warned, would happily work with the Gestapo when war came. Donovan and Mowrer's thesis was one that would have a parallel in the postwar years, when the Soviet Union became the new bogeyman: domestic enemies were responsible for the German (later Soviet) victories.[42]

Harold Ickes was convinced that Nazi agents and Nazi organizations were preparing to overthrow the U.S. government as they had those in Belgium and France. He and others in the Cabinet thought that Nazis "inside the government" were more of a threat to the country similarly placed Communists.[43]

Howard Williams

Did anyone believe that Italian aliens were saboteurs?

No, it was just a suspicion. The Italians were so engrossed in this community, and had such widespread friendships that nobody was really concerned about them. But we had real fear of a possible invasion here. We had gun emplacements out on the beach and cavalry units stationed at Samoa patrolling the beaches twenty-four hours a day. The old Washington School, now the Senior Citizens Center in Eureka, housed an army unit. So there was a lot of worry around here then.

When you stop to think about it, though, it's kind of ridiculous. The easiest way to gain access to the waterfront, if they wanted to sabotage anything on the waterfront, would have been to become naturalized citizens and go down and blow up a ship.

IN MAY 1941, HUAC interviewed Richard Krebs—a reformed Comintern (Communist International) agent, a veteran of Nazi prisons, and author under a pen name of *Out of the Night*—describe Nazi espionage techniques in the United States. According to Krebs, Nazi agents in the United States were disguised as political refugees or were those who had families back in Germany held hostage to their cooperation. Anyone released from a Nazi concentration camp, he stated categorically, must pledge to work for the Gestapo.[44] This, apparently, became the catalyst for repression. The roundup of alien enemies in the United States began.

The first to be arrested, detained, or interned were the crews of Italian and German merchantmen charged with violating the Immigration Act of 1924 by remaining in the United States after their ships had departed. In another incident involving merchantmen, the State Department sent the Italian Naval Attaché packing, persona non grata, when it learned from a crew that the attaché had instructed them to cripple the engines of their ships in American harbors. The FBI cracked this case by holding the crewmen incommunicado until they confessed. Another version of how the government uncovered this plot is related by journalist David Brinkley in his best seller, *Washington Goes to War*. It seems the Italian attaché, Alberto Lais, was the happy victim of British super spy William Stephenson, who sent his American agent, the attractive Amy Thorpe (code named "Cynthia"), to solicit the information from Lais—horizontally. But the attractive pawn succeeded only in part; most of the twenty-seven vessels were blown up.[45]

Crewmen from the German merchantman, *S.S. Columbus* had already been sent to Angel Island in San Francisco Bay in December 1939 (minus five who escaped en route from New Jersey). They remained there for about a year before being shipped to Ft. Stanton, New Mexico. While on Angel Island, they were frequently permitted shore leave in San Francisco, which gave the natives the jitters. Perhaps they were afraid the crewmen would be enlisted in the service of the Nazi Consul General, Fritz Wiedemann, who reportedly moved his consular offices from their downtown location to a three-story, thirty-room brownstone mansion at 2090 Jackson Street in Pacific Heights. There, reported a neighbor, Wiedemann kept an eye on "everything that [went] on in the Golden Gate" with a six-inch telescope.[46] Before German conduct abroad made his presence a liability, however, Wiedemann had been a hit among the city's swells. The *Chronicle*'s durable society anecdotalist, Herb Caen, already writing for the paper at the time of Wiedemann's tour of duty in San Francisco, remembers "Dashing Fritz" as something akin to a "movie Nazi, wearing long leather coats and driving around in a glittering Mercedes roadster." He also belonged to the exclusive Olympic Club. Caen reports that when 165 Olympians threatened to give up their memberships (a hoax as it turned out) unless Wiedemann resigned, the club's directors "apologized abjectly."[47]

In May 1941, immigration officials, acting under the orders of Attorney General Robert Jackson, interned 70 Italian waiters who had been brought to the United States to work in the Italian pavilion at the New York World's Fair in 1939. Having overstayed the thirty-day grace period after the pavilion's closing, they were legally deportable. This was part of a nationwide roundup of illegal Axis aliens under the attorney general's supervision, an action that eventually netted 114 additional Italians at the World's Fair, arrested while celebrating the fifth anniversary of the Ethiopian conquest on May 9. Nothing, if not cocksure, Jackson announced that "the secret weapon of the Nazis has been the failure of nation after nation to recognize and deal with...non-military invasion."[48]

One alien who worked at the Italian pavilion in New York escaped the attention of authorities for more than a year after the fair closed:

Alfredo Cipolato,
Missoula, Montana

Originally, I'm from Venice. As a young man, I worked in Libya at a hotel owned by the Italian government. My brother who was in Libya at the same time had arranged to work at the World's Fair in New York City in 1940, but when he was unable to go I came in his place. I arrived in New York on April 25th, and went to work in the restaurant at the Italian Pavilion. Just a few months later Italy joined Germany in the war. When the Pavilion closed in October, I went to Miami, Florida, to work at the Roney Plaza Hotel, and it was there that I was arrested by the FBI one afternoon in July 1941. They wouldn't even let me change out of my shorts and T-shirt because, as they said, "I would be gone for only a short while...." Some of the other prisoners in that Miami jail tried to shake me down for money, but I only had thirty-five cents, so they made me shine the prison bars and sing Italian songs every day.

ONCE THE WAR started, the pressure to fight Fifth Columnists intensified. A federal judge in California implored newly sworn citizens to watch out for subversive activities among their former countrymen and to report them to the government: "Be on the alert, because in a democracy like ours we breed what is known as the [F]ifth [C]olumn. Our doors have been thrown open in the past to all kinds of people. Some of them now seek to harm us."[49] Perhaps some of those new citizens, whose faith in America had led them—with some difficulty—to the courtroom that day, could have given the judge a lesson in civics, rather than the other way around.

It is deceptively easy—with the advantage of hindsight—to make light of the threat posed by American Fascists, Nazis, and their sympathizers before Pearl Harbor. But history cares not whether the danger was real, only that Americans in 1940 believed that it was. There may have been no militant, organized Fifth Column, but the existence of ethnic

ghettos and the reluctance of Italian Americans to denounce Mussolini
and Fascism—until Il Duce made his bargain with Hitler and Italy joined
the Fuhrer's war—heightened native Americans' suspicions. Then,
spurred by the popular press, ignorant of the sentimental ties within hy-
phenate American communities, duped by the Fascists' propaganda, and
possessing little faith in the power of their own ideology, it became the
turn of the politicians and the military to treat the threat as genuine.

Mr. and Mrs. Lorenzo Maniscalco, San Francisco, ca. 1905.

Zelindo and Elena Picchi, the parents of Lily Boemker, Arcata, California, 1947.

Frances (Chicha) Trezza, Pittsburg, California, ca. 1942.

Albert Mangiapane, Monterey, California, ca. 1943–44.

Pete Maiorana, a change of clothes in the sack over his shoulder, heads for his boat, *Diana*, on Fisherman's Wharf, Monterey, California, 1940.

Pietro (Pete) and Giuseppa Maiorana, the parents of Anita Ferrante, Monterey, California, 1946.

Steve Antongiovanni (*left*) with his parents, Celide and Paul, Scotia, California, ca. 1944–46.

Angelo Vanni, Arcata, California, 1982.

Ida Ghera (*right*), the mother of Ernesta Dunn, with her daughter, Marie (*left*), and niece, Elizabeth, Eureka, California, ca. 1940.

THREE

"We can't fool around"
The Order to Evacuate

This matter of evacuating the Japanese and other enemy aliens is only one of the things we have to be tough about. To see this war through, we shall have to take on, in many directions right here at home, a degree of toughness that subordinates everything to victory. If we do not, we shall have masters who will be tough.
—*San Francisco Chronicle*, March 1942

IRONICALLY, JUST AFTER the attack on Pearl Harbor, when the United States was most vulnerable, there was no hurry to rid California of its enemy aliens. Not until the hastily convened Roberts Commission (named for Supreme Court Justice Owen J. Roberts, its head) released its report nearly two months later—hinting that Japanese Americans on Oahu had aided Japan's air assault—did the cry to do something about Axis aliens on the mainland commence in earnest.[50] And from the start, nearly everyone who had an opinion on the subject of alien restrictions wanted the Italian and German aliens treated exactly like the Japanese.

As political temperatures in California rose, the federal government escalated its policy of restrictions on enemy aliens. There were four critical dates: December 7, 1941, Pearl Harbor; January 25, 1942, the commission's report; January 29, when the Justice Department issued its first enemy alien relocation order; and February 19, Executive Order 9066, which authorized the army to exclude *anyone* from restricted zones along the West Coast.

To Californians reading their newspapers in those first desperate days, weeks, and months of the war, it was obvious that the United States was not winning. Thus, the political pressure that drove alien policy paralleled the bad news from the Pacific, culminating in the surrender of Bataan and Corregidor in April 1942. In the confusion, desperation, and panic, the politicians were extended an unlimited mandate to act. Resolutions from citizens, city councils, chambers of commerce, boards of supervisors, Congress, and law enforcement officials urging swift action were stacked higher and higher each day on the desks of responsible officials, including the president's. Probably no politician could have resisted. It made no difference that not a single case of Fifth Column activity on the West Coast could be documented, even in December and January when any competent sabotage plan might reasonably have been expected.

The *San Francisco Chronicle* typified California's earliest press reaction to the sudden attack on Hawaii, warning its readers to be on the lookout for "witch smellers"—letter writers proposing "witless" forms of torment for the Italians and Germans. "Persecution of innocents won't win the war," lectured the *Chronicle*. "It comes down to a question [of] whether we are going to act as civilized Americans or as barbarians." A month later, just before the release of the Roberts Commission report, the *Chronicle*, still upholding "civilization," told the assembly's Un-American Activities Committee to keep its bloodhounds away from the aliens. Early on, the nationally syndicated columnist, Dorothy Thompson, identified the "monstrous [F]ifth [C]olumn" in the United States not as enemy aliens, but rather those who accused others of disloyalty in order to camouflage their own unwillingness to aid Britain and the Soviet Union. But just two months later, in a remarkable turnabout, Thompson trumpeted the reality of a "vast" pro-Fascist network along the West Coast, working in collaboration with the Japanese. "When will this country wake up and make war on its enemies right here?" she demanded to know.[51]

In December 1941, Washington officials reportedly believed that Fifth Columnists had already contacted enemy forces, who were in turn using the information given them to prey on West Coast shipping. It mattered not to a San Diego man that the FBI later showed these reports groundless.[52] C.K. Schoell wrote to Rep. John Tolan of Oakland:

> We *one & all* would like to see precious Time Saved, & potential danger removed by migrating the aliens *one & all* to Interior Concentrations Camps, Pronto. We Americans could lose this war by continuing to be soft-hearted and soft-headed about American born Japs in particular, but Germans and Italians also.... This is no time to try to weed out the sheep from the goats.... FEAR is creeping more & more into the hearts of people we contact. So let our govt. do something, definite, & now.[53]

The governor of California, Culbert Olson, agreed. Two days after the release of the Roberts Commission report he told General DeWitt that federal action was imperative. If nothing was done, Olson predicted, "the people may take things in their own hands." In Washington, Major Karl

R. Bendetsen, then working in the office of Provost Marshal General Allen W. Gullion, told DeWitt on January 29 that the California congressional delegation was "beginning to get up in arms" and had scheduled an informal meeting the next day to formulate resolutions. Bendetsen attended the meeting, where he expressed DeWitt's view that the army was willing to take control of the aliens from the Justice Department if DeWitt were assured that the army had the authority to force other agencies to cooperate. Subsequently, the congressmen unanimously approved a resolution calling for the evacuation and internment of *all* enemy aliens and dual citizens, regardless of the fact that their children may have been American-born.

This resolution, which the delegation sent to the War Department, did not refer specifically to the Japanese. The leader of the group, Rep. Clarence F. Lea of Santa Rosa, stated that evacuation would be only the first step; that ultimately all of the aliens would be humanely "resettled," initially in Civilian Conservation Corps (CCC) camps. Rep. Martin Dies (D-Tex), the chairman of HUAC, predicted that, "Unless the government adopts an alert attitude there will occur on the West Coast a tragedy that will make Pearl Harbor sink in significance." All of this suggests the truth of what Eric Bellquist, a professor at Berkeley, wrote in April 1942: "What must everlastingly be driven home is that the intolerance of native prejudices are just as much a part of subversive activity as Japanese sabotage, Nazi spies, and Communist intrigue."[54]

On January 29, the Justice Department announced that on the recommendation of the secretary of war, after consultation with General DeWitt, all enemy aliens would be required to vacate specified areas of the West Coast by February 24. For his part, Governor Olson swore he would revoke the aliens' business and professional licenses, keep them out of the food handling and liquor business, and kick them off the state's payroll. In the meantime, they would all have to apply for new identification cards. Attorney General Earl Warren eventually ruled against Olson's plan, due largely to the prestige of the Bank of America's Italian-born president, A.P. Giannini. By the 31st, Attorney General Biddle had named more areas programmed for evacuation by February 15.

Having now decided, on the basis of rumor alone, that the danger was more serious than in the days just after Pearl Harbor—and feeling a bit more "barbaric" than he had earlier—the editor of the *San Francisco Chronicle* crowed on January 31st:

America's long-ridiculed attitude of sweetness and light to enemy aliens has been blasted out of existence.... Hundreds of thousands of

Japanese, German, and Italian nationals...saw for the first time, the grim specter of concentration camps, mass evacuation of families, revocation of business licenses, doctors and dentists thrown out of work, a savage hunt to crush secret organizations.

An early February meeting between California Attorney General Earl Warren and law enforcement officials from across the state, convened for the purpose of using California's Alien Land Law to remove Japanese aliens from strategic areas, turned into a debate about what to do with the Italians and Germans. Contra Costa County's district attorney boasted that after finishing with the Japanese, "We are going after the Italians and Germans and do the same with them." A minority of delegates (one-eighth) felt that the group's formal resolution calling for the evacuation of Japanese aliens ought to apply to the European aliens as well. The San Diego County district attorney suggested ironically that more danger could be expected from the Italians and Germans than the Japanese: "You can always tell a Jap when you see one, but as for a German or an Italian, they can get by. They are the ones who are most difficult of the three to detect."[55]

The exchange continued. Attorney General Warren and others argued that the Alien Land Law could not be applied to the Italians and Germans because the "Japanese problem" was unique to California. But the district attorney of Stanislaus County countered, "When we go to recommend action to the Federal Government, I think we would be very glad to say it is the sense of this group that they ought to exclude every enemy alien, Japs and all the others from this area.... Our Alien Land Law is inadequate. We can tend to the Japs with it, but we cannot the Germans and Italians. I think it would be very reasonable to say they ought to remove all enemy aliens."[56] Still, a resolution favoring only the removal of Japanese aliens went forward to the secretary of war with the conferees' expectation that the federal government would eventually find a way of dealing with the Italians and Germans.

The mayor of Los Angeles, Fletcher Bowron, also harbored strong feelings about the potential threat posed by the Italians and Germans. In a radio address broadcast on station KECA on February 5, Bowron acknowledged that most Italians and Germans were loyal, but a few had come to the United States to spread Fascism and Nazism and had taken out naturalization papers to camouflage their treason. He proposed that such "agents" be identified by virtue of having remained citizens of Italy or Germany after 1933 (the year Adolf Hitler came to power), and that they be drafted into non-combat service. Not about to be out-bigoted by the mayor of Los Angeles, and offering no proof of its assertion, the *San*

Francisco Chronicle proclaimed that, "Some of the most savage enemies of America and liberty have come disguised as refugees from Hitler." Since there was no foolproof way to separate the guilty from the innocent, the editor simply hoped that "by the process of individual justice the mass injustice of an emergency war measure will be abated." But he admitted it would be "problematical."[57]

Local governments were among the first to act. Seventeen counties, along with the statewide County Supervisor's Association, urged alien evacuation in formal resolutions. The Los Angeles County board was the first to take the plunge on January 27. More than two-thirds of the relocation demands from California counties have been traced to a resolution circulated by the state association and first passed by Ventura County on February 20. Another motion before the Association recommending evacuation of non-Japanese enemy aliens was defeated. Assistant Secretary of War McCloy would shortly refer to the pressures emanating from local sources in California as "drastic" and "unintelligent."[58]

Mayor Fred J. Moore, Jr.
Eureka

I was appointed Humboldt County Clerk, July 3, 1940; war was declared December 7, 1941. Being county clerk, I was secretary of the Humboldt County Defense Council, which each county had during that period. The defense council consisted of the county department heads, representatives of services like fire and police, and the chairman of the board of supervisors. I was secretary of the council because the chairman of the board was a member, and during an emergency, the chairman would render proclamations on policy. Every one of those had to be written down and confirmed by a majority of the board.

Humboldt County had several colonies of Italian people. We had quite a "Little Italy" in Wildwood and Rio Dell out near Scotia [35 miles south of Eureka]. Italians are still there in business. We had quite a few Italian natives in Eureka; there were quite a few in Korbel [5 miles east of Arcata]. Most of them were laborers in the mills; some were commercial fishermen.

I don't think the evacuation order was very effective because I don't recall any order excluding the Italian natives who were not naturalized. I do remember that the Japanese were impounded, but I don't remember anything impounding the Italians.

I was raised in the Korbel area, and there were a lot of Italians in that community, many of whom moved to Eureka later. I don't remember any problems with the Italians at all; they were a part of our community and we accepted them. I don't even remember that there was a prohibited zone from the Mad River to the Eel River along highway 101. In Eureka there were a few houses between Wabash and Washington Streets, west of 101, and commercially through the city on 101—Fourth Street going south and Fifth going north. If they put everyone out north of Fourth Street—well, there aren't many residences in there. I don't think that the people who had to evacuate that so-called "critical" zone could have been very many. When you think about that area, heck, there's nothing down there. If anybody was under that kind of an order, they would have voluntarily got out before.

Do you recall any increase in FBI activity?

No citizen could be aware of what the FBI was doing. I do recall something, though. When the Volstead Act was adopted, the 18th amendment, prohibiting liquor, the Italian people in this region made some of the best vino grappa, "speakeasy" wine. Some of the Italians were recipients of what we called the "dry squad," which was some extra employees under the sheriff who made raids and closed down those illegal distilleries. I remember most of the people on it. We had quite a bit of activity of the dry squad. The board of supervisors challenged the sheriff in court for hiring these people and funding them. You see, the sheriff was cooperating with the DA's office. The DA, an ultra dry by the name of Arthur W. Hill, Sr., organized this dry squad and the supervisors denied him funds. He took the Board to court and won the case, so the county wound up having to pay for his dry squad. Principally, it was the Italians that received visits from the "dry squad" and had their holdings confiscated. So, as a nation and a people, that's the worst thing I can think of them doing.

The Italians were accepted in the community?

Sure, sure. No problems with the Italians.

Did the board of supervisors have any connection with the County Supervisor's Association of California?

Yes. Every board of supervisors in California is a member of that organization. I was affiliated with the County Clerk's Association of California. Each county office had its own association.

The County Supervisor's Association sent a resolution to federal and state officials recommending that "all alien Japanese and their descendants be evacuated and interned." Did the Humboldt County Board of Supervisors take a stand on that resolution?

Yes, I remember that. Quote: "There were no Japanese in this county." We cooperated with it fully, but there was no real effect here; there were no known Japanese here. People were extremely anti-Japanese because of Pearl Harbor.

Was the German situation different than the Italian? I read about a German man who committed suicide in Eureka because he couldn't get his naturalization papers in time.

What was his name?[59] The reason I ask is, because as I told you, I was the clerk of the superior court, and I handled naturalization and passport questions personally. So I'm very familiar with anybody filing an application for either first or second papers, and guiding people, about who was eligible. I was in the courtroom on naturalization days to swear in the new citizens. This German who killed himself probably couldn't acquire naturalization papers because he was a German, and had just come over. Possibly he had a certificate of lawful entry for permanent residence, but was ineligible for naturalization, as any citizen of Germany, Japan, or Italy would be.

UNLIKE MOORE, SOME county officials were worried about *all* the aliens. In Imperial County alien enemies were registered, fingerprinted, and prohibited from engaging in any way (except as laborers) in agricultural work. Supervisorial resolutions from Placer, Orange, and Yolo counties called for the removal of enemy aliens, including their descendants "who are loyal or may become disloyal." (No one suggested how authorities were to determine which descendants might become disloyal, or why.) San Buenaventura's city council proposed that all dangerous enemy aliens of any country be relocated 200 miles from the coast, while the Exeter, California council specified east of the Sierras. The urgency felt in San Benito County was even greater. There the chamber of commerce exhorted the army, navy, FBI, congressmen, Governor Olson, and Attorney General Biddle to "get all enemy alien citizens [whatever that meant] and Japanese-American citizens out of the entire Pacific Coast area." It was reported that in southern California "aroused" organizations were planning reprisals against enemy aliens. Tom Clark, working in the Justice Department's Antitrust Division, but sent to the coast by Biddle (at DeWitt's request) to coordinate alien policy with the general and California politicians, reported the situation in Los Angeles as being "pretty hot."[60]

This mounting wave of vigilantism struck state and federal authorities as a menace to their own, more "efficient," anti-sabotage efforts. The *Chronicle* sympathized with federal officials and, with no small touch of irony, called the localized alien hysteria "mostly imaginary." There must be no witch hunts like the last war produced, the editor counseled: "Government is taking very vigorous steps. But it is the Government, facing facts, not politics, reflecting popular hysteria." Part of that hysteria was reflected in letters like the one Rep. Knute Hill (D-Washington) received from a man in Orange, California: 90 percent of the people he knew, he said, wanted all enemy aliens moved away from the coast. In Pittsburg, a fishing and industrial city in Contra Costa County with a large Italian alien community, a local judge urged Kiwanians to help the government by discouraging criticism of the February removal order. The judge, a member of the Contra Costa County Defense Council, claimed that the county was the third most dangerous enemy alien area in the state, just after Los Angeles and San Diego: "The war is not a joke." Five frightened citizens—who cared not one whit for logic—wrote the Western Defense Command, "To evacuate the Japanese alone would create exceedingly difficult international problems in both Asia and Europe. *Discrimination is dynamite*. Many white Americans believe that Nazi and Fascist aliens are a greater menace than Japanese."[61]

And there was growing dissatisfaction in Congress with the Justice Department's and the FBI's handling of matters. Many in the Congress agreed with Mayor Bowron that the children of foreign-born Italians and Germans were potentially more dangerous than their parents. Senator Frank Van Nuys (D-Indiana), chair of the Senate Judiciary Committee, refused to rule out passage of legislation permitting the arrest of American citizens.[62]

This restiveness became specific on February 13 when the Pacific Coast Congressional Subcommittee on Aliens and Sabotage adopted a resolution— forwarded to the War Department and Roosevelt—calling for the immediate evacuation of anyone determined to be dangerous to the defense of the United States. (This resolution anticipated by a few days Roosevelt's Executive Order 9066.) The congressmen defined strategic areas as military installations, war industries, water and power installations, oil fields and refineries, transport and other essential facilities, and perimeter areas large enough to serve as protective buffers. The subcommittee called on the president to solicit the cooperation of the appropriate government agencies in the operation.[63]

On the eve of what would be President Roosevelt's portentous decision to turn policy over to the army on February 19, the American Legion voiced its opinion about what ought to be done in letters to Secretary of War Stimson, Rep. John Tolan, and General DeWitt. The Legion clearly had no faith in the Justice Department's ability to handle what it termed the Axis aliens, agents, and sympathizers residing in California, and it demanded immediate action—exclusion from the state—to prevent another Pearl Harbor.[64]

To anyone believing that the Japanese were perceived as the only threat to American security early in 1942, the convictions of law enforcement officials across California provide more shattering revelations. Just before the promulgation of a federal enemy alien policy, California Attorney General Earl Warren telegraphed a critical question to city police chiefs, county sheriffs, and district attorneys: can the danger be contained by treating all enemy aliens alike, or should we differentiate? The 116 responses can be summarized as follows: 1) those who believed that all nationalities should be treated alike, 2) those who believed the Italians and Germans were the most dangerous and should receive harsher treatment, and 3) those who believed the Japanese were the main problem.

Not surprisingly, nearly half the respondents, fifty-four, identified the Japanese as the most dangerous; only four believed that either the Italians or Germans were the greater threat. But nearly 25 percent, whether they thought the Japanese more dangerous or not, believed that all three groups should be treated alike, although some of these men (eighteen) also thought that the Japanese were more dangerous. The examples that follow reflect the confusion of the time. Emotion, not analysis, drove policy.[65]

Some lawmen argued that, although the Japanese were a greater threat, the Axis countries were ideologically linked. The only solution, therefore, was to evacuate all enemy aliens immediately. In the city of Madera, the mayor, city attorney, and police chief did not consider Italian nationals to be "aliens." Unlike the Japanese, they said, the Italians in Madera were so well assimilated that the loyal ones would report the disloyal ones. Because the Italians were white, officials were convinced they could predict the Italians' behavior but not that of the "inscrutable" Japanese. This argument proved to be the central racist motif of the relocation story. It was used in part to justify Japanese relocation, not only by local functionaries in cities like Madera, but by top government officials in California, such as Earl Warren, and by some in Washington, including Secretary of War Henry Stimson.

On the other hand, the sheriff of Merced County said to lock them all up; it was impossible to pick between "good" and "bad" aliens. Los Angeles's police chief opined that the small number of Italians and Germans in that city was "somewhat offset by the intelligence and viciousness of the German aliens," and that all three classes of aliens should be "concentrated."

The Madera County district attorney, however, did not concur with his colleagues. Yes, he acknowledged, the Japanese—all of them—had to go, and other enemy aliens as well, though not from all the areas subject to Japanese evacuation. He suggested that classifications be established based on nationality, citizenship, and individuality.

The district attorney of Marin County thought the Germans were the greatest threat, even the naturalized ones whom he was convinced were still loyal to Nazi Germany. Fullerton's chief of police suggested that the Italians and Germans should not be overlooked simply because of exclusive Japanese involvement at Pearl Harbor; the European aliens were still dangerous, and they could mix with the general population more easily.

Others reported that the Italians were the least dangerous of the Axis groups. The district attorney of Santa Clara County reminded Warren that many of the older Italians had come to California years before, raised families there, and were loyal Americans. Moreover, many of the young men joining the army were of Italian descent. "Before we move their parents," he counseled, "consider what it would mean to their sons in the armed forces."

Another suggestion was that loyalty boards in each county look into individual Italian and German cases. If the Italians and Germans could not prove their loyalty (by renouncing their allegiance to their mother countries), they should be shipped out of the country. And if the aliens could not be shipped out, they should be sent somewhere (ill-provisioned concentration camps) where they could not compete with "Americans."[66]

Not satisfied that the Japanese posed a greater threat than the Italians and Germans, historian Morton Grodzins notes that in California in 1940 there were 7,194 more foreign-born Italians than the entire Japanese American population of the state, and eighteen thousand more Italian aliens than Japanese aliens. No proponent of exclusion pointed out that the Japanese were barred by law from citizenship, hence assimilation. "Virtually every statement made concerning the special danger of the Japanese minority," Grodzins writes, "could also have been made against Germans and Italians." That they were not shows "how completely western proponents of mass evacuation sifted the nation's enemies through a racial screen."[67] But the question of relocating Italians and Germans was influenced by more than just racism, although racism was an important reinforcing element.

Racial screen or not, the most vocal Californians in late February and early March 1942 wanted all of the enemy aliens out without delay. Washington officials were warned on March 3 that opinion in the major Los Angeles and San Francisco dailies revealed an ugly public mood and the possibility of mob violence if the army did not move swiftly. The Los Angeles Council of California Women's Clubs petitioned General DeWitt to place all enemy aliens in concentration camps immediately, and the Young Democratic Club of Los Angeles went a step further, demanding the removal of American-born Italians and Germans—U.S. citizens—from the Pacific Coast.[68]

THE ANTI-ALIEN phobia, both before and after December 7, 1941, had an immediate and profound effect on policy and the lives of the aliens and their families. Early in February 1942, after contentious negotiations between the Justice and War Departments, in which the latter emerged victorious, the government decided to relocate all enemy aliens fourteen years of age and older away from strategic areas on the West Coast. An earlier, more cooperative mood between the two departments to avoid an overreaction to alien enemies in case of war vanished overnight.[69]

The most persistent advocate of a sweeping relocation and internment policy was the War Department's man-on-the-scene in San Francisco, Lieutenant General John L. DeWitt. The general, a sixty-two-year-old army bureaucrat, whose only combat experience came during the Filipino "insurrection" (1899–1902), had spent much of his career in the quartermaster corps. He initially recommended to his superiors in the War Department that Italian and German enemy aliens be interned simultaneously with the Japanese. Rebuffed, DeWitt then urged that the European aliens be placed in camps after all the Japanese were removed. This suggestion got a better reception in Washington. General DeWitt may have been a reluctant recruit to the notion of relocating the Japanese, as earlier historians and others have shown, but he consistently led the way in pushing for the relocation of Italians and Germans.[70] Only the repeated objections of his superiors finally stopped him. DeWitt's recommendations, at times couched in rather peculiar logic, suggest that the general regarded the aliens under his authority as little more than faceless but available relatives of the distant enemy, who had to be moved from place to place as one might shuffle supply warrants on a desk top.

Two contemporaries have given contrasting views of DeWitt. Robert E. Mayer, who acted as FBI liaison officer at weekly meetings with General DeWitt, remembered him as a "kindly, sensitive, religious man, visibly suffering under the burden of an order to make a recommendation to Washington." Mayer added, "With General DeWitt, there was no vengeful or punitive purpose, no hysteria, and no racism.... There was nothing but calm, deliberate appraisal of the situation." On the other hand, Alfonso Zirpoli, an assistant U.S. attorney in San Francisco in 1942, believed that DeWitt had no sympathy whatsoever for enemy aliens or Japanese Americans.[71] Had DeWitt prevailed, as he very nearly did amidst the bureaucratic chaos, tens of thousands of Italian and German aliens would have been moved, very likely alienating the loyalty of hundreds of thousands—even millions—of their relatives. Such an eventuality would undoubtedly have presented the government with a grave domestic crisis.

In light of the demands made by DeWitt, politicians, law enforcement, the citizenry, and the prewar ideology and activity of some Italians and Germans (who arguably posed more danger to American security than the smaller number of Japanese), it is curious that the Europeans were not relocated en masse. Historic white hostility toward the Japanese in California only partially explains why they alone were relocated. Only after months of confusion, misinformation, and bureaucratic infighting did the government decide not to move all the European aliens. Significantly, an official commission that reviewed the evacuation in 1981 concluded that "the less harsh controls faced by [Italians and Germans] in 1942 did not emerge simply from a more benign view of their intentions."[72]

WHEN THE UNITED States declared war against Japan on December 8, 1941, President Franklin Roosevelt ordered the arrest of Italian and German aliens whom the FBI and other agencies had previously determined were dangerous to American security. (The Justice Department's and the army's respective internment and exclusion programs are detailed in Chapter 9.) Attorney General Biddle vowed not to disturb the mass of enemy aliens so long as they obeyed the law. "At no time," he pledged, would "the government engage in wholesale condemnation of any group."[73] Perhaps nothing the attorney general said in the next few months so clearly revealed his naïveté.

The well being of the enemy alien population took a turn for the worse when, less than two weeks after Pearl Harbor, General DeWitt gave in to panic, apparently because of some scare stories about the activities of Japanese on the West Coast. He recommended to the War Department—the first of many such occasions—that *all* enemy aliens, fourteen years of age and older, regardless of nationality, be removed to the interior. FBI director Hoover sympathized, although he thought the army was acting a bit too "hysterical." The historian Peter Irons discovered that DeWitt's superiors, believing that the West Coast alien enemy population included about a half-million people, simply ignored him.[74]

From late December to early January, the War and Justice Departments were locked in a struggle to control the aliens, despite more harmonious days. Both the FBI and the War Department wanted Justice to take tougher measures. DeWitt, in fact, had been asked to recommend that the War Department (meaning DeWitt personally) assume control of the aliens from the Justice Department. Major Karl R. Bendetsen, a uniformed lawyer in the judge advocate general's office, advised DeWitt that unless the attorney general agreed immediately to a program of enemy alien restrictions enforced by the FBI at its discretion, "The necessity for seeking Presidential transfer of authority from the Attorney General to the Secretary of War is manifest." DeWitt needed little more encouragement. The next day he proposed that the FBI be given "blanket authority" to go after the aliens, whom he accused of disloyalty: *"I want to go in and search the house or residence and premises of every alien...right now....* We can't fool around." (emphasis added)[75]

Such pressure, combined with the deteriorating military situation in the Pacific, eroded the will of top Justice Department officials to resist the army's demands. After a series of civil but frank meetings, representatives of the two departments agreed on an alien policy on January 6 favorable to the military. In return for its promise to place more minor restrictions on the aliens and to step up enforcement, the Justice Department was able to divorce itself from the radical relocation program being pushed by DeWitt. It may surprise some that Attorney General Biddle and his aides were not displeased with this new face-saving arrangement; they personally wanted nothing to do with relocation. Their thinking appears to have been: "Let the army take the heat for this thing. DeWitt can't pull it off and in time we will be vindicated."[76]

Alfonso Zirpoli

Were you aware of the struggle in Washington between the Justice Department and the War Department over control of the aliens?

Yes, I was aware of it. Ed Ennis came out here as a representative for the Department of Justice, and I said to him, "Well, what did you do? You surrendered to the War Department. You turned over authority to the general." "Yes," he said, "that's what we've done." He didn't offer any rationale; he kind of accepted it, just as I accepted my responsibility. And strangely enough, Ed Ennis became chief counsel for many years of the American Civil Liberties Union. So, here are these liberals, people of this nature.

Did you believe that you were working for the Justice Department rather than the War Department?

Oh yes, absolutely. As long as General DeWitt had the power to issue proclamations, and we had the obligation to prosecute if they were violated, my responsibility was to see that the orders were carried out, that those who violated them were properly arrested, and that whatever was necessary to do was done. The first six months of that war we were in bad shape all around.

THE INCREASED AGGRESSIVENESS of certain War Department officials and the escalating public demand for action during the latter half of January, showed how much Biddle had underestimated his rivals. On January 25, the Roberts Commission released its report. Whereas before the public had been satisfied with the roundup of only the most dangerous aliens, citizens now put enormous pressure on authorities to protect the country from all "internal enemies." Stimson disclosed that the War Department was constructing camps in the interior for all enemy aliens, and DeWitt came to an astonishing conclusion: the absence of any sabotage to date proved that Fifth Columnists exercised a sinister control and were simply waiting for the right moment to strike.[77]

Faced with congressional demands to expel all enemy aliens and their families—an action supported by State Attorney General Earl Warren—and added public pressure, DeWitt concluded that all enemy aliens should be removed from the West Coast. The general trumpeted his new mood: "I do not feel that it is incumbent upon this country to be sentimental in this matter." Forgotten was President Roosevelt's earlier admonition not to repeat the Nazi technique of pitting "race against race, religion against religion, prejudice against prejudice."

On January 29, DeWitt announced that he was prepared to take complete charge of the alien program from the Justice Department. This led Stimson to declare that enemy aliens would have to move out of Category A prohibited areas (primarily waterfront locations and areas surrounding and adjacent to defense industries, power plants, reservoirs and the like) by February 24. There would be no exceptions. But the Justice Department's man in California, Tom Clark, complained to Washington that he had neither the expulsion notices telling the aliens what to do, nor the personnel to post them. "What is the plan?" he asked plaintively. There was none, only more interdepartmental intrigue and delay. Where the aliens would go was entirely up to them; the government had nothing in mind, either in the way of supporting relocation—other than a vague reliance on the Federal Security Agency—or in monitoring its progress.[78] And no public official had questioned the wisdom of removing all enemy aliens.

When the possibility of moving American citizens came up, the ever-resourceful Bendetsen offered a tactical ploy to thwart the Justice Department's constitutional objections: they might accept a policy of excluding aliens and citizens from prohibited and restricted zones, if such a program provided for licensing selected residents to return later. That way, Bendetsen calculated, the overly squeamish civilians in the Justice Department would not appear to discriminate against a particular class of people. DeWitt mused that Biddle and his men were just "trying to cover themselves" by criticizing the army. He boasted that the job of removing Italian, German, and Japanese aliens—as well as Japanese American citizens—would not be too big even if it involved as many as 100,000 people (a low estimate as it turned out).[79]

The FBI, on the other hand, began to back away from the army's grandiose plans. The Bureau had concluded that Italians and Germans would be harder than Japanese to pick out of the general population, increasing the difficulty of DeWitt's proposed mass relocation. It was at this moment that the delegation from the Committee to Aid Italians Loyal to the United States in San Francisco warned a member of DeWitt's staff that moving Italians was a significantly greater logistical problem than relocating the smaller number of Japanese, and the group threatened litigation.[80]

In Washington, officials continued to struggle to find a way to match these realities in California with their own requirements for national security. Assistant Secretary of War McCloy tried to bring DeWitt closer to heel: "There are so many that would be involved in a mass withdrawal, the social and economic disturbances would be so great that we would like to go a little slow on it." DeWitt appeared to concur, saying that for the time being he would deal with the Italians and Germans as individuals and concentrate on getting the Japanese out.[81]

McCloy's point having been made, federal and state authorities took the hint. Most of the California congressional delegation did not favor the mass expulsion of Italians and Germans. Earl Warren told the California Joint Immigration Committee that it would be "disruptive of national unity" and a "crime" to expel Italian and German aliens, for despite their governments at home, they were just like "everybody else"—that is, they were not Japanese. Attorney General Biddle, knowing Roosevelt's political instincts, told the president that the hysteria on the West Coast was beginning to affect Italian and German morale in New York and Boston. But, he warned Stimson, "The evacuation of all enemy aliens from [these areas] would...present a problem of very great magnitude."

Biddle's reluctance to endorse General DeWitt's plan to relocate the bulk of enemy aliens received the endorsement of a trio of respected lawyers. Backed by the attorney general, they issued an advisory recommendation—clearly isolating the Japanese from the other enemy nationalities—that accurately forecast future policy:

> Persons of Japanese descent constitute the smallest definable class upon which those with the military responsibility for defense would reasonably determine to impose restrictions.... The Japanese problem is a special problem.... Similar dangers of disloyal activities by citizens of other racial stocks cannot, and, in fact, need not be handled in the same way. It would...present an insuperable problem of administration, not to mention the consequent disruption of defense production, to bar the millions of persons of German and Italian stock from either seacoast area.[82]

In other words, who should or should not be removed came down to a question of the number of people involved.

The War Department proceeded on this understanding. By February 11, Stimson had decided to recommend to the president that Italians and Germans not be expelled for the time being. Roosevelt, who, according to Stimson, supported this idea in principle, shied away from a personal commitment, telling the secretary to do what he thought best under the circumstances. Perhaps no one has better described Roosevelt's administrative style—which fits the relocation decision precisely—than journalist David Brinkley, at that time a youthful reporter in Washington:

> [Roosevelt] wanted to make only the great, historic decisions, yet was always reluctant to delegate power to those who could relieve him of tedious details. And so issues remained unsettled until they became more troublesome, more expensive, and finally had to be dealt with, usually hurriedly. This weakness would in time be costly to Roosevelt and the country, and the cost would be counted in the coin of delay, confusion and waste.[83]

McCloy informed Bendetsen that the president had deferred to the secretary of war, and in turn, Bendetsen advised DeWitt that Stimson probably would not approve a recommendation to evacuate the entire coastal strip. Stimson then met with McCloy and Clark to formulate a strategy to derail DeWitt's ambitious plans, and told them that DeWitt was asking for too much if he expected to expel 120,000 people from the West Coast. "This is one of those jobs," Stimson cautioned, "that is so big that...it just couldn't be done." Army historian Stetson Conn estimates that had DeWitt's recommendations for Category A areas been accepted, it would have necessitated the removal of nearly eighty-nine thousand enemy aliens, nine-tenths of the West Coast Germans, nearly three-fourths of the Italians, but less than two-thirds of the Japanese.[84]

In a resigned mood, Attorney General Biddle decided that, if it had to be done, he preferred to let the army do the dirty work of relocating the aliens en masse. But he gambled (wrongly) that the military was neither willing nor able to carry out such a program. Unsure of the extent of the War Department's plans, yet realizing that he, a junior member of the Cabinet, could not thwart the politicians and Stimson at the same time, the attorney general proposed to mitigate the army plan. He advised Stimson, as Bendetsen had predicted he would, that the army could expel everyone from a specified zone, if a "military necessity" existed, then license some to return.[85] In effect, Biddle had dared the army to act. And it did.

On St. Valentine's Day, DeWitt submitted his final report on the West Coast situation to the War Department. He anticipated expulsion of 133,000 people—perhaps all enemy aliens—from expanded Category A zones (now termed military areas). Ironically, most of those residing in or near the most sensitive strategic points were Italian and German aliens, not Japanese.[86]

Thus, the momentum had swung back to the extremists. The political pressure from the West Coast, DeWitt's buoyant and sweeping recommendation, sympathy at the highest level of the War Department for removal of the Japanese, and the abject surrender of Attorney General Biddle were powerful persuaders that left the president few options. Not even Biddle's closest aides realized the depth of his capitulation. A final series of conferences between the two departments provided Roosevelt with the consensus he needed to act. The attorney general kept his counsel and remained a team player. Despite his reservations, Biddle disingenuously told Roosevelt that "no dispute" existed between the Justice and War Departments, since his office's "practical and legal" jurisdiction was limited to alien control. Thus, because alien relocation was not presented as a matter of interdepartmental controversy, the War Department's recommendation never received a thorough presidential review.

In approving a draft of the relocation order, Stimson confessed in his diary: "I have no illusions as to the magnitude of the task that lies before us." Some officials—Biddle for example—believed the order only affected the Japanese. But a postwar investigation conducted by the War Department concluded that when the president signed Executive Order 9066 on February 19, some officers believed it applied to the Italians and Germans as well. Governor Olson thought so, and certainly the Italian and German aliens believed that they might still be relocated.[87]

The unseemly and debilitating squabbling within the government that had characterized policy to this juncture continued for several more months. This delay, the result of petty bureaucratic maneuvering for advantage, was responsible for the extended relocation period endured by the aliens, while doing nothing to enhance the nation's security. As the two departments wrangled, General DeWitt ruled the West Coast unchecked. Virtually unnoticed, the lives of the aliens had been turned upside down. What did they think about their place in America now?

FOUR

"What'll happen to our Papa?"
The Impact of the Restrictions

There is a heavy responsibility upon us to shield these friendly peo-
ple—enemy aliens though they be—from abuse and persec[u]tion. We
cannot abandon the democratic principles we are fighting to defend
by denying them to minorities in our own midst.
—James H. Rowe, Jr., February 1942

T HE COLLAPSE OF France in June 1940 spurred the American
government to act against potential domestic enemies. It was
widely believed in the United States that France and other countries were the victims of Fifth Columnists. In a matter of days that fateful June, President Roosevelt transferred the Immigration and Naturalization Service from the Labor to the Justice Department and Congress
passed an alien registration act (the Smith Act). All noncitizens fourteen
years of age and older were required to report to the nearest post office to
be fingerprinted and registered. Rep. Vito Marcantonio (Am. Lab.-New
York), himself of Italian ancestry, claimed that this "Hitler-imitating
spectacle" had been "blitzkrieged" through Congress as part of a "so-
called national defense program." He thought it unlikely that "spies and
saboteurs [would] report to a Post Office and submit themselves to fin-
gerprinting." The director of the Alien Registration Division of the Justice Department in 1941, Earl Harrison, pleaded for sanity and respect for
the law as the country dealt with the issue of "disloyalty." His successor,
Donald Perry, concluded in 1942 that the government knew more about
the aliens than it did anyone else: age, sex, occupation, marital status,
military experience, organizational affiliations, arrest history, literacy,
progress toward naturalization, residence, when and where they entered
the United States, and why they came. One student of the registration
process claimed that if nothing else, registration helped to temper intolerance by showing that an overwhelming number of aliens were loyal and
law abiding; there was no Fifth Column menace—period.[89]

In the first days and weeks after Pearl Harbor, enemy aliens in California were treated more as a nuisance than a serious threat. The government immediately began to round up so-called dangerous individual Italian and German aliens on December 8, but allowed naturalization to continue for those who had already obtained their first or second papers. The president urged fair play in the workplace, and Justice Department officials expressed optimism that the United States would not repeat the hysteria of the First World War by imposing repressive acts akin to black and brown shirt behavior in Italy and Germany.[90]

But hints of greater severity were not long in coming. The Justice Department warned enemy aliens in mid-December that they would have to give up their firearms or be interned. Two weeks later it was cameras and radios. The government promised solemnly that when the war was over the items that had been turned in voluntarily—not confiscated—would be returned, a subtle distinction that was lost on some aliens.[91]

Benito Vanni

My dad, [who was interned], was picked up at the produce market on a rainy Saturday morning. When the two men from the FBI and my dad came in the front door, my sister and I were there to greet them. We were scared stiff. Once he was in the house, they asked him if he had a short-wave radio. He told them yes and showed it to 'em. They took out that portion of the radio. Then they asked my father if he had any guns, and being honest he said yes. He could have said no and they never would have found them.

He brought them down to the basement and they took two shotguns, two rifles, a handgun, a beautiful saber, and a pair of binoculars. The only rifle that wasn't taken was a .22, and that happened to be under my father's workbench; I found it much later. He didn't know about that one he had forgotten about it. He was cooperating 100 percent with them. They told him that he would get all of it back after the war. They were kind of gruff. They didn't rough him up, but they weren't giving any loving care either. I just remember that when he left we were crying.

When my father was released, he was very upset. We went up there after the war to reclaim his personal property. They asked us where the receipt was, but none had ever been given to us. They were supposed to give the guns back to him, but they were gone. I think the FBI figured they were nice pieces, worth a lot of money, so they divided them up, "One for you, one for me," and that's it. We went up there to get the receipt, and they said, "Receipt for what?" I was twelve years old at the time. What did I know? People like my dad, being born and educated in Italy, whatever the government told you, you'd do, because you figured they wouldn't do you any wrong. And that's what the Italians did. They bought it; they took them at their word: "Don't worry, you'll be able to pick all this stuff up at the end of the war. You go up there, just give your name, and you'll get all your stuff back."

We went up there, and what'd we get? Empty hands. I'd still like to find out who the arresting officer was, just track him down. I'm sure they wouldn't give their names out, but they split the goodies among themselves.

Harry Massagli,
Eureka

Shortly after the war started, the noncitizens found out about the restrictions. My dad wasn't a citizen. He had even served in the war—in Italy—when he was younger. My mother was born in France, so she wasn't included in the restrictions; she could go wherever she wanted.

You didn't live in the prohibited area, but your father was still subject to a curfew wasn't he?

He was. And not only that, but we had firearms and radios taken from us. The sheriff's department came with their subpoena and asked what we had in the way of firearms. We showed 'em, and they removed all of our guns and radios. They figured that we might do something to give the "enemies" our position along the coast some way or other.

It was quite restrictive. No lights at night. After six P.M. you pulled down your shades so the light from inside the house couldn't be noticed on the outside. At my age, I felt a little bit afraid of all these restrictions. Dad was a little upset because they confiscated the valuables and things like that. Since his children were citizens, he thought they would make an exception, but no way. He was a little bit irate at first, but he got over it. After all, there wasn't much he could do about it.

Did they keep your guns until the end of the war?

We don't know what happened to 'em; never did get them back. We had a radio, three .22 rifles, and I think a .12-gauge shotgun. My brother and I hunted small birds with the .22s. Dad hunted birds so they could make stew out of them—for their polenta, or whatever they needed a sauce for. They liked those wild birds. The sheriff's men didn't give us a receipt; just came with their subpoena. We thought we'd get 'em back at the end of the war, but they didn't even know where they'd put 'em.

Don Raffaelli

Our family didn't feel any impact from the restrictions on Italian nationals, other than being Italian and living in an Italian ghetto, so to speak. In my case that meant not being able to speak English, something we didn't do until we went to grammar school. Because my family wasn't affected by the restrictions in 1942, we became the guardians of all the hunting rifles and shotguns in the neighborhood—probably for twenty or thirty families in the group of Italians down near Broadway Street.

People either had to get rid of their guns or they were confiscated. Radios that had shortwave capability were confiscated. When people had to get rid of them, they were assigned to my mother and father. The authorities knew we had them, and they allowed it. I think the reason for that was that in Eureka at that time, which probably had a population base of ten to twelve thousand people, at least ten percent was Italian.

There was some annoyance with the fact that they couldn't go certain places. But I think the majority of people—by the simple fact that they became naturalized at the first opportunity—realized that they were being treated the way they were because their native country was an Axis power. They were aware of what was happening to the Japanese to the degree that that was being publicized. We did get the Italian newspaper every day from San Francisco. Of course, it was always a day or two late. So they were aware of current events. I think their anger was tempered by their realization that they had had an option [to become citizens], and they hadn't exercised it.

THE NEW REGULATIONS swamped local officials; they had no advance warning. In San Francisco alone, the aliens surrendered nearly 5,000 radios and cameras the first day. Soon to be added to this deluge were ammunition, explosives, maps, photographs of the exteriors and interiors of defense plants, signaling devices, codes or ciphers, and "papers, documents or books in which there may be invisible writing."[92]

Implementation of the new policy was excessive, often ridiculous, and at times cruel. Beer and wine sales by aliens were halted in Monterey. The commander of the Northern California Defense Sector told the mayor of Monterey that unregulated "vice resorts" (bars run by aliens) might impair military efficiency and become nests for treasonous activities. Elsewhere, wives turned in their husbands to facilitate divorce proceedings. An Oakland car dealer and civic leader, who also happened to be an Italian alien living in the United States since the age of six and had sold $35,000 worth of automobiles to Alameda County, was told that he could not collect the $5,309.50 owed him on five cars the county had purchased four days after Pearl Harbor. The reason? A 1917 federal law barring "trading with the enemy." Three Italian-language schools in San Francisco—affecting 300 students—and the office of the Italian Chamber of Commerce were shut down by Sylvester Andriano, an Italian and chairman of the schools' board of directors and president of the chamber. He thought it unsafe for the children to be out at night during the blackout. A German man whose father had been tortured and then killed in the Buchenwald concentration camp was not allowed to join the U.S. Navy as he had requested after Pearl Harbor.[93]

At Monterey, purse seiners (fishing boats with nets that close at the top like a purse) were required to have "all American crews," despite the fact that most Monterey boat owners were natives of Italy or of Italian descent. They had telegraphed President Roosevelt pledging $50,000 in defense bonds ("our first contribution") and had donated an eighty-foot diesel craft to the navy. Italian crab fishermen in San Francisco offered 250 boats for coastal patrolling.[94]

Of no small inconvenience was the ban on travel further than five miles from home or work. Again, applicants seeking permits flooded the offices of local authorities. Most inconvenienced were traveling salesmen. "Necessary business" qualified one for a pass, but it was made clear that this did not include skiing, weekend visiting, holidays or other "pleasure trips." Officials in San Francisco barred a woman from a friend's funeral in the next county. When another woman was apprised that her plan to visit her fiancé 200 miles from San Francisco was forbidden, she looked U.S. Attorney Frank Hennessy in the eye and said, "Mr. Attorney, I guess you just don't understand this love business." A German man was refused a travel permit because he had received Nazi propaganda publications at home, although he had not asked for them and such publications were readily available through the libraries of information of practically all United Nations countries in the United States. Alfonso Zirpoli, an assistant attorney in Hennessy's office, remembers, however, that the travel permits were easily obtainable and at times issued in lots of ten or twenty.[95]

On January 15, Attorney General Biddle ordered the nationwide re-registration—between February 2 and 7—of approximately one million enemy aliens fourteen and older. With that announcement, the government handed local agencies another monumental task; San Francisco's postmaster, for example, was expected to register 19,500 aliens in five days. And this sign-up promised to be even more detailed than the general alien registration of 1940. The new regulation required enemy aliens to carry identity cards with fingerprints and a photograph. Additionally, they had to report any change of employment or residence. Some saw in the aliens' predicament an opportunity for their own pet projects. An Alabama congressman had introduced a bill in December that would have required a similar registration of *every* American citizen age sixteen and older.[96]

The most stunning blow came, of course, with the government's successive announcements in late January that it was establishing eighty-six prohibited and restricted zones on the West Coast to be cleared of all aliens to aid the "national defense" and to "protect" the aliens. Italians in Illinois thought their countrymen in California were being put into concentration camps. The army predicted that between 200,000 and 226,000 enemy aliens and their citizen children in the three Pacific states would be removed to locations east of the Sierras (including 100,000 alien Italians and 71,000 Germans).[97]

Alfonso Zirpoli

As I mentioned earlier, Italians who were not citizens were ordered to move out of the area north of Beach Street [in San Francisco]. One Italian came to see me; his son had been killed at Pearl Harbor. He wanted to know what he should do—should he move? So I turned to Tom Clark and I said, "I want you to listen to this man's story." Clark said the general still wanted everybody from the north side of Beach Street excluded without exception. I had a big argument with DeWitt's aide, Bendetsen, that Beach Street should still be open to aliens since it was the main street on which the municipal railroad carried passengers downtown. I finally convinced him.

I only talked to the general once, and that was when they said the lights had to be out after sundown. The Marina shipyard was working night and day, and they had their lights on. DeWitt came in and wanted me to issue warrants for their arrest. So I did. Well, Washington apparently complained when I did that and the general was told to behave. Then, when a member of his staff asked me to have the complaint dis-

missed, I said I wouldn't dismiss it until I had the general's approval in writing, which we got. He was a difficult man to convince.

The whole period was a sad time for so many Italians, certainly for my father. He died about six months after Pearl Harbor, and, as I said, he saw the war coming. As far as the Italians were concerned, except for those ordered out of the area, there was nothing out of the ordinary in any way. They had to have curfew permits; it's true. Otherwise, there was nothing extraordinary that happened. Oh, the fishermen, they all had to move. That part was true. But those were noncitizens.

Did noncitizens ever appeal to you?

No, they never did. The only one was the man who I said came to me and told me that he had been [forced to move] *and that his son was killed at Pearl Harbor.*

Angelo and Nida Vanni
Arcata

Nida: *The order to move came in the papers. General DeWitt ordered it. He did it for the Italians and Germans, and who else was it—the Japanese. 'Course we didn't have any Japanese here. We had a certain date that we had to move. G Street [highway 101 through downtown Arcata] was the street that was OK on the other side. It was crazy...crazy. Everybody that I knew in Arcata was just dumbfounded. The Italians were suddenly enemies because of the war. It was just the idea of this general. I don't know how he got it passed. That's what baffled everybody.*

My mother, who lived here, too, was born in France, so she was able to stay in her house, even though she was Italian. I was able to stay because I was born here. But my dad and husband had to go across the street. They both lost their jobs. That's why everybody became a citizen in 1942. They tried to take out their papers right after the law was passed. My dad had been here since 1902; nobody ever bothered you, so you didn't become a citizen. He was working night and day and he just didn't have time to study. It was a hard thing to do. You had to learn all that Constitution. Everybody was trying to learn, and they were teaching it to each other and going to school. They finally got their papers; my husband got his in 1942.

Angelo was working at the Barrel Factory in Arcata, but he had to leave our house and his job and work at Korbel. For a month, he lived with my aunt in a little cabin. He slept there because she didn't have any room. Then we found a little house up on the hill, right below the college. We were gone three months altogether. We read in the papers that we could come back.

My mother took the Italian paper that came from San Francisco, and she would read everything that was going on down there. It was really bad because in San Francisco they put thousands and thousands on trains and sent them back to concentration camps some place, just like they did with the Japanese.[98] I don't know if you ever heard of the Sons of Italy; that's a big organization. Well, there were quite a few in San Francisco who were very active in it. They thought maybe they were Fascists. So, they were sent away on a train, out in the Middle West some place. Even us here, you know—the papers would say, well, "they might send you up to Trinity County and make a concentration camp," all kinds of rumors. We didn't know what was going to happen. But at least they didn't take the Italians that were born here. They didn't touch us at all. We were lucky here that nobody was shipped out. The Japanese are still fighting for their money.

Angelo: *And the United States makes Japan rich. That's what gets me now. It makes no sense.*

Nida: *It was sad, because if your doctor was on this side of G Street* [the restriction line in Arcata] *you couldn't really go unless you knew somebody who would say, "OK, you can go for an hour." You just couldn't do it. You had to get a special permit over where the police station used to be, across from where the fire hall is now. Our dentist happened to be on this side, but my husband only had to go one time. But a lot of poor people—I tell you, there was this family that had two boys that were born in Italy. We were poor. My son, Fred, would go tan barking up in the hills, to make a little money; he was just a kid. And he got poison oak. He was so sick; he had arms on him like this—just terrible. And Angelo couldn't come home and see him. He was so sick we had to take him to the doctor.*

Angelo: *One of the kids was sick one time, I forget who it was. So I went to the chief of police. He said, "No, you can't visit him. I'll put you in jail."*

"I married an American citizen. How can you speak like that?"

Nida: *Well, they didn't care then. In those days, the law was so strict. But it didn't last. We lived through it. On weekends, I'd go up to my aunt's with some food and we'd eat together. That's what we did for that first month or so. And then when we moved into that other little house we were all together. The kids and I could go anywhere; Angelo just went to Korbel and back.*

Angelo: *I got a job at Korbel in the machine shop. Getting that job wasn't hard. Almost everybody got a job that wanted it. I was a sawyer then. I won't brag, but I was one good sawyer. I made money for the company, and they were mad because they sent us over the line. There was no reason to send us over there. I had worked at the California Barrel Factory since 1924. I remember the general manager of the factory was mad because he lost a lot of good men. They sent us to see the sheriff, who I used to know well. But there was no way to get out of it; his hands were tied. He says, "I know you. I know all of you. But what can I do?" I felt bad about the law, but what could I do? I never did anything wrong, always worked in this country. I was upset, but not angry against the government. The Barrel Factory replaced us, but they wanted us back.*

Nida: *There was another thing. We were so in the dark we didn't know how long this was going to last. I remember the last night he spent home. I was standing right there when he went that night. He said, "All the work that I did in this house," 'cause he built it. "This land that we have here, all this, and I'm going to have to move and I didn't do anything. I don't know whether I can ever come back." That was it. He was crying when he left.*

There were lots of rumors, about the Japanese, about the Italians. Every day the paper would say something different. The Italians in San Francisco didn't know how long it was going to last. In fact, the ones that they took out to the Middle West were gone a long, long time.

We never once thought that anybody was out to get us because we were Italian. The town was smaller in the forties, and we knew each other. We didn't have this influx of people that we're having now. Everybody just felt sorry for you. We understood. I think all of the Italians I've talked to, even the ones who were shipped to the Middle West, figured it was a mistake. They never felt any resentment toward the government at all because everybody knew it was just the general.

Angelo: *We weren't upset that the government put out that law. General DeWitt did it.*

IN PITTSBURG, CALIFORNIA, where one-third of the population was about to be relocated—three thousand persons, including half of the city's fishermen and ninety-seven-year-old Placido Abono, the oldest living pioneer of the city—Boy Scouts dutifully posted the evacuation notices in Italian, German, and Japanese. The government prohibited the entire city to the aliens. Those who had hoped to move to adjacent Antioch found it off limits as well, although some elderly Italians had already made down payments on homes or paid rental deposits in Antioch.[99]

Mary Riccabuono, eighty-three, a Pittsburg resident for sixty years, had operated a combination general store and saloon on the waterfront with her husband. Her cows supplied the town with milk, and her savings had brought many Palermo families to the community. She could not understand, she said, why the government wanted her to move: Though not a citizen, "I helped build the town. Without me it still might be nothing but mud flats." City clerk Frank Taormina, who later would lead a delegation to Washington to plead the aliens' case, complained about the indignities being heaped on his own family: "We were welcome when we came to Pittsburg. My family helped to build it. Pittsburg was just a mud flat when we came here. My father was illiterate; he couldn't read or write Italian or American." Taormina's mother and brother were aliens. The latter had bought $750 in defense bonds. "Now he hasn't any ready cash to go anywhere."[100]

Some of the Pittsburg Italians who sought homes in nearby towns were given the cold shoulder. Those with sons in the armed forces reckoned that perhaps their families' sacrifices made them more loyal than those who were making their lives unbearable did. The funeral of a Pittsburg woman who died in a Monterey hospital had to be held in Oakley so that her children could attend.[101]

Mary Cardinalli,
Pittsburg

I was born in Detroit, Michigan, but my husband was an alien. He and I had to move in 1942. He lived with his mother and his sister in Brentwood. My mother was an alien, too, but with five little kids. They had to go to Oakley, and I had to go back and forth from my mother's house in Pittsburg to see my husband in Brentwood and my mother in Oakley. I had to bake bread once a week, twenty-five pounds of flour—bake bread for my mother; cook it in Pittsburg and bring it to Oakley; go to see my husband in Brentwood and bring him some food.

It was about five or six months we were out. My mother came home sooner, but not my husband. She came home because she had her boys in the service. My brother talked to the chaplain in the Navy, and he said, "What am I doing here when my mother's out? She's got two sons in the war and she's out as an alien." The chaplain wrote to Washington, I think, and then we got a letter and they sent my mother home earlier with her little kids. They were all American-born, the kids.

It was really a struggle; I really had it rough. I had all that "freedom." [laughs] My husband and mother couldn't come to Pittsburg. If they'd catch 'em coming to Pittsburg, they'd get arrested. So I had to help my mother out because there was no stove over there to bake bread for the kids to eat. First make it, and then bake it. Yeah, the kneading—oh boy! When my mother was sick my brother Joe used to knead for her. And it was always twenty-five pounds at a time. Roll it, lay it away to rise, put it in the oven to bake. That was a lot. I did that once a week.

There was no washing machine to wash the kids' clothes in Oakley. It was just a little cabin, and she had those five little boys. There were a lot of dirty clothes. She had a nice home in Pittsburg, but I had to stay there and do all that stuff and bring it to her. Plus I'd go see my husband in Brentwood. And I did that three or four times a week.

I had a little boy, nine months old. I had to carry him back and forth with me in the car. And then my husband finally went to see if he could get work because we had no money. We were starving. Before he moved, he was a contractor in the canneries. He used to work in the cook room, stacking up cans and all that stuff. Then he was out of work for about six months after he was put out.

Did your husband eventually find work?

Yes, a day job in Isleton, and he moved there, into a small apartment, by himself. Isleton's on the other side of the Antioch bridge, about twenty-five miles. You had to pay a fare to cross the bridge. We had a car, and I could drive, so I kept the car because I had to go back and forth. I was taking care of my mother and I didn't want to leave her stranded. I used to bring my little boy back and forth to Isleton, and one time we almost got killed. He was throwing up in the car and we didn't have car seats in those days. I had him right next to me. I was watching the baby throwing up, and here I was going to have a wreck. And it scared me to death. I didn't like to go back and forth too much.

Ratzi Trezza

We were fourteen children. I was born in Pittsburg. Both my folks were born in Italy. In 1940, my father became a citizen, but my mother was an alien, so she had to go out, and my dad went out to be with her. We got a notice through the mail. I know they got it through the mail. You had to go where they told you; you couldn't go where you wanted to go.

The aliens all moved out of Pittsburg. They were forced to go. I had two brothers in the service during that time and they still chased my mother away. My brothers didn't like the idea at all. They were moved over to Oakley, about five miles east of here. There must have been thirty families there we called it "Little Italy." My brothers and sisters, the ones who weren't married, stayed in the house in Pittsburg. Oakley was nice, except it was a little town, maybe a couple of thousand people. They didn't rent homes. They were little cabins out by the tracks and the waterfront. It was "Little Italy," maybe twenty to twenty-five families. We'd go and visit 'em every Sunday. Every Sunday it looked like a holiday. Everybody was going to visit their folks. There were regular visiting hours. With all the kids and everything, there were about 500-600 people every Sunday afternoon.

There were a lot of aliens. There must have been about three to 400 in Pittsburg. A good 60 percent of Pittsburg was Italian then. The population was about ten thousand. I imagine every family had a son in the service; some had two, three, even four, and still they had to go out. What got me mad at the time was, what the hell, didn't the big shots in the White House notice that there were a lot of foreigners' kids fighting for the United States, and they were throwing their mothers out?

Dad was a commercial fisherman; it was seasonal work. At the time he left he didn't want to go fishing any more and leave her alone, so he was retired for a while, till they came back. They had to go in '41, I think. It took 'em a couple of years before they let them come back. When my mother left the house, she was crying like a little baby. She'd always cry when she thought about the house. And she'd cry when we visited on Sundays. What could she say? "It's not right, them chasing me away." I was mad about it, but what can you do? She couldn't come back. If she had they would have grabbed her and done something worse. I used to think about it. My mother came over here, she raised fourteen kids, never was in trouble, and they chased her away. I was peeved, yeah.

When the war broke out, and the United States started drafting, I was one of the first guys called in. So when I went to the draft board I told them I was essential; I was a commercial fisherman. That's when they deferred me. If they hadn't, I'd have been one of the first in there. Maybe I wouldn't be here today. I fished the river here, and I used to go to Alaska for salmon. And that's the only job I could do, 'cause if I'd done any other job they'd have grabbed me and put me in the service. I told them about my mother, but they didn't care. There was always one man that wanted me in the service. I'll never forget his name. There were five on the board, and every six months I had to go before them, 'cause they'd classify me 1-A again. I told them I was going to Alaska to fish. And this one man, when it came to a vote he was always against me. I'll never forget him. He lived here; he had a bar in Pittsburg. I don't know why, but he wanted me in there. The other four voted against him all the time. So I got out of it, but my two brothers went.

PITTSBURG'S FISHERMEN WERE not the only Italian seamen idled by DeWitt's orders. In 1930, the California Chamber of Commerce had estimated that Italians managed 80 percent of the state's fishing business—some ten thousand employees. Among those affected by the relocation order were 1,400 of the 2,000 employees of San Francisco's half-a-million-dollar-a-year fishing industry. On Fisherman's Wharf children wondered, "What'll happen to our Papa?" There was Luciano Sabella, seventy-one, a fixture on the wharf for fifty-four years, unable to write and with a son in the army; and Luciano Maniscalco, fifty-eight, a fisherman for forty years, whose head was, as he put it, too hard to learn how to become a citizen. He had four sons in the armed forces. Giuseppe DiMaggio, sixty-nine, father of baseball's "Yankee Clipper," came to San Francisco in 1898; his wife, Rosalie, sixty-four, in 1902. The DiMaggios had nine children, all of them American citizens. Both had filed their first papers, but the war ended their hopes for eventual naturalization. Like many of the fishing families of the wharf in San Francisco, the DiMaggios could neither read nor write English. Both were proud but bewildered Americans, citizens or no. Although their home was not located in one of DeWitt's prohibited zones, and thus they were not required to relocate, Giuseppe could not work out of Fisherman's Wharf or eat at his son Joe's restaurant.[102] The ban on fishermen included East and Gulf Coast ports as well.

Joseph Maniscalco

[My dad] had a fishing boat when the war started, and he kept it docked at Fisherman's Wharf. He would go down there and, with my older brother, just take a look at it during the day to make sure that it wasn't being mistreated in any way. Nobody objected to his being there; there was no retaliation. Guards patrolled the wharf continuously—twenty-four hours a day—because they wanted to make sure the Italian fishermen were not abusing the law, and that they didn't go out in their boats.

He was always friendly toward most people in San Francisco. As a matter of fact, he was very prominent in city hall. He had lots of political friends because many of the politicians loved to have crab cioppino,

*and they would always call the king of the crab fishermen, Mr. Lorenzo
Maniscalco. He was called the king of the crab fishermen—*il campione,
which means, "the champion. "

*No one would go out into the sea as far away as my father. He'd go
beyond the Farallon Islands, and no matter how stormy the night he did
a tremendous job. Most other fishermen thought he was out of his mind
even to attempt to go out on a stormy night. He lost two boats, and
when his third boat capsized, he was saved by two men, including the
father of Joe DiMaggio, the baseball player. My father also saved many
people from drowning during the wreck of a freighter. He was a very
daring man. I don't think there is anyone who could deny the fact that
he would do anything, go anywhere, and defy anybody. But as the war
came upon him, he was very hurt. It was a great insult to him to have to
be restricted from fishing. This was his livelihood.*

*Many people were antagonistic toward the Italian people. They thought
that they should all be incarcerated. These were people who were perhaps very pro-American, including some Italians; my wife can verify
that. They were citizens who felt that the aliens should be sent to Alca-
traz.*

*I sensed the indignant feelings that my father had about the govern-
ment, but by the time that I got out of the navy, he was already employed by the Bank of America. A.P. Giannini, who was a friend of his,
and Mr. Cuneo, who was a brother-in-law of A.P., got him a job, and
they were very lenient and considerate. They had loaned my father the
money for his home in the marina district. And having no income when
he was restricted, he couldn't pay the mortgage. He bought the property
at their suggestion before 1929 when he thought he could become a
multi-millionaire in the stock market. Many of his friends wound up
jumping off the bridge after the crash. He was very hurt, but he was so
pleased that he had a job—and at the main branch of the Bank of America on Montgomery Street, which was an honor. He was so happy that
people liked him. Here he was, in the financial district, a man who had
no education, who spoke only broken English, and who was always so
courteous toward the people who came to see him.*

*That twelve months when my father was restricted was really a
tough period. The family was without sufficient income, and it was very
hard financially for them. My mother had great faith. She was a very
deeply religious woman and always felt that there would be some provisions, and that God would take care of her needs. She just felt that
something good was going to come out of this. Primarily, she wanted to
make sure that my father was not going to lose his head. She was also
an outstanding woman. She was chosen Catholic Woman of the Year by*

an Italian community services organization, and given great accolades for the charitable work she did and her wonderful upbringing of her family. She was really the pillar.

When my father lost his third boat, which was called St. Christopher, or, in Italian, San Christofero, he was really angry. It was the most beautiful boat he ever had. He got it from a couple of boat builders as a prototype diesel boat. They said, "Lorenzo, we want you to have this boat, and because it's a prototype we're going to give it to you for what it cost us. We want you to try it out." Well, it worked just beautifully. It was inexpensive because it was diesel and not gasoline. So when he lost that boat, or thought he lost it—it capsized out towards the Cliff House—he came home enraged, and he was saying words in Italian, cursing and saying, "Why did this happen to me? My boat! I lost my boat." My mother was trying to calm him down, and said, "Take it easy, take it easy. You're lucky you're alive. You've got your life." And he said, "Who cares about my life? My boat, my boat."

IN SAN FRANCISCO, the post office couldn't register alien applicants fast enough. By February 5, only nine thousand of an expected thirty had been processed, with just two days remaining until the deadline. Local photographers were putting in sixteen- to eighteen-hour days.[103]

Alessandro Baccari, Jr.,
San Francisco

As a little boy, I witnessed the trauma of those of Italian origin who were not American citizens during the outbreak of World War II. At the time, my father had a photographic studio. To the studio came nearly a thousand Italians to have their photographs taken for placement on their alien registration papers. I would witness my mother attempting to console them as they waited for my father to take their photographs. And, after their picture was taken, they would say in Italian, "But I'm not a criminal. What have I done?" "I've lived here forty years I love America." "I'm not intelligent enough to pass the citizenship test." "Why do I have to be in at eight o'clock?" "Why can't I go to my boat? What kind of living will I have?" "They take my sons into the service, but I'm considered an enemy. What have I done Signor Baccari?" It was very difficult for my father to answer these people.

I never forgot their sadness, their tears. It was a very emotional experience for me. And of course I got to see it daily because of my father's photography. My parents also wrote letters for them in English to *explain their feelings. Many had no relatives here, just themselves. They couldn't turn to anybody. There was no social agency. There was no one to go to. It was a very trying time.*

The only organization that helped was the Roman Catholic Church. Saints Peter and Paul Church on Filbert Street became a sanctuary for these Italian aliens. At the church, mass was said daily in Italian so that the people would not feel that they were being forsaken.

I'll never forget Mr. Maniscalco. He was a fisherman, the most respected at the wharf. I went to grammar school with his son, John. One day, I was visiting their house and he greeted me by saying, "Alessandro, I can no longer go aboard my boat at the wharf." Italian aliens were compelled to remain fourteen blocks away from the waterfront. He couldn't comprehend. With tears in his eyes, he told me, "I'm gonna breaka the law. My boat is my life." He would sneak out to see his boat and the waterfront.

Fishing with him was an experience. I remember going out the first time, and he said, "You gonna getta seasick, but I'm gonna put you in the front where I'm gonna be cooking the cioppino. And the fumes will make you more sick and you vomit a lot, and you gonna be all right, and you sail and never be sick again."

Another time while returning to port, we ran into rough weather in an area called the Potato Patch. The location is just a few miles west of the entrance to the Golden Gate. I asked, "Mr. Maniscalco, how are we going to get back?" He replied, "Don't worry," and gently placed his hand on the crucifix hanging on the wall. "That's been my compass since day one."

Nobody could sail like him; what a fisherman! The best. He could do things with the boat that nobody else could do. He was an amazing man. Devout—mass every morning—but swore like a trooper. He was a man of unbelievable courage. And when he was happy, God, the whole world was happy. He expressed himself with such gusto and love and pride.

AROUND MONTEREY BAY, there was also nothing gentle about the forced removal of families, friends, neighbors and relatives. The relocation order touched the lives of nearly everyone on the peninsula; between 2,500 and 3,000 had to leave, the local newspaper reckoned. Moving and transfer companies did a land-office business. Most of the 2,500 Italians scattered to new residences in seventy-five towns throughout the state; 300 others remained within fifty miles. The pastor of the Italian Evangelical Church said that out of more than thirty families in his parish, only four would be left after February 24. More than anything else, people wanted an end to the confusion and uncertainty in their lives. Reportedly, some Italians even preferred internment to their doubtful enemy status. One Italian with a sense of humor wrote from his new residence in San Jose, "What has Monterey come to?—San Jose." And there were the inevitable tragedies in Monterey similar to those of Pittsburg and San Francisco. One of the most poignant was the case of Rose Trovato, who was told that her son had been lost on the U.S.S. *Arizona* on December 7, but whose second son, Mike, had enlisted to "take Tommy's place."[104] Others had these recollections:

John Spataro,
Monterey

What happened after Pearl Harbor?

I got drafted nineteen days after I was married. That was in March of 1941. My wife was pregnant, and I was making twenty-one dollars a month. But we had to pay forty dollars a month rent, so we couldn't make it. I explained to them that I couldn't do that. No way. And I told them that they had to do something about it. I figured they had to support my wife, take care of her when she had the baby. She had my son, John, and I was discharged in September. They used to discharge a lot of people that worked on the farms in those days, and we fishermen were bringing in a lot of sardines—150-160 tons every day, six days a week. That's what got me discharged. They needed the fish just as much as they needed people.

Then, in December, as soon as they bombed Pearl Harbor, we had to move out of here. We went to San Jose; we had to be inland. My wife was an American citizen, but she had to move on account of me. I went to the authorities and inquired. I told them that I had been in the army. They said, "That's not going to do you any good." My mother-in-law had to move, too. She had just had an operation and had to be taken to San Jose in an ambulance. We put everything in a truck and went straight there. There were cherries, artichokes, and lettuce there to be picked. So I went to work in this factory canning asparagus.

When that finished, I went to this gas station. I said, "Can you give me a job? I need work. I've got a wife and kid."

"OK, but I can't pay very much."

"Whatever, you know."

One day I was pumping gas in some guy's car and he says, "Are you Italian?"

"Yes, I am."

"Are you the one that moved out of Monterey?" This guy was Sicilian. His father used to come to Monterey to sell oil in five-gallon drums for five dollars. "You want to come and work for me?"

"Doing what?"

"How much you make here?"

"Twenty, twenty-five dollars a week."

"You come with me. I'll pay you seventy-five cents an hour."

"Doing what?"

"We got a little factory. We get artichokes from San Jose, fifteen, twenty tons, then bring them to our factory." There were ten or fifteen girls working in that factory, all Sicilian, canning artichokes.

Well, I worked there four or five or six months, steady. There was no comparison with what I made fishing, though. I made so much money fishing I didn't know what to do with it.

Then there was this other boss there. He wanted me to be the godfather of his little girl. He wanted me to drive this truck to Castroville, said they would have all the artichokes in sacks waiting for me. "Bring them over here."

I told him, "You're goofy. I can't go more than five miles from here. If they catch me, they'll put me in jail."

"Oh, no," he says, "Nobody is going to put you in jail."

"What are you talking about? That's the law! I have to be in at eight o'clock at night, and I can't go out before six in the morning. I can't do it. I'm not going to jail for no reason at all. They catch me over five miles, they put me in prison."

Anyway, he insists, "Don't worry about it. I'm an alien too. I go on business from here to Chicago, New York, and I couldn't care less if they catch me." And he was doing it, too, I tell you.

I told my wife and she said, "Don't take any chances. If they get you, you're in trouble."

He kept after me. "Don't worry. If they put you in jail, I can get you out in ten minutes."

I said, "Who do you think you are, Al Capone?" Yeah, that's what I told him, "You Al Capone?" I didn't forget he came from Detroit. I don't know why he came to San Jose. Something wrong some place. Then I find out other things. But he was a gentleman to me, to all of us. I don't know about Al Capone, but he was connected with the Mafia, I can tell you that. One time my driver's license expired and I said, "I can't do anything now." He says, "You don't need it," and he made one phone call. I gave him my old license and a guy brought me another one without ever going to the courthouse. "Just sign here. You're fine."

When we were living in San Jose, I received a letter saying that they wanted to draft me again! They wanted me to come to the draft board here in Monterey. Well, I couldn't, so my wife went. And when they called "John Spataro," she got up and said, "I'm John Spataro's wife."

"We don't want you, we want your husband."

"He can't come here. He can only travel five miles." So they talked among themselves and finally said, "Yeah, she's right."

"Do you want to arrest him," my wife asked? "If you want to arrest him, I'll tell him to come here." They agreed that I couldn't travel the seventy-five miles from San Jose, and that was the end of it.

Albert, Nancy, and Peter Mangiapane

Albert: *I was born in Italy and came to Detroit in 1929 as a stowaway when I was eighteen years old. I struggled to get to America. I worked five years to pay for my trip. My father was here with some other guys in Detroit working on the railroads. Then something went wrong with my father's eyes and the doctor told him he'd better go back to Italy. He never came back. He had worked in Detroit for twelve years.*

I stayed with an uncle for one year in Detroit after arriving in the United States, but there were no jobs. Then some friends gave me a ride out here in their car in 1930, and I got a fishing job with my cousin. My father had told me he wanted me to go to Monterey where it was warmer than Detroit in the winter, and where the fishing was good. I had been fishing in Italy since I was ten years old, in San Vito Locapo, near Palermo.

In Monterey, I went to school for three years to get my citizenship papers. Three years, twice a day from two to four in the afternoon, and from seven to nine at night. During the day, I fished. Then, just when I was ready to take the test, along came the war. I was supposed to go in on December 8, but they stopped all naturalization and eventually all the aliens had to move out of Monterey. I still had my little boat, but I couldn't fish anymore. My wife could have stayed; my kids could have stayed; but I had to move to San Jose. I looked for a job up there, but with the law that you couldn't travel more than five miles from home, plus the eight o'clock curfew, it was tough.

Nancy: *December 8, 1941: I had one son and was expecting. My daughter—my oldest daughter—was born on January 8, and we had about a month after that to get out of Monterey. That week is something terrific! I've got five birthdays in the family that week.*

I was born in the United States. Here I was, pregnant, and I felt, "Gee, this doesn't seem right." It was hard for me to pack up and leave with my little kids. Even my mother and father had to go—they were aliens too, lived here since 1916—and my grandmother, who was over eighty. Two of my brothers were in the war already. We felt that with me a citizen, and two brothers of mine in the service, that it wasn't fair to put us out. There's a lot of things that run through your mind in that situation. All those old people, my grandmother, my parents, they came here when they were young. They had worked hard and built their homes and everything. They were secure. And then to be thrown out like that. It was an awful thing. They were all upset, but there were no ifs, ands, or buts about it. You had to go. Who was going to fight the government? You couldn't. So we did what the government said. We moved out and we did the best we could.

Peter Mangiapane (son): *We were in the same position as the Japanese.*
Nancy: *The only difference was they put them into camps. They lost more than we did.*

Peter: *I was pretty small at the time, but for some reason, in my mind, I still don't like San Jose. I have a lot of friends there who own restaurants and bars, but I don't like going there. I think what happened in 1942, when I was a small boy, sticks in my mind.*

Nancy: *We went to San Jose because we had friends there. They found us a place to live. We could have gone to Salinas but we thought it was better to be near them. We also thought Albert might be able to get a job in one of the canneries up there.*

We didn't have a house of our own. We lived together with my parents and grandmother in an apartment. We were there three or four months.

Albert: *I had a small fishing boat. I moored it to a buoy and somebody I knew in Monterey promised to look after it. I didn't get a job in a cannery in San Jose. I worked in a pottery factory instead for twenty-two fifty a week. It was hard work for me. I was scared.*

I stayed there for a month, and by that time they had changed the law, so I could come back to Monterey. I still couldn't fish, and that lasted for a couple of more months, so I went to work in a sardine cannery.

I got my citizenship on December 8, 1942. I still have that date written down on an old piece of paper here in my wallet. I was really glad to become a citizen. I've been here fifty-eight years now.

I tried my best to learn the laws and the Constitution. I wanted to stay here. As long as I was single, I was afraid that immigration might catch up with me and send me back to Italy. After I got married, every-

thing was all right. I got all the right papers and went to Mexico to clear things there with the American Consul. I had to go out of the United States and re-enter legally, on foot, because I had first come as a stowaway. So I went to Mexicali, Mexico, in 1938, and came back in as a legal immigrant.

THE GOVERNMENT HAD decided to inform each alien of the relocation order personally. But when the large number of aliens involved made that impractical, authorities switched to a mass mailing of notices. That idea, however, was quickly vetoed by the already-overworked post office. Instead, eleven-by-fourteen-inch instructional placards in Italian, German, and Japanese were tacked up by the thousands in the restricted areas on February 11.[105] None of the interviewees remembers learning about the relocation order from these signs, however.

Mayor Fred J. Moore, Jr.

Do you remember seeing any evacuation notices posted on telephone poles?

No, because as I say, there were no known enemy aliens in that area [north of Fourth St. in Eureka]. As a matter of fact, people suspected of being Russian communist sympathizers were more numerous than any possible anti-American Italians.

Alex Frediani

We lived in Samoa at the time [of World War II]. My dad was a citizen. My mother had applied for her naturalization papers in either 1939 or 1940, but when the war came along, she was not a citizen; she had not gotten her second papers. I think it was in January of '42—what's his name, General DeWitt? Yeah, it was Lieutenant General DeWitt who wanted the enemy aliens, as they were called at the time, to [be put out].

I was a freshman or sophomore in high school. I remember that Sunday afternoon when we got notified the Japanese had bombed Pearl Harbor. And just prior to that, they [the government] had built a tower out on the sand dunes. If you know where the Samoa store is, it was straight west of that, where L.P. [Louisiana Pacific] now has lumber yards. It was about a two-story tower. I guess they were waiting for the

*Japanese to land on the beach over there. It was mainly World War I
vets who manned the tower, but I used to pull duty up there, too. As I
think back on it now, it was a joke. These guys were ready to hold off
the invasion of the Japanese right there on Samoa! It reminds me of that
movie,* "The Russians are Coming! The Russians are Coming!"

*February I was when we found out about it. I remember this guy
coming up, and he was an Italian, an Italian-American, knocking on the
door—it was a Sunday:* "You gotta get out of town right now!" *Dad
was working and my mother said,* "Why?"

"Because otherwise they're going to arrest you and throw you in a
concentration camp!"

"Where can I go? I have two children." *My dad came home from
work and he said,* "Gee, I just don't believe they'd do that in this country."

At that time, the General Manager over there [at Hammond] *was Mr.
Birmingham. He told my dad,* "Don't worry. Nobody's gonna arrest
her. You take your time. If there are any problems I will take full responsibility for any people here." *I took that to mean that if the sheriff
came over and put her under arrest, we could go to Birmingham and
he'd bail her out, or do something. Actually, this Italian fellow had
misunderstood what the paper said. They announced that the Italians
had two or three weeks before they had to leave, and he thought they
had to get out that day.*

Lily Boemker

*The law came that people who did not have their citizenship papers,
and who lived on the west side of G Street* [highway 101 in Arcata] *had
to move. This must have been in January or February of 1942. I was a
senior in high school. Where were we going to go?*

*We decided to move to Eureka. I wanted to graduate with my old
class, so I commuted back and forth to Arcata High School until June of
'42 when I graduated. My mother and father couldn't attend. My mother
could have, but she wasn't well. My uncle and aunt brought me over,
and I went through the ceremonies and everything. Then I went back
home to Eureka.*

How did you first learn that you had to move?

*Well, the Italians in those days would visit. People would meet in one
home and just visit. One evening, our friend down the street came and*

said, "The news is on the radio that the aliens have to move." I went to
the post office and found out for sure. At the time, we thought of just
moving to the other side of G Street. But my dad was working in
Eureka, and we thought, "Well, it would be better for him not to have
to commute back and forth," so we moved to Eureka.

Was it because your father couldn't travel more than five miles that he
didn't attend, or because the high school was across the line?

*It was across the line. Yes, that's why. There were quite a few of us—
Joe Nieri, Marino Sichi—and you were looked down upon, let's face it.*
*I would stop at the old house—we rented the house out—and collect
the rent for my parents. We didn't have a car or anything like that. Let's
see, we moved back—I think August of '42, we moved back to Arcata.
Yes, it was in August, because my uncle died in May—he was from It-
aly. I graduated in June, August we moved back, and September is when
I met my husband.*

Did anyone ever say what you might do that would be dangerous?

*At the beginning, no. We found out in Eureka why they wanted us to
move. They were afraid that we were going to give signals to subma-
rines and things out in the ocean or bay. Nobody official ever told us; it
was just rumors.*
*And you know, my sister and I became air wardens. There was one
night I remember. The wind was blowing; it was a rainy stormy night.
My sister looked at me, and I looked at her, and she said, "Do you think
we should go out?" When the air raid sirens started, you were supposed to go out. So we decided, no, we're not going to go. And then we
thought, "What if something happens? We gotta report it; you have to
write everything down." So we walked up K Street, went down J, up
Eleventh, down J, up Tenth. Then we saw something on the sidewalk.
My sister and I both thought, "Gosh, what's happening?" And here
was this man. We thought he was dead. His pants were torn, his leg
bleeding, and oh my gosh, we didn't know what to do.*
*We started screaming. Everybody around there came out of their
houses. I can still see it, right in front of the Roberti's house. Finally,
Mary said, "We have to call in something happened. A car hit this fellow and he's dying." We weren't too sure what to do, so we found a
phone and called an ambulance. I think it was an ambulance—we called
somebody. They came and put him on a stretcher and took him away.
Come to find out—you know what they pulled on us? What they had*

done, they got a beef tongue and slit it. You know how a tongue bleeds. And they ripped his pants open, put the tongue inside, and he was "bleeding." That's what they did to us. We had to report it. Just think if we hadn't gone out that night. They'd have known we weren't on the job.

Let me get this straight. At the time you were forced to leave your home in Arcata, you were actually working for civil defense?

No, but we were asked to be air raid wardens for four blocks in our neighborhood. You were asked to donate a certain amount of time. But we had to stop, of course. We also took turns as lookouts up at Redwood Park, where they had an observation station. We were keeping watch!

Was it difficult to find a place to rent in Eureka, and somebody to rent your Arcata home?

No. Some American people rented our place and we didn't have any problems. It was not a financial burden on the family. Dad was never out of work.

As a high school student, what did you think was going on?

In those days, when you're a teenager, you wouldn't even let people know that you spoke Italian! I was very, very angry, and I'd get angry with my dad. There's no two ways about it; I would get angry with my dad. He hadn't become a citizen. He lived and thought as though he was still in Italy, but he was over here. And I can still remember saying, "Do you think you're going to live forever? You have to change; you have to change." And he would say, "I'll never change, never."

Did you blame him for what happened to the family?

In the way he thought, yes. But in his personal being, no. He was such a loving, kind man. I only saw my dad cry once, and that's when we had to leave our house in Arcata. We had a cellar, and he had made wine. He had a hose, and he brought the hose down into the cellar and put it in the barrel to put his wine in gallon containers. Evidently, he walked away, the hose came out of the container, and his wine went all over the backyard. Tears just poured down. It hurt him so.

George Mori,
Eureka

One event involving my grandfather made a mark on my mind. His name was Erminlindo Rosaia. I can't remember whether it was three days or one week after Pearl Harbor. I was fourteen years old. I remember so clearly my grandfather picking up the newspaper. It was around seven o'clock at night. We had just finished eating and everyone was talking about how Italy had declared war on the United States. He was one of the last ones to look at the paper.

My grandfather and I were still at the table that night. My mother, my aunt, and my grandmother were in the kitchen doing the dishes, everyone had been working at the store. He picked up that paper and these headlines were in red and great big headlines. He looked at those and tears came to his eyes. As God is my judge. He didn't use his glasses very often, but that night he did. And he put down his glass of wine and left his pipe on the dinner table, which is something he had never, ever done. And he walked straight to bed. He didn't say anything he was a very quiet man, the most gentle person you could ever meet. We used to drink together at the cantina downstairs. If he'd made new wine, he'd take me down there—me, only seven or eight years old.

Along about two or three in the morning I was awakened by my mother. She told me that my grandfather was dying. I heard her tell my dad that she was going down to his bedroom on the bottom floor. We lived on the third floor, the Pasquinis on the second, and my grandparents had the ground floor flat. In those days, it was one family under one roof, the old Italian way. My mother came back upstairs around three or four, and I heard her telling my father what grandfather had said to her: he was going to die; take good care of your mother, and the business, and the children—things of that nature. When I woke up the next morning, he was gone. The mortuary people were already there and had taken his body away. I had been a pallbearer at age six or seven because I lost a buddy. But nothing hit me quite that much.

He had never been ill. He was eighty-one, eighty-two, somewhere around there. My mother said that he died of a broken heart, because he so loved Italy, of course, and he loved America. He loved this region especially. She also told me of a story about him when I was very young, around 1930, 1931, during Prohibition. They heard that the police were coming to see how many gallons of wine he was making, to test it for alcohol content. He knew, of course, that some of his prize wine was very high in alcohol. My mother said that she remembered going to the cantina and found him pouring his wine down the drain. And he was actually crying. He very seldom cried. In fact, the only time I saw him cry was the night he died. That's probably why it made such an impression on me.

Gino Casagrande

My mother was Vittoria, and my dad, Angelo. They had a bakery where Gilhooye's [restaurant] is now. My mother was the alien, and dad had to find a place for her to live south of Fourth Street. He found one at the Evans Hotel—or Apartments—at Fifth and A Streets. It's still there. He found her an apartment there because there were two other ladies that lived there who were in the same situation. So she had a little company. It created a bit of a hardship because we had a business here that she helped my father with.

Did you ever hear your parents comment about the restrictions?

They were kind of put out; that was only natural. It was an inconvenience, a hell of an inconvenience. When you split up a family it's bad. The thing is, nobody ever came around to apologize to them or anything like that. It was just one of those things. Ship 'em out, and when they say, "OK," go back. That's it.

Did your mother ever come back to the house while she was restricted?

Never. And I really don't remember her ever going anyplace. I don't know the reason. I used to go up to see her every day. In fact, I had lunch with her most every day, and I'd go there for supper. She might have gone downtown; I don't know. My dad probably did her shopping.
    What kind of burned me up was when the draft started. I had to sign up along with everybody else between eighteen and thirty-six. But here they are, they take my mother and ship her south of Fourth Street, and I was subject to the draft. I was bummed out, but there was nothing I could do about it. I was eventually drafted.

Did anyone say, "We're sorry, we know we've inconvenienced your mother, but you are a citizen and this is your duty"?

Never. It's so asinine. You take Eureka. I'd say ninety percent of the aliens that had to move were women. They thought these women were going to send signals to the birds out there in the bay, I guess. Take my mother. At that age, with all that family. She wasn't Tokyo Rose or anyone like that. That's what I mean. Even with the Japanese, they panicked. I mean they didn't know what the hell they were doing, so they said, "Well, let's get 'em out of here," without sitting down and thinking. I don't think the Japanese were going to bother anybody.

Mrs. Casagrande: *That was one of the worst things I think we've ever done. To tell the truth, I didn't realize all this happened until after I was grown up. They didn't have to do that.*

Gino: *Over the years, you never heard anymore about this because I think they wanted to keep it suppressed. Not that there was going to be any retribution or anything like that, but I think that they made such asses out of themselves they just didn't want people to know it.*

MOST OF THE Italians knew, of course, that the relocation order had been issued because they or their parents were not American citizens. But for one woman the reason for the breakup of her family seemed not to fit the general pattern:

Ernesta Dunn,
Eureka

Dad became a citizen when we were in Korbel. My mother was going to adult education here in Eureka to become a citizen. But she had to move anyway, south of Fourth Street, of course. It would have been different if mother hadn't been going to school. But my recollection is not that my mother had to move because she was an alien. We always felt that it was because the Jehovah's Witnesses used to come to the house. During World War II the Jehovah's Witnesses were almost "enemies" because they wouldn't salute the flag. They didn't believe in it. This is what we always felt. They came to our house with these Italian records about God and sang. Mother didn't know a thing about what the Jehovah's Witnesses stood for. All she knew was that here were these records and they spoke about God and sang. They spoke Italian. To her it was just pleasant. My mother had a good sense of humor and she liked people. This was such a pleasure. Here she was having these lovely records and conversations. I thought it was the Jehovah's Witnesses that caused the trouble, and how our country felt about them at the time of the war. I didn't realize there were questions about her loyalty. I didn't realize that, because she was Italian, she was considered an alien. Later, I became aware that it was because she was an alien.

*Daddy had to support two homes. He had to get extra beds and extra
things. This has always been a bitter recollection on my part. All these
years I have resented it. My resentment actually has been against the
Jehovah's Witnesses. I blamed them, mistakenly, so I now have to admit.
We had our home, and then she had to go and live across Fourth Street,
and daddy had to support another home. He rented a place. And he
worked, of course. The boys would stay in the new house all night, and
my sister and I slept in the other house. Dad kept up the other house,
but he stayed with mother. She cooked the meals and what have you. She
wasn't allowed to go back and forth across Fourth Street, and we always felt very bitter. Then the Japanese raised all this fuss about getting money. I thought, "This is so unfair. What about the people who
weren't Japanese who were deprived of certain things, too?" We're such
an emotional people anyway. I was bitter, but I don't really recall my
mother or father expressing any bitter thoughts. I felt we were discrimi-
nated against. That's uninformed youth for you!*

AS FAR AS the Italian aliens of Monterey and San Francisco were concerned, economic life ground to a halt for the remainder of 1942, when,
in late February, the coast guard barred all enemy alien fishing in bay
and coastal waters for the duration of the war. Appeals to the Justice Department got nowhere; Biddle's staff passed the buck to the War Department. The restrictions idled 75 percent of Monterey Bay's small boat
fleet, and in an insulting slap at the aliens, the state health officer ordered
all state-licensed canneries to keep aliens from operating food steriliza-
tion machinery.[106] Soon, the army and navy began to requisition the
fishermen's boats and industry-related property.

Salvatore Ferrante,
Monterey

When World War II began, you were an American citizen. Tell me about
the fishing boats the government confiscated.

*Right after Pearl Harbor, the army and navy requisitioned most of the
best fishing boats in Monterey and San Pedro. The fleet was then left
with the poorest boats. Most of the boats that were taken were sent
down to Latin America—and down the Atlantic side also—for patrolling.*

How did you know about this?

I had just completed a canning plant in Port Hueneme. That's by Oxnard. The navy requisitioned the entire harbor, and my plant along with everything else. The idea was that they were going to use the harbor as an assembly port to ship war material and men to strategic places. I was given three months to vacate everything that they didn't require. They wanted the building I had just completed, and most everything in it that they could use. I came back to Monterey and bought a piece of property and transferred all the equipment the navy didn't take up here. I was compensated, eventually, but it took quite a while. I had to go out and borrow the money to do the building here.

All the Italian fishermen were sent to Salinas. But by the time the season opened in August, all of those fellows were cleared and went back to fishing. It was considered that the canning of sardines and mackerel and what have you were needed for the war effort.

The men came back, but did the navy keep some of the boats?

The government took most of the best boats, but there were still enough of the small boats available that the army and navy did not need to keep the sardine and mackerel fisheries going. The owners were eventually compensated. When the war ended most of them were returned and rehabilitated. The army and navy kept them until they could replace them with new boats of their own.

They took boats from fishermen in Monterey who happened to be Italians. Was it because they were Italians?

No, they just had to have boats, and they wanted the best ones that were in the fleet. It didn't matter whether a man was a citizen. They took my plant; I was a citizen quite young. I came here when I was twelve, and as soon as I was of age I became a citizen. But they took my plant and everything in it that they could use. We were at war. We understood that. We just cooperated to the fullest extent as to what was needed for the war effort. It was just as simple as that.

What about the letters that were written in behalf of people who had to leave here? Were you aware of those efforts?

There was a lot of effort put into bringing the people back that were needed, such as the fishermen. Letters were written to their congressmen. Sardines and mackerel were considered essential items. Therefore, those who were cleared could go back to work. It didn't take too long to

clear all of the Italians who were not citizens. They were good peo-
ple—just didn't happen to be American citizens—and they were needed.
As a matter of fact, there wasn't one that wasn't cleared who was con-
nected to the fishing industry here. Most of them were back fishing by
the opening of the season on August first in whatever boats were avail-
able.

If you weren't a fisherman, if you weren't considered essential, were you
also cleared?

Most all of the wives were not citizens, and they and the children were
all cleared. They went back home, went about their business, and
worked for the war effort. In San Pedro, it was a little different. There
were a lot of Japanese there, and of course we all know what happened
to the Japanese. Some had boats; they weren't confiscated, but they were
taken for the same reason as the Italians', and those people eventually
recovered the value of their boats.

Did the government keep your plant until the end of the war?

As a matter of fact, they still own it. I never went back. I came back to
Monterey and bought a piece of property on Cannery Row and rebuilt
the plant here.

Giuseppe, Vitina, and Joe Spadaro,
Monterey

Giuseppe: *I came to the United States in 1920, from Sicily. I was en-*
gaged to be married when I came the first time, then I went back and
got married. When the restrictions came in 1942 I was a citizen but my
wife was not, so the family moved to Salinas. I came back to Monterey
every week to fish, and to check the house.
     Then the government took our fishing boats. We had to fish to earn a
living, so some of the other fishermen and I went up to Seattle to char-
ter boats. With those, we were able to call out our crews again and
resume fishing.
     The government kept my boat for about two years. But when they re-
turned it, it was in very bad shape. I spent a lot of money to repair it so
I could fish with it again, but it was no use. I had to moor it to Wharf
No. 2 and continue to fish with the rented boat.

One night when we were out fishing a sudden squall came up and we had to go up near Santa Cruz. The weather was so bad we couldn't come back to Monterey. The storm broke the anchor chain on my damaged boat and it was swept up on the beach. The insurance company tried to pull it off the beach and refloat it, but it was a total loss. The bottom was so broken up it kept sinking.

Vitina [daughter]: *The coast guard called my mother during the storm, telling her that the boat had broken its mooring and was headed toward the beach. My mother was panicked because my father was out fishing and there was no way to get in touch with him. The fleet was anchored at different points out in the ocean where the water was a little more calm. I remember telling the coast guard that my father was out, and I asked if there was anything they could do. "No," they said they had no orders to go there and do anything about it.*

Giuseppe: *I called the shipyard to see if they had any idea how to salvage it. A man from there worked on it a little bit, but he said it was too expensive for me to have it fixed and offered four thousand dollars for it. What was I going to do? I couldn't fix it myself. So I sold it to the shipyard for four thousand. Soon after that the men from the yard rigged some canvas to cover the bottom of the boat and somehow, with pumps, managed to raise the boat and tug it to San Francisco where they fixed it up real nice.*

I asked the man from the yard if he would sell it back to me. I offered thirty thousand, but he said it would cost me sixty. I said, "No, I'll build a new boat for less than that!" To be fair, it cost them some money to have it fixed up; probably thirty thousand just to replace the engine. I got some insurance money for the loss, but that went toward the attempts to refloat the boat before I finally sold it.

Did the government pay you for using the boat?

Six hundred dollars a month. While they had it, the navy paid the insurance and taxes, everything. I didn't have to pay anything, and they sent me a check $600 every month.

Vitina: *The fishermen were told that the government needed their boats to patrol the Panama Canal and other areas. So all the fishermen were left without their boats. But this was their livelihood, and they had to make a living for their families. So my father, my uncles, and others went up to Seattle and rented boats. That meant another loss for the fishermen. They usually worked with shares the boat gets so many shares. So when they rented from another company all of the profit went to them.*

My father experienced yet another loss by having to do this. When the government took his boat it wasn't properly maintained like a fisherman would do it. So it was returned to my father, but it was in such poor condition he was unable to use it for fishing again. All the boat owners—the fishermen in Monterey—had already chartered other boats; they had contracts for which they were responsible. So they tied up their boats here in the bay and continued fishing that season with the rented boats.

When the boat crashed on the beach, it was like losing a member of the family. Because my father fished on this boat day and night, and put all his love into it, it was such a sadness for him. I think that was the only time I actually saw him cry. We were all bitter. I was a child, and then to see my parents cry, and to see everything dad had worked for was gone. Because they owned their home, everything else went into the boat. It changed everything. But after a while he decided to build another boat. He called his second boat the New Marettimo. *The first boat was just* Marettimo.

Joe [Vitina's husband]*: It means "small ocean."* Mare *is ocean, and* timo *is small.*

Vitina*: When my father had the second boat built, it cost much more than he paid for the first one. He managed to get a bigger loan, but that meant more headaches and responsibilities to pay the loan off. The seasons were good, though, and through the years it was paid.*

To tell these families to leave their homes and go somewhere else and rent, that meant extra expense. To charter different boats when they already had their own fishing boats, and then the loss. We were losing money all the way around.

We also heard what was happening to the Japanese. Then somehow the word got around that they were going to do the same thing to the Italians. My mother always lived in fear that the Italians were going to be put away. That's why she was so nervous about being home in the evening by eight o'clock. There was talk that they had spies out in the street, or things like that. Really. And she never wanted to go out. Of course, she never thought of coming to Monterey to check on her home. So I think they lived in fear all that time.

Vitina*: I was in grammar school in 1942, and for a time, it was very confusing. There was so much news going out that all the aliens were going to concentration camps. Thank God the Italians were not. But we were told to leave Monterey because it was considered a war zone, and so my family decided to move to Salinas.*

It was very difficult for my father and mother because my mother had to leave her home. I remember leaving my schoolmates and saying good-

bye to everyone. What I really recall was how difficult it was to find a place to live in Salinas. When we did go out looking for a place to rent, and the owner found out we were aliens, we were turned down. It was difficult as a child to accept something like that.

There were a lot of people from Monterey, including relatives, moving to Salinas. They chose Salinas because it was approved for the aliens, and yet it was close to Monterey. My father owned a fishing boat, a purse seiner, and he fished for sardines here in the bay. So, from Salinas, it was convenient for him to go to Monterey to fish during the week, and then come back to Salinas on the weekends. Other people moved to San Jose.

My parents owned their home in Monterey, and we kept that while we lived in Salinas. My father and I used to come back here on weekends to check on the house and pick up a few things that we needed. He came back here to fish during the week the only day they didn't fish was Saturday.

My father owned a car, so that's how he got back and forth. He would leave my mother and me Sunday afternoon because they started fishing Sunday night and worked until Friday.

How long were you in Salinas?

I think from January to June. I remember June, because that was the month I came back to graduate from grammar school with my classmates.

I also remember that the aliens were told that they had to be in their homes at night no later than eight o'clock. We would be having dinner at a relative's, and my mother was so nervous, looking at the time, making sure that we left that house and were home before eight.

Joe: *I was young at the time I went to Salinas: nineteen. I worked there in a [frozen food] plant. We heard of other aliens who couldn't fish who had to work out in the fields picking fruit and vegetables.*

I was single, so I moved in with a group of five single men, and we rented a house. After three months, when there was no more work in Salinas, I moved to San Francisco and was there six or seven months. Even after the aliens could come back to Monterey, they still couldn't fish, so for me it was better to stay and work in San Francisco. I worked in a freezer there; we froze turkey and vegetables for the government. I went by there the other day and it's gone.

While I worked in San Francisco, my mother still lived in Italy. I received a letter from her after about two and a half years, through the Italian Consulate in Portugal. They forwarded it to me. One day while I was at work an FBI agent came up to me and started asking a lot of questions about how I got this letter from Portugal. I had to explain where my mother was and what was in the letter. They were checking us very, very close to see if we did something wrong.

When I got back to Monterey, I received a card from the draft board; they wanted me to go in the army. I didn't want to serve in Italy. I had a good skipper who depended on me a lot, so he went with me to the draft board and got me a deferment. Since fishing was so good, I was considered to be in an essential industry. Our cannery sold directly to the government, not to commercial stores. The soldiers needed the food, so I got to go to work again.

I finally became a citizen in 1946 and bought my first car. On April 18, I got my citizenship papers, and on April 27, I married my wife. It's a month I don't think I'll forget.

Anita Maiorana Ferrante

When the war broke out in 1941, my mother was not a citizen but my dad was. I was a citizen through my father, so I was qualified to stay in Monterey. But my mother, being an alien, had to leave. All the Italians that were in this area had to move twenty miles inland. The closest place they could go was to Salinas.

How do the authorities specify twenty miles, or did they say, "Go to Salinas"?

No, no. It was twenty miles inland: "You must be away from the sea, twenty miles." So we packed our belongings, very cheerfully, and everything was put into a moving van. We owned a home on Larkin Street. The house next door was vacated too. Moving vans were moving the people out, some to San Jose. Most of them that had husbands who were citizens were moved to Salinas so that the husband could come in and fish. So we established our residency there, and we were there from February to May. I was in the 7th grade, so I don't remember too many details. But it was a very, very sad thing.

How do you remember that it was those months?

Well, because the war broke out in '41, and I was in the 7th grade at San Carlos School. I had just started Catholic school, and I remember how hard it was for me to leave. I remember it was right after January that we had to pack up and leave my classmates, my new school; it was very, very hard. But over in Salinas we had a lovely home and made new friends. We rented the house in Salinas, and kept ownership of our house here. My dad was coming over here, and he could check the house, though it was totally vacant. Every piece of furniture was moved out and brought over to Salinas. He went back and forth every day in our car, and fished every day. My dad knew people who were well known in the community, so he was able to have letters written saying that "this is a good family" "they should not be taken out of this area" "they should come back." I remember my father saying, "We got some nice letters that will bring us back home." So we were one of the first families to go back because of our contacts. I really do think it was through my father's wonderful friends, and through those letters that went out saying we were a good family, and so forth. I got a chance to be with my classmates before the end of the school year. My friend Vitina said she got back in time to graduate with her class in June. We left together, but we came back to Monterey earlier than she did.

BY LATE SPRING 1942, all the army's restrictions were in place. In rapid succession during the month of March, General DeWitt issued a series of proclamations that, while aimed primarily at the Japanese, hinted that when the army was finished with them the Italians and Germans would be next. New bureaucratic machinery was established to coordinate the removal of the three groups, the most important being the Civil Affairs Division of the Wartime Civil Control Administration, headed by the ubiquitous Colonel Bendetsen.[107]

By early April, the Japanese were on their way to Manzanar and other relocation camps as far east as Arkansas, while the Italians and Germans who remained in California continued to suffer silly indignities. Governor Olson suggested that enemy aliens be denied parole, except of course to inland states, and then only under the most extenuating circumstances. When reminded that San Quentin lay in a restricted area, Olson remarked that he didn't think General DeWitt would object to the continued presence there of enemy aliens who were already locked up! One Italian got six months in the Alameda County jail for failure to register as an enemy alien, possession of a short-wave radio and camera, and making a false claim of citizenship. The man was superstitious and thought he would be protected by the elk's tooth he kept in his pocket, or by the judge in the case who, like himself, was a member of the Elk Lodge.[108]

As weeks stretched into months, the Italians discovered—to their dismay—that hostility toward some of them existed within the Italian community as well as outside it.

FIVE

"He was a stool pigeon"
Neighbor against Neighbor

*The rule caused a lot of hubbub in this town. All the young ones were
citizens because they were born here, and all the older ones, they
liked to go down to Second Street. There were two or three saloons
down there run by Italians.... And they couldn't do that anymore. I
tell you it hit them pretty hard.... There was a lot of jealously.... The
ones that stayed home didn't go out because they were scared, so
they turned in the people that were out. It made a lot of hostility.
That's why it was such a bad law.*
—Mary Tolomei, 1986

BETRAYAL TOOK SEVERAL forms in 1942. The government
betrayed the faith that most aliens had in America, including the
some of ideals for which the nation professed to be fighting
around the globe. But what the aliens may least have expected was what
happened in their own neighborhoods. While curfews might appear reasonable and uncomplicated restrictions in wartime, that of the late winter
and early spring had an unforeseen twist: Italian American citizens exor-
cised their own fears and old grudges by reporting friends and neighbors—even family members to the authorities. Vigilantism became the
unseemly offspring of panic.

Attorney General Francis Biddle had established the first curfew for
the aliens on February 24 as the hours between 9 P.M. and 6 A.M. At
all other times they had to be at home, work, or somewhere in between,
so long as it was not more than five miles from home. Consequently,
hundreds of aliens descended on U.S. Attorney Frank Hennessy's office
in San Francisco to obtain permits to enable them to continue working at
night. General DeWitt superseded Biddle's ruling slightly in late March,
when he extended the curfew from 8 P.M. until 6 A.M., but this did not
help those who worked the graveyard shift. The FBI was given the responsibility of enforcing the army's new edict. From March until October, when restrictions on the Italians were lifted, the FBI periodically
picked up Italians and Germans who, for one reason or another, were

reported to have violated the curfew or to have unlawfully entered a restricted zone.[109]

Nelo and Lena Dal Porto
Arcata

Nelo: *Well, I was born here, so I'm no alien, unless you're an alien if you were born in Arcata.* [laughs]

Lena: *We lived on the side of the street that was OK, so we didn't have to move. But Nelo worked on the other side and I couldn't go to the store at all. I was an alien.*

Nelo: *I worked right next to where Don's Donut Bar is now. There used to be a grocery store in there. That's where I learned the grocery business. We had just been married and had lived there about five years. Our son was born in 1941. It wasn't long after that that the orders came through that no enemy alien could cross highway 101* [through downtown Arcata].

Lena: *So his mother and dad, being that his dad was an alien, moved in with us.*

Nelo: *My brother-in-law was an alien, so he had to cross over. They rented a house close to the college. At that time, 101 was not a freeway like it is now. So he just moved on the other side of 101.*

Lena: *I don't know how many years this lasted.*

Nelo: *It was over a year, I know.*

Lena: *They really disrupted a lot of families. I remember my brother got married in San Francisco, and I couldn't go down without a special permit.*

Nelo: *The only way I got a travel permit for her was from the postmaster. He was the only government representative we had in Arcata.*

What was his attitude?

Oh, fine. Of course, I knew him for a long time. Most of the general population felt kind of bad about it. We were all neighbors. They lived with us; our kids grew up together.

Lena: *To get back to the travel thing, just to tell you how scared they made you, I went to the wedding, and who the heck would have known it if I'd stayed up till midnight. There was an eight o'clock curfew. Believe it or not, I went home at eight o'clock. That just about broke my heart. I was afraid somebody would turn us in. People did that, you know. There were a lot of those.*

Nelo: *They used to do a lot of snooping. I had a cousin who was an alien. Well, he married another cousin, and they were going together at the time. And he'd sneak over to see his girlfriend. And this one guy turned him in. I don't know if he thought he was being patriotic, but they put him in jail. He was only a few years old when he came over here. But anyway, this one guy, his name was _____, and he was an assistant deputy sheriff. And he was a stool pigeon. Boy, if he could turn you in, he'd turn you in. He belonged to the dry squad from Prohibition days.*

Lena couldn't go where I worked, but she could go to any store on this side [of the line]. *And the movie theater was where it is right now, so she could go to the movies.*

Lena: *But I had to be home by eight o'clock. They patrolled the streets at night. I remember one night I went to the show, and I was scared. I didn't want to stay after eight o'clock, so I had to leave in the middle of the picture. I had to get home and I was scared somebody would see me and turn me in.*

Nelo: *She'd go to the matinee, like on Sunday, and I'd go in the evenings so we had somebody to stay with the kids.*

Lena: *We could never go together.*

Nelo: *Yeah, you always were afraid somebody might squeal on you. But that's the only guy that I know that squealed on anybody during that period.*

Alex Frediani

Did anyone ever report curfew violators to the authorities?

Oh, sure. Especially down on B Street, where a lot of people [aliens], *like my mother, were living. People knew who they were. They would say, "Watch out for So-and-So." You'd go over to the neighbor's house, and you had to make sure that you got out of there by ten minutes to eight so that you had time to walk across the street and be in your house. I'll tell you who treated us the worst were some of the Italians who were naturalized, who thought they were a little better. It was generally the guy that was trying to feather his own nest. There were just one or two that I can remember, and one of them was really a "stoolie." I wouldn't tell you his name because I really don't know. But I do remember people saying, "Hey, watch out for So-and-So, he's a stoolie." I knew whom they meant. This person would try to be one of the gang, but nobody'd have anything to do with him, even after the war.*

Joe Nieri,
Arcata

My grandparents emigrated to Sao Paulo, Brazil, where my dad was born. They stayed there for about six months, then went back to Italy. Consequently, when my parents were married my brother and I were born in Italy. My dad came over here in 1924 and worked for two years, and then sent money for us to come to the United States.

We came when I was three years old. The family settled here and dad worked in the lumber mills and camps. Along comes the war, World War II. My dad was not considered an enemy alien, because he was born in Brazil. He got his citizenship, I'd say, after the war; I can't remember what year it was. It was after we came back from the army, though. But my mother and my brother and I had to relocate across this imaginary line—G Street, the old highway 101.

We heard about the order, and we read it in the newspapers; but the official word came from the local police department. They came around and explained to us what we had to do. We were living at Eleventh and K Streets, about five blocks too far west. So we had to relocate to the east side of G Street. I was seventeen and a senior in high school. It really hurt me 'cause we had all gone to school with these kids from grammar school on up, and of course, we knew everybody and they knew us. I was supposed to graduate with them, and was looking forward to it. Well, my brother and I lost that year of high school. I had to go back to the class of '43. But when the class of '42 had their reunions, they always asked me: "Well, you were in our class, right?"

"Yes, but if you remember correctly they had this enemy aliens thing, and we weren't supposed to cross the line." 'Course those people now, they say, "Oh well, it was a stupid thing to do to a person." There were three of them that I talked to; they kind of forgot what happened. But I said, "Do you remember when we had to go across that imaginary line?"

"Oh God, yes, we forgot about it."

"Well, I didn't!" So I have to go to reunions with the kids that were behind me. It comes up every time and it brings back old memories. It bothers me, it really does. You kind of forgive, but you can't forget. It's embedded too deep.

I was on the first string basketball team, and that's another thing that hurt me. I was going to get my second stripe and then a sweater. I could have walked around school with two stripes on my sleeve! I couldn't participate in sports in '43 either, because technically that would have been my fifth year in high school, and they only accepted four years of athletic eligibility. That's something that really hurt. I couldn't even get into the yearbook, my pictures or anything like that. I didn't try to argue with them, but I explained, "It was five blocks from this imaginary line. What harm is it going to do? Just let me go to school for another year, until the end of June."

"No. We've got orders to relocate you, and that's it. You have to go."

It happened during basketball season, I remember that. I was sitting on the high school gymnasium steps, when the principal came and told me I had to leave school. That was my last day. I still remember sitting on those brick steps and thinking, "This is it. Three-thirty's coming." I had a big lump in my throat, and I said good-bye to all those guys. But I got to go back to school the following September.

The whole family moved. We rented a house on Ninth Street, near where the Arcata ballpark is now, right across from the fire station. It wasn't really difficult, other than moving. But we had to pay a higher rent, which hurt. We couldn't travel across the imaginary line. If we had to go to the dentist or a doctor—they were on the west side of the line—we could cross, but we had to get a police escort. To go from our house to the doctor or dentist they had to call a police officer to come and pick us up after we were through. Just like we were in jail. I thought it was really foolish, or stupid, or whatever you want to call it. The dentist and doctor were on the plaza. They thought it was kind of dumb, too, but they had to go by the regulations. They were all sympathetic. Besides not being able to cross this line, we had to be on our property by seven o'clock at night. No later. And if we were out, well, there were two or three spies around—neighborhood people—who would report us to the police. There was one guy that we know who turned us in; the police chief told us.

We snuck up to the show after dark, through a lot of alleys and backyards. We'd jump across peoples' yards, hide in the bushes, then go in through the back door of the theater. That was an awful thing, you know, sneaking around like that. If we didn't go to the show for entertainment, though, we were stuck at our house.

I couldn't get a job; all the jobs were on the west side of the highway. All we could do was sit around the house. We used to love to go clam digging, but that was too far for us to travel. And on Sundays, all the grocery stores and other stores were closed. Before the war the family used to go on picnics out at Camp Bauer or Blue Lake. And we couldn't even do that; we had to sit at home. The Japanese were in concentration camps; I really felt sorry for them. But we were just like in a concentration camp, too, but for a short time.

Mom felt sorry for us. She wasn't too concerned about herself. Most of the time she'd keep to the house, clean and cook and all that stuff. 'Course we liked to wander; you know kids. But we couldn't go out on dates or anything.

They made us go in the army. We had to register for the draft, even being enemy aliens, which I could not comprehend. Course at that time I didn't understand too much of what was going on. Whatever they told us, we did. So we registered, and I said, "Well, I'm not going into the draft because we're enemy aliens. We're not supposed to be in the army or the armed forces." We registered anyway, and got a notice to report to San Francisco. But we didn't go. We were that bitter. So they sent a sergeant, or somebody, and the local police. They came over to our house and gave us an ultimatum: "You will go down for a physical and if you pass, you're going to go in the army or you're going to prison." So we didn't have too much of a choice. We talked it over and thought about it, and decided we didn't want to dirty the family's reputation. So we said, "Don't ruin the Nieri name. We'll go." So we did. We went in the army on May the third of '44.

At first we were in the artillery down at Camp Roberts. About two months later they took all the aliens—mostly Mexicans—over to the county seat at San Luis Obispo. They swore us in and gave us our citizenship papers. They couldn't have an enemy alien in the army, so we had to be citizens. Later we found out that because they needed more infantry for the Normandy invasion, we would have to convert to the infantry. But of all the places, we were sent to Italy! And we got into the fighting there, just above Rome. Yeah, it wasn't very pleasant, but it was the last two weeks of the war. Still, when those bullets buzz over your head, and you don't know if your name is on it, it's terrible.

I saw all the aunts, uncles, cousins. In fact, I even saw the house and the room I was born in. The people were really glad to see us. When the Germans made a final push up there by Milan I got hit in the back with mortar shrapnel. And of all the places to be sent, I was sent back to Lucca, my home village, to the field hospital. My brother was hit, too. We were in the same foxhole. They sent us to this field hospital in Lucca, and we were talking to this civilian who knew my uncle and he told him and the family came over and visited us. That's how we got to know where they were.

Anita Pera

There was a nine o'clock curfew; the stories about that are funny. My grandparents had a house on the corner here. All the men that were moved out of "North of Fourth [Street]" boarded in this area. At about six–thirty every evening they would congregate at my grandfather's. Dan Banducci was one. I can't remember all the names, but they were all friends of my grandfather. The minute it got to be a quarter to nine you'd see it—wipe out; everything just went dead all over the neighborhood. The kids would still be out playing, but all these men would have to go into the houses and be locked up. I guess that was pretty hard on their egos.

Some of the naturalized citizens were tattles, you know. There was one lady, and she was definitely your dyed-in-the-wool American, who had very little use for anybody that wasn't American, except Vilma. She loved Vilma I don't know why. She had no use for me. I was a little brat, a little sister, and I thought I should be able to get away with everything. But anyway, I'm sure she did a lot of reporting on those men that were out a little after the curfew. I'm sure she did. They knew of one lady that they said did some reporting to the government, and boy, they gave her a bad time. She was a naturalized citizen, and she had not had to struggle for it like my mother and others. She was the proverbial witch. She made sure she had some kind of dirt on everybody.

The names that the Italians had for the tattles weren't very nice. I can't remember 'em all; they were four letter words. I remember people narcking on the non-citizens somebody narcked on my grandfather and the FBI came to the door at two o'clock in the morning. I don't know what they reported, because he worked down at the Roma bakery, which was on the correct side of Fourth Street. I remember that morning because my sister used to sleep with my grandmother when grandfather was at work. And I remember them coming and waking us up. My grandmother was just petrified when she saw two policemen and an FBI agent, but they were just asking questions.

"Where's your husband?"

My sister said, "Why, he's working."

"Are you sure?"

"Yes. I know my father took him to work."

"Are you positive?"

"Well, you can go down to the Roma bakery and see for yourself."

They never did, which I cannot understand.

Did anyone ever say what the restrictions were for?

The only thing that I can think of was the bay, and maybe they thought that we'd put bombs over there or something. I have no idea. What on earth could Georgia Massei or Dan Banducci, or any of those that lived down there, have done that would have been destructive? I can understand that they might have been a little apprehensive about the East Coast, but on the West Coast? This is the funny part. Look [pointing out the window], *there's Broadway* [Street] *down there. Do you know what used to be down there? Swamp. It was swamp from there clear down to Field's Landing. We used to go over there and pick blackberries. The Stump House was there, but behind it—nothing. There wasn't a building or anything, and yet they were restricted. What on Earth was north of Fourth* [Street]*? Fishing. What can you do with fish? That law was made in Washington where no one had any idea what was going on in half the states. And yet they stood over there and made those laws, from the president on down. You can quote me on that.*

Marino Sichi

My dad came over in 1920, and my mother and I came in 1922, when I was two. Right after Pearl Harbor, General DeWitt issued an order. That son-of-a-bitch, I hope he rots in his grave. Anybody of Japanese, German, or Italian descent could not live west of highway 101. That was the demarcation line. We had applied for our citizenship papers, and were in the process of getting them. My parents hadn't gotten theirs because they couldn't read or write English. If my father had gotten his, then I would have automatically been a citizen before I was eighteen. [Sichi's reference is to "derivative citizenship," which was provided for in Sec. 339 of the Nationality Act of 1940.] *But he didn't get his in time, so we had to apply individually. Then, with the war on, they froze it* [naturalization] *and we had to move out.*

We owned a chicken ranch, here, on this property. We had to sell out close to five thousand chickens. My dad took a beating. Five thousand hens he sold to Seely & Titlow for twenty-five cents apiece. They were all laying hens, not for breeding. After all this happened he got back into it after a fashion, but his heart wasn't in it. Anyway, we had to move out [when the war started] *and some people across the street took us in. We lived there for a few months. Then we got a little cabin, a little three-room shack about halfway up the road to their house. We could look over here* [at the old house], *but we couldn't come near it. We weren't too happy about it.*

I was courting my wife at the time, and we weren't allowed out after eight o'clock at night. We had to be inside, but I figured, "Oh, to hell with it." I'd go where I'd want. Went all my life, so why not now? I was twenty-one at the time. Well, somebody turned me in. Called the FBI. A so-called "friend." Wore one of those dollar-a-year badges. Special police at dances, things like that. And next thing I know I had a real sharp looking young man knocking on my door. He was looking for my dad, then found out he had the wrong guy and wanted me. He says, "I understand you were out after eight o'clock?" What could I say? I said, "yes." So he arrested me for violation of the curfew; I forget what else he called it. This time they caught me. I was on the right side of the line, but I was out after eight. I'd go to the movies—sit right next to the police chief. He never paid any attention to me 'cause he'd known me practically all my life, and he figured I was just as safe as anybody else, so what the heck? I know who turned me in. He didn't wake up very good the next morning. Some friends went in and busted his head open, blacked his eyes, and busted his nose. He didn't recuperate very fast.

They confiscated all of our guns. I had a .22 and a .410, and my dad had a .22. That's about all the things that we had at the time. I had just bought my folks a brand new Zenith console radio, which I still have. We took it down to the shop and had the short-wave component disconnected. They were afraid I'd use it for receiving or transmitting some way. I kept one .22 long shell, which I made into a dum-dum. I intended to use it on a certain person. But I never had a gun to use it with.

The guy who arrested me was nobody local. Even the police chief said afterwards, "Heck, I've known you all my life. I never knew you weren't born here."

"No, I've been living here since I was two years old." I didn't know any other country, really.

So they locked me up in the county jail for five days, waiting for transportation, I guess. And from there, they took me—two marshals and another prisoner—in a car, a Chevy, I remember. They said, "We can be tough on you, or be easy. Whatever you want. If you want to cooperate we won't put handcuffs on you, but if you want to get smart, we'll cuff you." I said I wouldn't do anything. What could I do? So they let us sit in the back seat of the car. At Willits, they let us out at a Standard station to go to the bathroom, one at a time. They put us on our honor while they gassed up the car.

They brought us to what I think was FBI headquarters [INS detention facility] on Silver Avenue in San Francisco, a big mansion up on the hill with a big wall around it. When they turned us over to the man-

ager, he said, *"Well, what am I going to do with them? We have no
facilities to keep these people."* So he locked us in a big closet. We sat
there for quite a while, just sat on the floor. Pretty soon they opened the
door and let us out and loaded us into a paddy wagon. We didn't know
where we were going. It turned out they took us to Sharp Park, near
Pacifica. They had quite a concentration camp there, a holding camp I
guess you'd call it.

I remember the camp was divided in half. The Japanese were on the
left side as you went in, and we were on the right. I don't know; it
seemed like there were thousands of people; it was quite a large gather-
ing. There were Germans, English, French, Italians, every nationality
you could think of.

We didn't get to talk to the Japanese. They had us separated by a
double fence, big enough to drive a truck between, and they patrolled it
steadily, on foot and by truck. And barbed wire. It must have been at
least ten feet high with barbed wire coming up on the ends on both
sides. Couldn't get in or out.

We had barracks, mess halls, a camp bakery. Naturally, there was a
commandant's office, and everything was enclosed by a chainlink fence.
There were guard towers at every corner and all around the perimeter.
Those guards were armed; I found out the hard way. We were playing
baseball one day, and I was out in the field. Somebody hit a ball and it
got past me. I ran after it and everybody was shouting to hurry up and
throw the ball in. All at once, I heard a sound that made the blood kind
of stop. Heard a "click-click," and when I looked up, I'm looking down
the barrel of a .30-caliber machine gun aimed right at my head. I
wasn't more than five or six feet from the fence and he was right above
me, just motioning me off. He says, *"You aren't supposed to be near
this fence. Back off."* I tried to explain that I was just after the baseball, but he said, *"I don't care what you were after. The next time we're
going to shoot."* There was no next time. I didn't go near it again. I
wanted nothing to do with it. They claimed the fence was electrified at
night, but we weren't sure.

It was a summer camp as far as we were concerned. Conditions were
good. Still, we were locked in at night, about nine or nine-thirty. We
had a chance to go to the latrine, and then we were locked in. Doors
and windows were barred. And that was it. We didn't get up until seven
o'clock the next morning. If you had bad kidneys, you were in trouble.
We had some relatives in San Francisco, and they'd come out on Sundays to visit me, through the fence.

Everybody had to work. We were asked what we could do, and I had
been a baker, so I was assigned to the camp bakery. There was a big,

fat German, a prisoner. He spoke with a real heavy accent. "Ya, what's your name?" *he said.*

"Marino Sichi."

"You're a goddamned wop"—*just like that.*

"No, I'm Italian."

"I don't want no wop working for me. Get the hell out of here."

So I said, "Screw you," *and left. I went back to the barracks and stayed. The next day the guards came after me and wanted to know why I wasn't working. I told 'em.*

"You got to work."

"I ain't gonna work with him. He don't want me, and I'll be damned if I'm going to work for a damn Kraut if that's the way he feels about it. I ain't gonna work for him."

The next thing I know I got hauled before the camp commandant, who had me stand at attention in front of his desk—all that baloney. He said I'd have to work for the baker, or else.

"What the hell you gonna do? Throw me in a damn concentration camp?" *His face got the color of your jacket* [red]. *When he calmed down a bit he says,* "Go on back to your barracks." *So I did. But the next morning they marched me over to the laundry. My job was to fold the sheets as they came out of a huge machine. We worked until about ten o'clock, and then they'd come in with coffee and hot pastry from the bakery and we'd have a break. We'd sit around, fifteen, twenty minutes a day. Same thing happened around two o'clock. After that, we had the rest of the day for recreation. They had a gym, but you could do anything you wanted. Baseball, horseshoes—anything you wanted. They had a library; they had everything.*

We got paid, too. When I was in the laundry a guard came in and asked if anybody knew how to press a shirt. I pressed shirts at home, so I figured I could press his. He said, "Can you run that mangle?" *I said,* "No, but if you'll show me how it won't be any different than a steam iron, I imagine." *He showed me how to press it right down the middle of the pockets, right across the button. He gave me two bits. After that, I spent most of my time pressing shirts for the guards. I made a pile of money. Heck, I didn't care whether I went home or not. Probably making more money than I did in civilian life. But no, I didn't want to stay there. All kidding aside, it wasn't any fun. We hired a shyster lawyer who took us for $200 dollars, but I got out. When I came back, I was really careful. I didn't want a repetition of it. Shortly after that they removed the restrictions and we were able to move home again.*

I had mixed feelings about this country. I wanted to stay here. I wasn't too happy about the situation because I figured I wasn't doing anything wrong. So I was born on the wrong side of the ocean. It wasn't my fault. I had applied for my citizenship papers and, if things had been different, I would have had them. But it just didn't work out that way. So, just because of a technicality I was thrown in the hoosegow.

I didn't like that, and I wasn't too happy about being drafted, later on. By then, I was back at work at the bakery on the "right" side of Fourth Street. I was even classified as essential labor. They didn't seem interested in me, then all at once they started after me. When I went down to San Francisco I said, "What are my options. I'm an enemy alien." The marines refused me. They had a desk with three people: army, marines, and navy. The second man, the marine, took one look at my papers and said, "I don't want no damn enemy alien." I thought, "Thank God." He threw my papers over to the navy guy and he said the same thing. "Thank you," I said, "You can't dig a foxhole on the deck of a battleship." And he threw me to the army guy who said, "We ain't particular. We'll take you." So I went in the Army. I went down a number of times before they finally took me in February of '44 because I was classified 4-F. I had problems with my stomach, and the doctor was treating me for ulcers. And then when I got in the service I found out it wasn't ulcers, it was colitis. I got discharged on that.

One thing though, the army handed me my citizenship papers with an M-1 rifle. When I passed the physical, I asked what my options were. They said you can refuse induction and you'll never be a citizen. We may ship you back to Italy. Or you can sign up and you can get your papers. They didn't tell me I'd go to jail, just that they might ship me back to Italy. I was already a draft dodger from Italy. They had called me up to serve in the Ethiopian campaign when I was seventeen, and I said, "Go to hell. I don't owe you anything." The Italian Consul in San Francisco called me up. They were calling all the Italian citizens who were born in 1920. They called it the Class of 1920.

If I tell you how I got my citizenship papers, though, you'll laugh. If you could see it. Camp Fannan, Texas, middle of summer. They told us to put on our Class A uniform. We were going to town and become American citizens. They loaded us onto these six-by-six trucks and headed for the county courthouse, Deaf Smith County, Tyler, Texas. We went up to the judge's chambers, and there was a character strictly out of Judge Roy Bean: boiled white shirt, string tie, white suit, planter's hat lying on the bench next to him, and a big mouth full of chewing tobacco, which he spit into a spittoon. I remember him saying, "You all swear to uphold and defend these here—spttttt—United States of America—sptttttt—?" And he'd clang that old spittoon every time. You wouldn't believe it unless you saw it. I got a little slip of paper that said I was now a citizen of the United States. That's all there was to it. There were Germans, Italians, you name 'em—Austrians, French. We went down on the courthouse lawn and we rolled and we laughed; it was the most hilarious thing. This was supposed to be a solemn occasion, and here was this judge with his "sptttt." He could hit that damn spittoon from six paces.

Ugo Giuntini

I went to visit Marino. I had a brother who lived in San Francisco, and my wife and I would go down quite often to see football games and for my wife to visit with sisters in the Bay Area. Then my brother and I would go down to this place and visit him.

The very first time my brother and I got to this wire compound, we saw him. It does something to you. It's just like looking at animals caged in a pen. We'd visit with him, and then come back and report on his condition to his folks. When I left, there he was on the other side of that wire. You could just read his thoughts: "Why? Why?" And it kinda did something to you, because after all, he was one of our family friends. I sympathize with those poor Japanese. By golly, they had it rougher. I don't know how they were treated except what you read and see in the pictures they made available to us. But I know that Marino didn't suffer. I mean he wasn't mistreated, let's put it that way. He just had a boundary beyond which he couldn't go, that's all. But those poor Japanese. Wow.

Mary Tolomei,
Eureka

My mother was an alien. We were living in the area that was considered off limits because they were afraid of sabotage. That made it a little hard. We had to move. My mother was sick at the time. She had a nervous breakdown not too long after my father's death. My husband worked on the railroad, and he was gone all week. My father died in '36, and when we got married, we lived with my mother. When my dad died, my husband said, "Let your mother live with us." So she did.

January of '42 was when we had to move. The sheriff came to the house to say we had to move. He got his orders from Sacramento. He told us they were afraid we were going to be doing some sabotage. That's the word he got from Sacramento. He knew all the Italians, and he thought it was a crazy idea too. But what could he do? That was an order. He was carrying out orders, so we had to go. I don't know whether it was six months or eight months before they realized it was a crazy law. I don't know who thought of it; boy, it was crazy. Mother thought it was a crazy rule. She said, "What could I do? Even though we live close to the bay, what could I sabotage? What is there to sabotage in Eureka?" She couldn't figure it out. I tell you it was a crazy thing.

We were fortunate enough to get an apartment on Fourth Street, on the "right" side of Fourth, a block and a half away from where we were living because we had chickens and rabbits and we had to go back and forth. We kept the house on Third and W. We kept it empty. My mother didn't want to rent it. We didn't take any furniture or anything, just our bedding and our clothes, pots and pans. My mother couldn't go back and forth; she had that nervous breakdown. We had an awful time before we could get her out at all.

I remember there was a curfew—eight o'clock, and everybody had to be in. Sometimes a lot of the Italians would be five minutes or so late. The rule caused an awful lot of hubbub in this town. All the young ones were citizens because they were born here. And all the older ones, they liked to go down to Second Street. There were two or three saloons down there run by Italians. They'd go down there and have a game of cards or something like that, and sit and talk by the hour. And they couldn't do that anymore. I tell you, it hit them pretty hard. The ones that didn't go out stayed in all the time, and they would tell on the ones who were out. There was one man, he was scared to go out anywhere, so he wouldn't go. Even if he could be back by eight o'clock, he still wouldn't go. And then somebody would be out late. Oh boy, there was an awful uproar. There was a lot of jealousy. Everyone wanted to be treated alike. The ones who stayed home didn't go out because they were scared, so they turned in the people who were out. It made a lot of hostility. That's why it was such a bad law. This man would run right to the sheriff, tell the sheriff, "So-and-So was out." The sheriff knew what it was all about; he'd been sheriff for years. He knew everybody and knew what they were doing. He would just go to the house and warn them; he wouldn't arrest them. The law caused a lot of jealousies—hostilities amongst the Italians. It made enemies; it really made enemies. Anything like that would. Whoever thought up that law had screws loose somewhere.

My mother applied for her second [citizenship] papers. She had to learn the Constitution and all that. She was to start school in September. Well, that's when she got sick. She got this nervous breakdown and we couldn't do a thing with her. So the doctor said: "Don't force her to do something you might regret for the rest of your life. When they're that way, they're on the borderline. It could go the wrong way." And so we didn't; that was in September. In December, the war broke out. She was in the midst of it really. She was real bad. Mother never became a citizen. She got mad. She got mad about having to move and all of that. She was just mad. She said, "I'm not going to bother with it. If they send me back to Italy, I'll go back to Italy." She figured, well, they don't want me, so I'm going back. She never did, though. She'd never go over there to live. My father would have gone back, but my mother never wanted to go 'cause she had a hard life over there. She had to go to work when she was nine years old. Mother always said, "It's better to be poor in America than to be rich in Italy."

Did any of you ever think they would come to the door some night and say you had to go back to Italy?

No, we thought all the uproar would stop them. I think they got scared in Sacramento with all these people being so mad and upset. But we never complained to Sacramento, just to the sheriff. He got all the complaints, poor guy. And I think it was terrible what they did to the Japanese, too. They didn't have to do things like that. That wasn't necessary.

ALTHOUGH IT MIGHT not have seemed so at the time, the aliens were not forgotten. Even as the Italians and Germans were packing and looking for new homes, influential politicians, bureaucrats, and ordinary citizens began a drive to reverse the relocation order.

Giuseppe Spadaro and his family and friends christen his second purse seiner, *New Marettimo*, San Francisco, California, 1944. Vitina (*center*) carries flowers and the traditional bottle of champagne.

Giuseppe Spadaro's first purse seiner, *Marettimo*, on its maiden voyage from Tacoma, Washington, to Monterey, California, 1936.

Fr. Gabriel Zavattaro, San Francisco, California, on the twenty-fifth anniversary of his ordination to the priesthood, 1959.

John Spataro (*right*) and Frank Cefalu take a break aboard Pete Maiorana's *Diana*, Monterey, California, 1936.

Dan Banducci stands in front of his Fourth Street establishment, known then as the Sportsmen's Club, Eureka, California, ca. 1944.

Navy seaman Rocco Buccellato at home on leave with his mother, Catarina, and sister Mary (Cardinalli), Pittsburg, California, 1943.

Joe Nieri, Arcata, California, 1943.

SIX

"There is absolutely going to be discretion"
In Defense of Italian Americans

Treat these children (of aliens) right so that when they grow up they will understand the advantage and benefit of being born and raised in a democracy, and understand what it means to be raised under the cruel dictatorship of Hitler, Mussolini, and the Mikado.
—Fiorello LaGuardia, February 1942

THE ALIENS' ANTAGONISTS were not the only voices heard that spring. Those who kept their moral bearings lobbied the authorities on behalf of the aliens. Their misgivings led first to piecemeal exemptions for certain categories of aliens, and then to outright repeal of the restrictions for all Italians and Germans by the end of 1942.

The concern that mattered most at the highest level of decision-making was, of course, political; the vote counters who eventually wrote finis to General DeWitt's plans. For Franklin Roosevelt and his electoral strategists, there had been at least one disturbing trend in the otherwise satisfying victory over Wendell Willkie in November 1940: Italian American voters were drifting away from the Democratic party in the large urban centers of the East. No doubt, this was due in part to the reluctance of Italian Americans to have the United States join Italy's enemies abroad, especially Great Britain. But events like Pearl Harbor and the cries of the mob never completely brushed aside the president's disquietude. Rep. Carl Curtis, a Republican from Nebraska, was overheard to say during the Tolan Committee hearings in March 1942 that the Italians "will all be Republicans...when they find out what is going on."[110] In time, FDR's political instincts assured that the downward spiral of Italian American support for the Democrats did not continue, even if it meant refusing to allow the military to dictate the terms of the relationship between the aliens and their adopted homeland. But second-guessing the army was not an easy thing to do during the first critical months of the war.

Even before the Italian aliens were ordered out of the prohibited zones, sympathy for them had developed in two ways: an unprecedented expression of loyalty to the United States from within the Italian community, and an apprehension among authorities that restrictions might slow the economy and hinder war production. Alan Cranston had written early in 1941 that job discrimination in defense and nondefense industries might "seriously curtail the supply of skilled labor necessary to the defense program."[111]

The applause in Congress during FDR's "date of infamy" speech following Pearl Harbor had scarcely abated when, in San Francisco, 200 new Americans swore an oath of loyalty to the United States, a great many of them Italians and Germans. Contra Costa County experienced its largest jump in citizenship applications ever; the city of Pittsburg headed that list with twenty-two. The day Italy declared war on the United States, December 11, 500 union garbage collectors in San Francisco (the Scavengers' Protective Association)—all Italian aliens or of Italian descent—delivered sand to every block in the city to fight incendiary fires. They then purchased $10,000 in defense bonds. Scavenger Tony Barbezalata posed for newspaper photographers in front of a sign that read: "ITALIAN BLOOD IS IN OUR VEINS, BUT AMERICA IS IN OUR HEARTS. WE HAVE ENLISTED FOR THE DURATION. GOD BLESS AMERICA. SCAVENGERS' PROTECTIVE ASSOCIATION." The fledgling anti-Fascist Mazzini Society, including 100 members in San Francisco, pledged its support as well. The cannery workers union in Monterey gathered $15,000 in defense bonds, which they sent directly to the president. This ongoing contribution, garnered from 6,000 members' union dues, eventually reached $19,000. And sardine plant operators in Monterey agreed to double the pre-war amount they were paying for the fishermen's' war risk boat insurance since canning was now considered a "defense industry."[112]

Alfonso Zirpoli

The Italians were very cooperative. But you have to remember that when the curfew went into effect most of the bakers were German and Italian; they did their work at night, and they had to have permits to be out after sundown. John Molinari was the lawyer for the Scavengers' Protective Association. They were all Italian. He had to come to me to get those permits, and I would grant them in groups, one permit for each person. The chefs in the restaurants were Italian. For instance, Fior D'Italia. I gave the chef of that restaurant a permit, and after that, whenever I ate there, he would take very good care of me. He would cook up special things for me. When I was there, I knew that I was liked, and I ate there quite often.

A DAY OR so after Pearl Harbor, Governor Olson, who could invariably be counted on to overreact, proposed that, as a way to avoid rioting, all enemy aliens be placed under house arrest. But the California State Defense Council, not known for its moderation when it came to alien enemies, vetoed the idea because it feared the scheme would jeopardize food production and distribution. A justice of the peace and former congressman from Half Moon Bay tried to get Tom Clark to intercede with DeWitt so that Italian truck farmers could finish the artichoke season. Santa Cruz agricultural officials had also told DeWitt that relocation would result in serious financial losses to that area.[113]

A branch of the Office of Production Management, the Labor Supply Committee of Northern California and Nevada, composed of representatives of industry, labor, and various federal agencies, charged that many employers with war contracts were allowing anti-alien prejudice to slow production. There were reports that aliens and citizens were being fired simply because they had foreign names. No law barred the hiring of aliens during wartime, except where war work was classified confidential, restricted, or secret, and discrimination against alien employees across the country perplexed Attorney General Biddle and the president. Biddle argued that only six in ten thousand aliens were even remotely dangerous and that most of them had already been incarcerated. Moreover, he warned, the Axis might use such examples of racial prejudice to foment disunity. "Everyone is alike before the law," Biddle reminded the country, a principle that had to be sustained "if we really love justice, and really hate the bayonet and the whip and the gun, and the whole Gestapo method as a way of handling human beings." Roosevelt applauded Biddle, adding, "It is one thing to safeguard American industry, and particularly defense industry, against sabotage but it is very much another to throw out of work people who, except for the accident of birth, are sincerely patriotic."[114]

But clearly, when the president said this he was thinking primarily of the more populous East Coast. On the eve of his decision to order thousands of people off the West Coast, the president expressed his concern about alien employment on the East Coast to the chairman of the U.S. Maritime Commission. Outright prohibition of employment of enemy aliens for marine work, the president wrote, "might have serious and immediate effects through the removal of a large number of qualified and undoubtedly honest men." The result, FDR surmised, would be a shortage of stevedores in Philadelphia and Boston, and he suggested that the most effective way of averting such an eventuality would be for intelligence bureaus such as the FBI and the Office of Naval Intelligence to conduct individual background checks.[115] But Roosevelt did not insist, and there was little likelihood that the maritime commissioner would chart such a course on his own.

Still, once the decision had been taken to relocate the West Coast aliens in the midst of the alarm over the Roberts Commission report, no one was certain who would have to go. Justice Department officials, including Attorney General Biddle, first said there would be no exceptions to the ruling, but then admitted that some might be granted where there were "compelling reasons" and a "suitable investigation." But initially, religious and political refugees, the aged and infirm, and even aliens living with naturalized sons or daughters could expect no favor from the government. When Alfonso Zirpoli, assistant to U.S. Attorney Frank Hennessy in San Francisco, told Tom Clark that one of the Italians ordered out of the city had lost a son at Pearl Harbor, Clark was unmoved; she had to leave with the rest of the aliens. Frank Taormina, the Pittsburg city clerk, was swamped by elderly Italians belatedly making out citizenship applications. In San Francisco a delegation of forty North Beach Italians, including lawyers, doctors, and a few city officials, called on state attorney general Warren to plead for consideration of "hardship" cases. Warren, who was in no position to grant any exemptions, nonetheless told the Italians that he thought federal officials would give the request a "thoughtful" hearing.[116]

Much of the concern for the aliens, which was both humanitarian and economic, had to do with the very large number of Italian fishermen who would be relocated. Estimates were that nearly all of California's independent fishing fleet was owned and operated by the foreign-born, most of them Italian. One anxious San Franciscan called the Justice Department's Alien Enemy Control Unit (AECU) to inquire what the city would do for its fish. The answer he got was cold and officious: "Remember, this is war."[117]

ALTHOUGH ATTORNEY GENERAL Biddle did not forthrightly confront the army, that did not mean he was without feeling or understanding for what alien relocation meant for the country. At a luncheon in early February, he solicited the president's support in his guerrilla-style skirmishing with the army. According to Biddle, "I emphasized the danger of the hysteria...moving east and affecting the Italian and German population in Boston and New York." It is not known how seriously Roosevelt took his chief law enforcement officer's warning; later the president would endorse Biddle's position completely, as though it had been his own from the beginning. But the point Biddle made was one that the politically sensitive president could ill afford to ignore. The attorney general did receive the wholehearted support of the Los Angeles branch of the Women's International League for Peace and Freedom, which decried the hysteria and prejudice sweeping the state. The ladies made sure that both the attorney general and the president received copies of their protest resolution.[118]

In Pittsburg, Italian civic leaders prepared to make a personal appeal for exemptions. Those affected by the relocation order, as well as other interested parties, raised three thousand dollars to send three men to Washington—city clerk Frank Taormina, former city councilman S. V. Cardinalli, and Joe Aiello—to plead for a district in the heart of Pittsburg for elderly and infirm Italians. The trio was emboldened by the encouragement they had received from state officials.[119]

John McCloy met the delegation in his office on February 16, as did Provost Marshal General Gullion in his. Gullion bragged the next day to DeWitt that he had "stalled them" in order to find out what Bendetsen and DeWitt thought of their plan. DeWitt coached Gullion that it would be impractical, as well as wrong, to award "preferential treatment to any alien irrespective of race." To be blunt, he added, "if there is one place where all the aliens ought to be out—then that is Pittsburg," where officials had planned a troop embarkation depot at the edge of town. "If you establish a precedent," DeWitt concluded, "then you are [through]."[120]

NEWSPAPER COLUMNISTS HAD engaged in a brief, belated crusade in behalf of the aliens after the relocation order was announced. Writers like Dorothy Thompson, who had already reversed herself on the alien question and was about to do so again, thought relocation played into the Nazi's hands. "While we are registering German and Italian democrats," she wrote, "the real pullers of Fascist strings [the America Firsters] are planning for the next Congressional elections.... We are following red herring scents." Chester Rowell believed the State Personnel Board's decision to remove from their employment lists only those who were "obviously" descended (meaning the Japanese) from enemy nations was racist and stupid. "The way to distinguish [F]ifth [C]olumnists, spies and saboteurs," Rowell wrote, "is to watch, not their complexions or their names, but their conduct. And the best way to defend the Constitution of the United States is to live up to it."[121]

AS THE ALIENS prepared to leave, a congressional committee, sympathetic to the plight of the European aliens, began public hearings into relocation and internment. It issued periodic reports of its findings and recommendations, and met frequently with Stimson's closest associate in the War Department, John McCloy. From February 21—two days after President Roosevelt signed Executive Order 9066—through March 12, the House of Representatives Select Committee Investigating National Defense Migration staged successive hearings in San Francisco, Portland, Seattle, Los Angeles, and again in San Francisco. The Tolan Committee, named for its chairman, John H. Tolan, hoped to exert a calming influence by publicizing the impact of the relocation program on the economic and social fabric of the West Coast.[122]

While the Tolan Committee fully supported the administration's decision to remove the Japanese, it clearly believed there was time to save the Italians and German refugees. Adroitly steered by the sixty-five-year-old Tolan, it sought to play a leading role in the drama. Tolan, born in Minnesota, a graduate of the University of Kansas Law School, Class of '02, and a resident of Oakland since 1914, personally knew many of the civic leaders and community organizers who appeared before the panel. He deftly extracted their testimony in a way that evoked sympathy for the Italians among committee members and, it appears certain, within the War Department.

To the witnesses gathered before the committee shortly after the commencement of the hearings, Tolan vouched for the loyalty of Oakland's Italians and insisted that the witnesses accept it as an article of faith. It was simply wrong, he said, "to treat alien mothers of soldiers...in the same way as dangerous enemy aliens." Edward Corsi, an expert on Italian Americans, estimated that in 1942 there were 400,000 young men of Italian parentage in the armed forces and thousands of Italian defense workers. The committee took as its special charge to determine whether there were extenuating circumstances in the cases of alien families threatened with disruption, which if not addressed skillfully, might arouse a resentment that would carry over into the postwar period.[123]

Frank Buccellato,
Pittsburg

I come from a family of eleven children—eight brothers and three sisters. My dad was an American citizen but my mother wasn't. She came to this country almost as early as my dad—1905. In fact, my mother's still living; she'll be ninety-five this year.

The war broke out and I was drafted. My other two brothers [who were of age] *were drafted. I was rejected and my brother Rocco, who was next to me* [in age]*, was also drafted, but he enlisted in the navy in 1941. He was in before Pearl Harbor. Then my other brother, Nick was drafted and he joined the navy, too. And both of them were aboard battleships—Rocco on the U.S.S.* Idaho, *and Nick on the* South Dakota. *They saw a lot of action.*

Right after the war broke out they started taking all the Italians and Germans out of Pittsburg. They sent notices to the house, letters. I don't remember exactly where these letters came from, but they might have been from the draft board. My mother said, "Well, I have two sons in the service."

"I'm sorry," they said, "but you have to move out of town."

She had her own home right here in Pittsburg, but we had to move to Oakley. I was married then. My father-in-law was an American citizen, but my mother-in-law wasn't. She had to move out, and she had two boys in the army. The whole family left; just left the house by itself. My in-laws moved with my mother to Oakley. Oakley's about fifteen miles [from here]*. "Why go* [just] *fifteen miles and stay there? What's the difference?" But that was it. We had to find 'em a place there. It was so much trouble, really. My in-laws didn't drive, or my mother. We had to go over there and get groceries for them and take care of everything.*

The two families lived in separate homes, next to each other. It looked like an army camp. They had these little shacks, and the families moved into 'em. It was like a migrant labor camp, across the tracks. Every summer people would move in there and harvest grapes, or peaches, or tomatoes. I had younger brothers; the youngest was nine. They were all going to school and had to transfer to Oakley.

There were quite a few Italians from Pittsburg living in that little camp in Oakley. And they used to entertain themselves. At night, Leo, my youngest brother, would play the accordion and everybody would sing. The kids would sing and dance around. Not the mothers; they were always sad because they had their boys in the service. But young kids, they'd have a ball. Oh, they used to enjoy themselves, because they were all from Pittsburg. There must have been, oh, ten or twelve of those little huts. Everybody knew each other. They didn't feel like they were alone. They talked about it [the relocation]*. My mother and my mother-in-law said this was really something: "We have to give 'em our sons to fight and they tell us to get out of our homes."*

I went to the draft board—in fact I told the lady, "This doesn't seem right. My family and my wife's family [each] *have two boys in the service, fighting for the United States of America. We're American citizens; we're all born here in this country. So what do we care about Italy, or*

Germany, or anyplace? This is our country, right here. Why would my mother or my mother-in-law want to sabotage this country?" It didn't make sense. They lived here since the early 1900s. In fact my father-in-law came over here before my dad—1877. He was an American citizen for years and years. It didn't really make sense at all. They said to me, "Well, we're sorry, but we can't do anything about it." And what gets me is now—you hear it coming up, a lot of times you see it in the news, where the Japs want to be paid back for all the problems they had and everything. All right, if they were American citizens, I don't blame them. But if they were immigrants, I don't think it was right for them either. We felt the same way. But still, the Italians and the Germans, they haven't made a move yet to be compensated for anything, for all the problems they had, and for having their own flesh and blood fighting for America. It didn't make any sense.

How long was the family gone?

It was quite a while. It was such a hassle. I know it was more than a year. The city itself told us it was all right to come back home. I visited the city managers and everything. In fact, at that time most of the city officials were American-born Italians. They said, "Well, we don't know what we can do about it." But in fact, there was a group of them that went to Washington. I think they did help quite a bit to get people back to their homes a little earlier.

Did the officials try to get a sense of community feeling before they went to Washington?

No, they didn't because they had the same thing happen in their own families, to their mothers and fathers. They didn't tell you where to go. "You just have to go so many miles from Pittsburg"—Oakley, Brentwood, Concord, but not to Antioch. Antioch was a little too close.

People couldn't get over it, 'cause I think the Italian people are so much a part of this country as it is. We've got heads of states that are Italians, and the heads of cities that are Italians, and here they go and tell you that you have to move because of your Italian descent and because you're not a citizen. If my mother was alone, it's fine to say, "Well, she's not a citizen she should go." But she's got eleven children, all born in this country. And they're going into the service. After that, they went through the Korean War, Vietnam. I had brothers in all of 'em. Five brothers that went in. I didn't go on account of a perforated ear drum. Three other brothers didn't go in because of the same thing.

And that was it, the rest of them went in. But they all came back. Thank God for that. They were real lucky.

It was a financial burden. We had to help, myself and my sisters—my sister who was married. I was the only one actually working in my family. When my mother moved she had seven children at home. They all went. It was really a hardship on her.

They got over it right away. They kind of held it against the government for doing it [moving them]. *As far as I was concerned, "I was born here, and they're doing this to my family, to my mother? My God, how terrible." I felt so bad. You feel, "Why should we go if they draft us?" Still, there were no Italian people from Pittsburg who refused to go to war. They all went. And a lot of them were killed.*

Rocco Buccellato,
Magalia, California

I was already overseas when I was notified that my mother had to move out. It was a letter from a family member. I was due to come home on leave, and when they notified me, I was kind of worried. They said the reason they notified me was so that I'd know where to find her. She was already out of Pittsburg, in Oakley, inland a little ways. I don't know when the navy was going to notify me, but before I went home, they let me know.

Did you understand what was behind it?

Well, not too much until I talked with the chaplain after I heard about it. I realized, of course, that with her not being a citizen, and with the war, why, they don't trust anybody. You can't blame them; when you have a war, you don't know what's going on. There I was in the navy; my brother was in the navy; and I knew the rest of them were going to go in. They were all in line, eight brothers, all born here.

Still, I wanted to find out what it was all about. Here I am fighting for my country and they kick my mother out of her home, the nicest person in the world. My father was already gone, so I really couldn't see it. It kind of upset me, but at the same time I wanted to find out what it was all about.

The chaplain told me he was going to look into it, and I don't know exactly who he called or what he did. He said that he thought it would be OK. He understood the situation. I explained to him how many little kids were at home. It wasn't very long after that, that they sent her back home.

It really didn't bother her too much; at least she didn't show it. Tough old gal, I'll tell you. Things like that she never did show. Every time I went home, it was happy days. I was always glad to get there and see her too. I did go home on my first leave. She was still in Oakley, and that's when I told her that I had talked to the chaplain and he was working on it. After that, when I went back overseas, they let me know that she was back home.

That Oakley—she and all the kids were in a cubbyhole, really. Little cabins. I was surprised that the place was so small and everybody just packed in there—all different cabins—the people and all that. A lot of people that I knew from Pittsburg were there, just shoved in these little holes. And yet, when I got home on that leave, why, we had a big feed and everything. It was wonderful, really, the way they kept their spirits up.

Vince Massei,
Eureka

I've lived in Eureka all my life. Born and raised here. In 1942, I was twenty-nine years old. Hell, I was thirty, born in 1911. We were living in the old Buon Gusto. My parents were part owners of the building. 'Course the whole family worked there at the time. I can remember that as a little kid my father had this hotel. It was a boarding house in those days, and he was partners in running it. And the families in those days always worked together. There was the Depression, of course. So we were a close-knit family, and we continued this all through those years. When the war came along, we stuck it out. 'Course, I'd enlisted in the service in 1941 at Hamilton Field, and my younger brother went in the service, too. My oldest brother didn't; he was too old. And I had a sister and a brother-in-law who also lived there, 'cause the whole establishment was practically run by our family alone. My parents were aliens at that time, although my father had passed away.

I was approximately a day and a half out of San Francisco when the war broke out. I was with the army air corps. Our destination was the Philippines, which we were fortunate we never reached at that time. We were turned back and went back to our old base at Hamilton Field. And we spent maybe a month or so there before we were shipped out again to the Fiji Islands.

Once I was overseas, the family sent me the local paper. I can't re-member ever picking up the newspapers out there, because we were in different islands all the time. We were an early outfit in the South Pa-cific. We were kicked along forward, and we never did get enough newspapers or magazines or things like that to keep up on some of these current events. But I always got sent the local paper. I'd get a gob of them at one time due to the mail situation and one thing or another. I'd just stack 'em up and go through them and see what I could pick up. I picked up this one paper and read that a veteran, an army sergeant in the service, his mother had been moved from her home out of the re-stricted area along the waterfront. So I keep reading and I find out it's my mother! It kinda floored me a little bit. I hadn't heard of it other-wise. If I'd heard of it, it probably wouldn't have floored me as much. And of course, the family never told me until a few letters got through. At the time, it really perturbed me. I figured, well, there I was. But we were advancing so much that every time I'd make a move my address changed. So, I just went along with the whole thing. 'Course I don't say I wouldn't have had to go into the service; the draft would probably have gotten me. But I enlisted on my own. When I came across this arti-cle I debated with myself whether I should go to my commanding officer and tell him the circumstances, and that maybe I should go back home and see what's taking place with my mother. But I didn't; I just carried on. I'd given it a lot of consideration, though. But I figured, well, if this is what it has to be, it's wartime, you know. So let it be. There were a lot of others in the same circumstances.

As far as any real animosity was concerned, there wasn't any that I can remember. I knew that there was no type of subversion in the family whatsoever. The Italian people in this town—and not only the Ital-ians—were a stable, rock-hard people. All they wanted was a home, something over their heads, something to say, "It's mine," and work and earn an honest living. I think that was true of most all of your for-eign people.

Gino Massagli

My next to oldest brother, Tony, enlisted in the Navy. Then my older brother Levio, he was the first call-up. He went into the Eighty-fourth Infantry Division, the "Woodchopper" division. And then Bart left. He became an ambulance driver in the Third Armored. I was still at home.

When the war broke out, all the [Humboldt] bay area was restricted. No aliens could live on the bay [north] side of our street. Even though *my dad was a citizen, my mother was an alien. The FBI and the Sheriff's Department came up and said to my mother, "OK, you have to move to the other side of Fourth Street." So dad found this house up on Seventh Street. It had exactly the same house number as where we were living. Within a week dad sold our house for $3,800, and he bought the new place for a thousand.*

It wasn't even a week later when the FBI came back and said, "Mrs. Massagli, we made a mistake. We didn't realize that you had three sons in the service. You can go back." Mama says, "No, we had an eleven room, six bedroom house. No way. I've got two bedrooms here; my sons aren't going to come home when they get out of the service. This is what I want. I didn't want six bedrooms, two stories, I'll stay right here." I'd say they came back after four or five months. I'm not real exact on that now.

There was so much to do to get everything moved; we had so much stuff to get rid of. My God, we left a lot of antiques there; it's just a shame. We just didn't have the room in the other house. We had three sets of big, old-time pitchers, the pitchers with the bowls we used to wash in. Folks just left them there. We even had one of those round Victrola record players. That stayed there. I cried; I cry every time I think about it. No, mom was happy when she got over there. She didn't mind staying there, she didn't mind at all.

What was your attitude toward the government?

I'll put it this way. We had a little flag, a little banner with four stars on it. We had it on the door. Very proud. Even my mother was very proud. Oh, yeah. In fact my dad had a fistfight with a neighbor one time. He was a garbage man. Hell of a nice guy, though. He made a remark like, "I wish this war would last a little bit longer. I can make a lot of money.'

My dad says, "How many kids you got in the service?"

"None, yet.'

"Well, I got four, so shut up!' And they tangled.

My dad understood that this was his country. There were no ifs, ands, or buts about it. Dad just went along.

How did you feel about Italy being at war with the United States? Did that divide your loyalty?

No. Gino Orlandi from Arcata and I were down at Camp Roberts together. We'd go out to the guesthouse, or one of the places there, and there were lots of Italians. They were all engineers, captured in Africa. We got to talking to a few of them. They asked if it would be all right if they came by our barracks once in a while. We didn't care. So, once in a while, we would meet them at the guesthouse. One said, "Hey, would you read this letter for me?' It was in English. It was from the post engineer's wife, writing to this Italian, warning him not to come by that night cause her husband would be home that weekend. "Don't drop by.' Things like that. Then the next time we'd see them, she'd say, "Come on up. He's gone for a month," or something like that.

They had to wear a green patch that said "Italy" on it. They were allowed off camp as long as they went with an American who spoke Italian. One Saturday afternoon, right after inspection, we got a call from camp headquarters: "Hey, there's a bunch of Italians to see you and Orlandi." We said, "Send 'em up." After they arrived you could hear the muttering in the barracks. Gene was transferring out, so it didn't matter to him. Those Italians came up and said, "Hey, we have a chance to go into town. Would you guys bring us?' I could hear my buddies, muttering. "Hell no," I said, "I've got to fight with these guys." Gene says, "Sure, I'll do it. Hell, I'm not going to be here. I'm transferring." So he took them out. He said they no sooner hit the gate when local Italians picked them up and put on a feast you wouldn't believe. Just spread the table for them.

We'd go down to the Italian barracks in camp for spaghetti or whatever they had. We went a couple of times. Hell, we'd walk in and half the mess hall would be full of American officers. But the Italian prisoners would treat us better than the officers [did] because we could talk Italian. And the officers would just look at us. That was something. But if I had been posted to Italy, I'd have fought the same way I did in the Pacific. It didn't make any difference; they were enemies of my country.

IN COMBINATION, THE Tolan Committee's witnesses addressed four issues on which the committee built its case for alien relief: 1) hardship, 2) should Italians and Germans should be treated differently or the same as the Japanese, 3) exemptions, and 4) did the army know best how to handle the situation.

For the first time since the crisis began in late January, civilian officials from Washington—not the army or its surrogates like Tom Clark—were to hear firsthand about the personal tragedies being played out on the West Coast. The same public that had pressured state and local officials to do something about the aliens was no doubt wondering what they would do for fish now and why their garbage was piling up in the streets. San Francisco attorney Chauncey Tramutolo, an acquaintance of Tolan's for twenty-five years, told the committee that 20 percent of the city's garbage collectors—the Scavengers' Protective Association—were enemy aliens who generally needed to begin work three hours before the end of curfew. Most of the alien scavengers (88 of 105) were working stockholders in the profit-sharing association, with average investments in the company of nine thousand dollars. Unless they could work, their investments were worthless. An identical situation prevailed in Alameda County.[124]

John Molinari

Five of us from the [Citizens' Committee to Aid Italians Loyal to the United States] were invited to the Presidio, but we did not get to meet General DeWitt, who apparently was busy with more important things. We met instead with one of the subordinate generals; unfortunately, his name escapes me. We had a very interesting conversation. He assured us that as far as he knew, there was no such action contemplated with respect to the Italians. We told him that we were pleased at his response. But lest there be any doubt of the feelings of the community—at least the leadership of the Italian community—we impressed him with the idea that moving Italians was a lot more of a logistic problem than moving the Japanese, who were, of course, a considerably smaller number [of people].

We reminded the general that, particularly in this area, up through northern California, the Italians were very active in many industries and commercial endeavors: the garbage collection, the farmers. We talked about A.P. Giannini being the president of the Bank of America. And we impressed upon the general that if you moved all of these people, the same thing would have happened that happened with the Japanese—that it would have included people of Italian descent who were born in this country. And we impressed upon him strongly that it certainly would disrupt the productive industrial and commercial endeavors in the community. We had already had some indication of disruption of commercial activities.

Fishermen were mentioned. Of course, the fishermen had already suffered from a different approach. You see, most of the fishermen were Italian aliens, and they had already been prevented from going out onto the bay because they were considered [enemy] aliens. In addition, by previous orders, Italian aliens could not live or be within a seven or eight block area of the waterfront and then there was the curfew. At that time I represented the Scavengers' Protective Association and, of course, our men used to go out at four o'clock in the morning.

As a matter of fact, to digress, I was [also] attorney for the largest fishing organization in the Bay Area known as the Crab Fishermen's Protective Association, which actually went out of business because most of its members were Italian aliens and couldn't go out fishing. So a good part of my time was spent dealing with the U.S. Attorney, who had the authority to grant exemptions from curfew regulations. He assigned a deputy in his office, Alfonso Zirpoli, who is now a judge of the United States District Court. He was of Italian descent and certainly sympathetic to Italians. The U.S. Attorney's policy with regard to the granting of exemptions was a liberal one. They were granted upon representation that the Italian alien was not a threat to national security.

Your committee was lobbying on behalf of Italian Americans whom you were afraid would also be relocated or interned?

Yes, plus the fact that we wanted to impress the government that there were Italians in all walks of life, some of them in very high positions at that time. We were loyal to the United States, period. We were unhappy with Italy's declaration of war against the United States. Our approach to the general [at the Presidio] was really two pronged. One, we wanted to impress him with the mass of Italians that would have to be moved and the effect that would have on the economy of the area. But we also gently hinted that, as far as the Committee was concerned, we would litigate the matter and urge the Italians not to go. We now know that meetings were held by community leaders of Japanese descent to decide what course of action they would take with respect to the evacuation order. They decided to comply.

Did this general seem to have any prior understanding of the problems you foresaw in an "evacuation" of Italians?

Well, you know how military men are? They're not very communicative. But I think he was aware of it. He probably didn't want to tip his hand or didn't want to put the general on the spot, so he was really noncommittal. I think if things had come to a sorry pass, our committee would have taken some affirmative action in the sense of filing lawsuits or whatever would be necessary. We pretty much made up our minds that we [Italians] were not going to go, and we were going to advise the Italian community not to go. It would have been a terrific disruption.

THE MAYOR OF Martinez, California, C.A. "Cappy" Ricks, a friend of Tolan's, pleaded the case for the Italians in that city. One example from Ricks's hardship list will suffice to illustrate his point: an Italian who had owned a shoe store in Martinez for twenty years tried repeatedly to get his final citizenship papers. But had been put off because immigration officials in Washington could not find the name of the ship he came over on. The man was forced to sell his store and move in with his son in San Francisco. "Are we safer with this man in San Francisco than in Martinez?" Ricks sarcastically asked the committee.

But Ricks also displayed a selective concern for the aliens, an unfortunate trait he shared with other witnesses. In a postscript to his letter to the committee, Ricks addressed his friend, John Tolan: "John—The Constitution can go overboard, if necessary, as regards to Japs. I do not think it possible to crystal gaze well enough to determine whether a local born Jap is loyal or not. Do it [relocate the Japanese] constitutionally if you can. If not possible, then we must win [the] war by dictatorship methods. 'Cappy'"[125]

The regional director of the San Francisco office of the Social Security Board hired Mr. Ottorino Ronchi, a former Berkeley professor of Italian and editor of *La Voce Del Popolo*, to survey the needs of Italians in the Pittsburg-Vallejo and Monterey-Santa Cruz areas. He reported on the widows who had nowhere to go and no work, whose sons had been killed at Pearl Harbor or were serving in the armed forces, and he described the plight of the Monterey fisherman whose boats had been requisitioned by the military. The committee, which naively assumed that hardship cases such as these would be dealt with automatically, got a gentle reminder from the Social Security Board's regional director, Richard Neustadt, that the committee's intervention would be necessary if help was to be forthcoming. "I thought one way of helping [you understand the situation]," Neustadt hinted, "is just to say it to you." Neustadt was particularly sensitive to the uncertainty in the minds of the evacuees. Though he pleaded against any mass expulsion, he was a realist. Make it clean, "surgical," he implored. Do not move them one place today then tomorrow another.[126]

Milano Rispoli of the Italian Welfare Agency cited unemployment, slipping morale, and the fear of future regulations as the principal difficulties facing the Italian community. What were his solutions? Put loyal Italians to work in all industries. Grant all the aliens citizenship, even the illiterate (providing they came to the U.S. after 1 July 1924, the commencement of restrictive immigration quotas). Provide federal relief in case of mass relocation. And inaugurate a program to lift the morale of all Americans involved in the war effort.[127]

Hearing case after case of extreme hardship had an impact on committee members. Rep. John Sparkman (D-Alabama), who no doubt spoke for the committee when he remarked after hearing about a particularly gut-wrenching case, "I believe we can feel certain that every effort will be made to see that all deserving persons receive full and proper consideration."[128]

Like the law enforcement officials queried by Earl Warren and discussed earlier, Tolan Committee witnesses were divided as to whether Italian and German aliens should be treated the same as the Japanese. Most thought not, but a few—for contrasting reasons—argued that they should. The committee even toyed with the idea of recommending identification cards for everyone entering restricted or prohibited zones. Some suggested the country as a whole might benefit from such a system.

San Francisco's Italian American mayor, Angelo Rossi, feared the restrictions would lead to "extreme hardship," the disintegration of Italian and German family life, and the disruption of city services and the economy. "Their problems," he concluded, "should be considered separately from those of the Japanese" aliens and disloyal Japanese Americans, who should be "removed from this community." He cited the example of what allegedly had occurred at Honolulu on December 7 and the general situation in the Pacific as reasons for treating the aliens differently. If the army deemed removal of Italians and Germans "imperative," Rossi recommended that they be allowed to apply to return home quickly. This view was a switch for Rossi, who, like many others in the early days of the war, had urged unqualified tolerance of the aliens.[129]

Leland Cutler, chairman of the Subcommittee of the Morale Service on Racial and National Problems in San Francisco, thought that the regulations would be harmful to "routine business" in the city and for that reason there should be "great flexibility" in the rules pertaining to Italians and Germans. Earl Warren agreed with Cutler on the need for flexibility. He was particularly impressed with the longevity of Italian residence in San Francisco and thought local authorities could determine their loyalty much more easily than that of the Germans and Japanese.[130]

The city manager of Oakland, John Hassler, believed the best way for loyal aliens of the Axis countries to show their patriotism was to follow orders and leave the East Bay. He wanted exemptions, however, for older Italians and Germans whose lack of education had prevented their obtaining citizenship, and for the parents of "fine Americans" serving in the armed forces. Hoping to reassure the witnesses, Tolan reported that there was a bill pending before the House Judiciary Committee that would give discretionary authority to the Immigration and Naturalization Service in cases where there had been delays. "We are going to try to take care of that," Tolan promised, "It is very, very bad."[131]

The highpoint—or lowpoint, depending on your perspective—of the discussion about discretion came during the committee's grilling of Tom Clark. Clark stuck to his previously stated position—which was obviously DeWitt's—that there would be no exceptions to the general's relocation orders. This did not satisfy the committee's staff director, Dr. Robert K. Lamb: "It isn't a question of loyalty or disloyalty. As far as this evacuation is concerned[,] it is a question of alien or citizen. You evacuate them because they are in a certain category."

Clark: "Yes, sir."
Dr. Lamb: "Appeal at this time makes no difference...."
Sparkman: "Not yet."
Tolan: "Oh, yes, it does. There is absolutely going to be discretion."[132]

In Tolan's mind there was "no question" that Executive Order 9066 made room for distinctions between the loyal and disloyal. He had been party, he said, to such discussions back in Washington before coming to the coast. Clark, however, kept insisting that General DeWitt alone would decide on the application of 9066 when it was time to do so. Hassler and some committee members were dumbfounded that a decision as potentially damaging as this one had not been taken before issuing the relocation order. The Oakland city officials agreed that since it was too late to do anything about the problem prior to the next day's restriction deadline, all of the aliens should leave temporarily, after which there could be reasonable tests for loyalty and some could return home.[133]

There were other witnesses, who, like "Cappy" Ricks, were willing to sacrifice some aliens to save others. Galen Fisher, advisor to the Institute of Pacific Relations and secretary to the Committee on National Security and Fair Play in San Francisco, warned that with all the attention being given to the Japanese, dangerous Italians and Germans might be harder to spot because they blended into the population. Thomas Mann, celebrated author of the novels *Buddenbrooks* and *The Magic Mountain*, and himself a refugee from Germany in 1933 and Czechoslovakia in 1938, called the refugees "the most passionate adversaries" of Italy and Germany. He and other reknown refugee intellectuals and artists—Arturo Toscanini, Count Carlo Sforza, Bruno Walter, Albert Einstein, Dr. Bruno Frank—had personally requested FDR to distinguish between potential Fifth Columnists and genuine refugees. Then Mann decided to throw the Japanese to the wolves to save the Europeans: "All of us know," he assured the committee, "that the burning problem on the West Coast is the question of the Japanese," who, unlike the European refugees, needed to be watched carefully.

No doubt, Mann was an effective spokesman for the German refugees, but in this instance, he was no humanitarian. Mann's testimony nonetheless impressed Tolan. He wrote Archibald MacLeish, head of the Office of Facts and Figures, that Mann's statements bared the "root of a crucial problem in our national life." The way the country chose to deal with that problem would "determine in large measure the problem of our national life both now and in the post-war period."[134]

The argument that Italians and Germans were more dangerous than the Japanese because of racial characteristics dissolved into the familiar theme articulated by Governor Olson and others: authorities could not distinguish between loyal and disloyal Japanese so well as they could Italians and Germans because the Japanese "all look alike." Olson refused to budge an inch. He insisted that even aliens with sons in the armed forces and those who had filed their final citizenship papers should be investigated thoroughly, with "full and complete hearings," before being allowed an exemption. Political refugees were different; Olson thought they should be allowed to stay put, if possible, and if not, a means should be found to permit them to return to their homes later.[135]

But those who thought that Italians and Germans deserved better treatment than the Japanese were not the only ones heard by the Tolan Committee. The Social Security Board's Richard Neustadt proposed exemptions for several categories of aliens: persons whose native citizenship had been canceled—the so-called expatriates; the aged and infirm; those with sons in the armed forces; and elderly aliens living with native-born sons or daughters, including the Japanese.[136] And the committee, which had already decided not to help the Japanese, was clearly embarrassed by the testimony of Louis Goldblatt, secretary of the California State Industrial Council, who denounced the pattern of ethnic discrimination ushered in by the restrictions. The incredulous Tolan wanted to know how Goldblatt would determine the loyalty of 120,000 Japanese if he were in DeWitt's shoes. Simple, replied Goldblatt, exactly as I would for Italians and Germans! Goldblatt feared that if second and third generation Japanese were gotten rid of, the Italians and Germans would be next. Speaking of alleged spies, Goldblatt said, "We don't care if he came over on the *Mayflower* or came out of the humblest Japanese home.... Get him and we [the CIO] will help out. But we don't want to see...a situation arise where this country will be divided against itself, where one-half the Nation will be standing on guard over the other half. Where is this to end, Mr. Tolan? We forget what was written on the Statue of Liberty. I have the words here. I would like to read them."

Tolan declined Goldblatt's offer, and instead patronized the witness: "I don't think you better. Did you ever intend to run for Congress? I think you are wonderful." Sensing Tolan's embarrassment, Sparkman changed tack, asserting that what was happening to the Japanese was their own fault because they had actively assisted Japan's attack on Pearl Harbor. But there was no large group of Italians or Germans on Hawaii, countered Goldblatt, and what happens now in California will automatically be extended throughout the nation.

"Not so," retorted Sparkman. The Italians and Germans hadn't pulled the same "stunt" as the Japanese. If they had, there would be the same indignation.

The only reason you want to evacuate the Japanese, Goldblatt rejoined, is because they "knifed us in the back." If the Italians and Germans do it too, then "away we will go and what a merry-go-'round that will be." Goldblatt finally got around to the CIO's recommendations:

1) Make no distinctions based on race or nationality.
2) Ferret out saboteurs no matter whom.
3) Establish hearing boards to separate Fascists from anti-Fascists.
4) Protect personal and real property from seizure, land grabbing, and racketeering.
5) Treat the evacuees humanely by not splitting families and by giving them useful work.
6) Do not set up concentration camps or a system of forced labor.
7) Switch night shifts so people can get around the curfew.
8) Give the Italian fishermen speedy hearings because of the vital nature of their work.
9) And allow the aged and infirm to live with their families in the restricted zones.[137]

The president of the California Council of Churches in Oakland, Dr. W.P. Reagor, found it difficult to believe that the government could remove the Japanese without also taking out the Italians and Germans: Since it would be impossible to remove all three groups, why bother with any of them? To the Japanese in Japan, Pastor Reagor suggested to the committee, it would appear that the United States was doing to their people here what Germany was doing to the Jews.[138]

The situation facing political refugees in California—a majority of them Germans—was especially poignant. Most had fled one or more Nazi-held countries in Europe after 1933, and now they faced another expulsion. In the haste to meet public demands for the mass removal of alien enemies in late January and early February, no one had thought seriously about the individuals who would be affected, particularly the refugees. Eventually the problem became serious enough for Secretary of War Stimson to send an experienced personal envoy to the West Coast to supervise General DeWitt's handling of the refugees (see chapter 7).

Emigre charitable organizations estimated there were five thousand European refugees in northern California, 3,500 of them in San Francisco. (The 1940 alien registration showed there were approximately nineteen thousand German aliens in California, half of them refugees.) Most had sought or obtained their first papers immediately after being admitted to the United States and had attended Americanization and English classes. Hundreds were serving in the U.S. armed forces.[139] Dr. Felix Guggenheim, a member of the board of directors of the Jewish Club of 1933, Inc., in Los Angeles, estimated that fully half of the German aliens in California—a majority of them in Los Angeles—were expelled and expropriated anti-Nazi refugees stigmatized as enemies of the United States. The French government, he noted, had turned away from its real enemy—Germany—to persecute anti-Nazi refugees. President Roosevelt's Advisory Committee had managed to save some of the better known emigres in France and bring them to the United States, but they were now classified as enemy aliens in this country.

Leon Feuchtwanger was such a man. An anti-Nazi writer forced to leave Germany in 1932, then interned in France in 1940, Feuchtwanger told the Tolan Committee that the Nazis would be pleased at his new predicament in the United States. By contrast, England—an example frequently cited by prorefugee spokesmen—had set up tribunals to verify and exempt bona fide refugees. This was the solution for California proposed by the refugee spokesmen. In a cruel twist of American church-state dogma, letter-of-the-law-man Tom Clark told a San Franciscan who had hoped to get a sympathetic hearing that, "In accord with our democratic principles, a question of a person's religion is immaterial. The status is determined by nationality." Hans Schwartzer, who was painfully aware of Clark's obstinance, implored the committee "to tell the military authorities about this [refugee] problem...to make it possible to make these decisions individually and not wholesale."[140]

One emigre told Monroe E. Deutsch, the vice president and provost of the University of California, Berkeley, that, "My wife and I would resort to pistols" if our lives are disrupted again. Deutsch clearly had a morale problem on his hands. Eight of the eleven Germans teaching at the campus were refugees and the other three were anti-Hitler. The two Italians on the faculty were also refugees. Deutsch eventually passed on this disturbing news to Supreme Court Justice Felix Frankfurter. Deutsch believed that the lives of these refugees would be "utterly ruined" if they were driven out. "If this order goes through," he warned Frankfurter, "I predict numerous suicides among the refugees.... Does the President realize how the army is acting?"[141]

Guggenheim, who had been in England when the war started, told Tolan and his colleagues that due to the "expectation of invasion" in May 1940, the English government had suddenly interned all male enemy aliens between the ages of sixteen and sixty residing in coastal areas, but exceptions were allowed. The government eventually realized that a majority of the German aliens were bona fide refugees, and after July 1940, it established procedures to identify and separate them from other aliens. Any one of 100 tribunals, staffed by a judge, a magistrate, and an experienced lawyer, investigated each case (between 60,000-70,000) individually. And while reviewing that number of aliens seemed a formidable task at first, each tribunal had only about 500 cases on its docket. There turned out to be so many harmless refugees that the tribunals had no difficulty. The British established three categories of aliens: the dangerous ones who were interned (569); those who could not convince the tribunals that they were refugees and were given special restrictions, or, in some cases, interned (6,782); and those who proved their status as refugees. From a maximum of 73,353 Germans and Austrians (of which 55,457 were eventually classified as "refugees"), and 19,127 Italians in September 1939, only 6,152 and 2,411, respectively, were still interned in November 1941.[142]

The American Civil Liberties Union urged Stimson to establish similar hearing boards in the United States. The organization suggested that the anti-Fascist and anti-Nazi refuges should qualify for an exemption if they had been in the U.S. for six or seven years. The ACLU charged that the naturalization office in Alameda County was thirty months behind in handling citizenship petitions and the U.S. District Court in San Francisco ten months behind. As a practical matter, a refugee had to have been in the United States six to seven years to qualify.[143]

Paul Armstrong, assistant director of the Immigration and Naturalization Service in San Francisco, confirmed the ACLU's claim. Over one-third of the three thousand naturalization cases pending (aliens who had already filed their first papers) in the district court on March 1 were "enemies." They were waiting for a variety of things to happen: expiration of the ninety-day waiting period; further personal investigation; personal interviews; or supplemental neighborhood investigations. An additional six thousand aliens, of whom one-third were "enemies," had filed their first papers and were awaiting an initial interview. Before January 1,

Armstrong reported, his office averaged about 400–450 applications per month, but the figure had skyrocketed since then to a thousand a month, of which 60 percent were alien enemies. There were well over 2,000 people (2,144 Italians and 400 Germans) in the San Francisco naturalization district who had filed their first papers before December 7 and were now classified as enemy aliens.

For friendly aliens, the naturalization period could last up to six months; enemy aliens needed three additional months. Armstrong believed that if his facility had been doubled in size a year before Pearl Harbor, about 1,200 more applications could have been processed. It would have been less expensive, he said, to provide those facilities than to evacuate aliens with government assistance. Relocation presented one more hurdle for petitioners: if a person was removed before he received his final papers, his petition would have to be refiled outside the prohibited area, and thus more delay.[144]

The committee heard testimony to this effect from Wolfgang Felix George Hallgarten, a refugee whose naturalization had been held up by federal agencies in the San Francisco Bay area. Hallgarten, who lost his citizenship in Germany in 1936, claimed to have been active in opposition to Hitler since 1921. Hallgarten said the restrictions cost him a research associateship at Berkeley, and the army had refused to allow him to volunteer because he was not a citizen. It would be disastrous, he said, for citizenship applicants if they had to start the process all over again because they could not attend courts in prohibited zones. He suggested that if the expulsion took place as scheduled applicants and their witnesses should be given permits and transportation fare to appear before their hometown authorities. Those who had filed their papers at least six months before Pearl Harbor should be exempt from the restrictions altogether, he maintained, since it was not their fault they were not citizens before the war.[145]

Mrs. Susie Banducci of Eureka wrote authorities in behalf of her restricted alien husband, Dan, whose business establishment was "just a few feet" inside the restricted area, across an alley from the Eureka police station. Susie's brother and a brother-in-law from the other side of her husband's family were both in the army. Dan had filed his first papers in April 1937, but his final papers, unfortunately, had not been filed before December 7 and were still pending. Mrs. Banducci hoped authorities would grant Dan "permission to attend to his business in order to support his family."[146]

Dominic Banducci

I was awfully young then. I was eleven years old in 1942. Before the war my father, mother, and my three uncles, Tony, Vincent, and Al, all resided at the Eagle House, in what is now the bar. It was owned by the Buon Gusto family. We all lived on the first floor. My mother and father had a little section with my brother and me. Al and Tony lived in another section, and my grandmother lived in the middle. My grandmother and father were not citizens, so when the war started they had to move. My mother continued to reside at the hotel. We stayed there with her, but we used to visit my father every night.

My grandmother's sister had a fairly large house on Summer Street, and my father moved in with her. That has always been odd to me because they were trying to remove us away from the harbor and [Humboldt] bay. Fourth and Broadway was the line, but Summer Street is only two blocks off Broadway.

There was a group of Italians that lived in that section. And of course, right after the war broke out the Italians who were not citizens could not be out of the house after sunset. We used to go down there and have our meals at my [great] aunt's house every night. We just visited, and then every night went home about nine-thirty or ten o'clock. And this went on for quite a while.

Grandmother was able to return to the hotel first. When my uncles, Al and Vince, went into the service, my grandmother thought, "I have two children in the service. Why do I have to go through this? I'm making my contribution to stay in this country by offering two sons." And she was able to return earlier than my father. She was gone, I think, about eight or nine months.

At night, when we visited my father and grandmother there would be a group of Italians there who were not citizens, and who found themselves in the same situation. I remember sitting in the big living room or in the kitchen in my aunt's house with its big diamond table. God, the poor lady—and she was a fabulous lady. I don't know if anybody ever paid her anything for her food. There'd be twelve, fourteen people at the dining room table at night. As a kid, I cherished those moments, even under the circumstances, because it wasn't like watching TV all night. There was a lot of conversation, a lot of discussion. We kids just sat in a corner eating—just sat and listened. It was really funny, really joyful; it was one of the best parts of my life. When you upset a child's routine, he enjoys the change. I enjoyed going out at night to visit my father, and sitting there and having these beautiful Italian meals with everybody around the table. I think we got more out of it than we lost. What kid ever could have enjoyed life more than I did, raised amongst the beautiful Italian immigrants and boarders?

My father owned a pool hall in an ice cream parlor. That was one of his businesses on Fourth Street. Of course, when the regulations came in he couldn't go to his place of business. It was really funny because he was a local character. He knew all the policemen, and the pool hall and the ice cream parlor were right in front of the old police station. The police would pick up my father in the morning and bring him to work, and then take him home. He had to be back at the house, I think, at sundown. He could go across Fourth Street. Up to a certain point he could walk up to the door, look in, but not step across the threshold. These Italians were no threat at all, so it got to be a joke. Here my Father would go to work in a police car and go home in a police car. I don't know if that was part of the federal government's regulations. I think it was just a local version. Nobody took it seriously, even the townspeople. There wasn't really a heck of a lot of animosity; there was a lot of sympathy. It was taken more in humor, you know, "the foolish American government." "What the hell are they doing?" "They don't know what they're doing."

My father was also in the fern business. He had some employees; most of them were non-citizens, too. He used to go into the woods and pick salal brush and ferns and bundle them into bales. They shipped them to the flower markets in San Francisco and Los Angeles. There were quite a few men who he kept employed, maybe twelve to fourteen. Of course, a lot of them lived at the Buon Gusto; I would say half of them. They had to move, although they did continue to work somehow. It really affected my father's business, but since he didn't rely solely on this, it didn't bankrupt the family. What really hurt him was that most of his customers in the flower markets were Japanese, and of course they were all removed. They were gone, so he lost all of his markets. It really curtailed his business a great deal.

Howard Williams

I was sixteen in 1942, in high school. My favorite story is one about Dan Banducci who owned Classic Billiards. It was a pool hall and soda fountain. We called it "The Club" since we used to hang out there a lot. We liked it; we liked Dan and he seemed to like us. He was a great big guy who didn't stand for any nonsense in his place. It was located right across the street from where Daly's is now [in Eureka]. Oh, let's see, I believe it's the Singer Sewing Machine shop, or the

Fourth Street Connection—where the Sportsmen's Club used to be, on the north side of Fourth Street, towards the waterfront.

Dan was not allowed to tend his business, while just down the street, on E Street—Fourth and E—was Teresa's Market, and that was owned by the Mori family. So Mr. Mori could run his business on that side of 4th Street, but Dan Banducci couldn't run his on the opposite side of the street. He used to stand across the street by Daly's and shout instructions to his son, Gino—who's now a well-known chef in this area—on how to run the business. Dan used to get pretty excited sometimes, but Gino was just a high school kid.

Gino Banducci,
Eureka

I was going to high school, and [my father] had a person working for him in the mornings at the pool hall. I would come up and work in the evenings for a little bit. [Dad] would give me directions from across the street—give me hell for not doing things right. You know where Daly's annex is? There used to be a little Mobil station at that corner. And he'd park in the lot and stand on the street and motion for me to come over. He never crossed the white line.

Did your father's customers ever ask what was going on when he gave orders from across the street?

No. In fact, they kind of kidded him about it. It was just a joke, my dad standing over there, and then somebody'd come in and say, "Your dad's over there, you better go over and see him." People used to say to him, "Hey, dad. Come on, come on, dad."

"Oh, yah, yah, yah. Come on, come on. Get me in trouble, huh?" But he abided by the law. He was a good citizen that way. Then he went after his second papers about a year or so after he could cross the line again. He never complained about it. He took it in stride. I think he blamed himself for not ever getting his second papers.

I think this thing with my father only lasted for about six to eight months. Is there any way I can get money out of this, like the Japanese? [laughs]

George Mori

I remember one story about Dan Banducci, who had his business across Fourth Street. Oh boy, he was a character, that man, I tell you. Great guy, though; great guy. Mean, but great. I'd vouch for him. He used to cuss at you, but he was soft on the inside. Oh yeah, he was a pushover, but he was also a big man, large. And guys like Jimmy Gregori would antagonize him. Jimmy Gregori owned a string of shoe stores. The Jewish people would antagonize Dan. But nobody ever got him down. But this fellow Jimmy Gregori was probably the biggest tease in all the world. Dan would say, "If it wasn't for 'Rosenfelt' [Roosevelt], I could go over there and go into my business." And Jimmy, standing right behind him, would reply, "If it wasn't for Susie," who was Dan's wife, "If it wasn't for Susie, you wouldn't even have the business." Susie had all the money.

THE RELATIONSHIP OF the Tolan Committee to its witnesses amounted to a "love feast": the committee heard what it wanted and from whom it wanted. Crucial among the points on which the witnesses agreed was that the army knew best how to deal with the aliens. One exception was Berkeley's mayor, Frank Gaines, who believed that local authorities could do a better job with friendly German refugees. M.C. Godfrey, mayor of Alameda, and Oakland's police chief, B.A. Wallman, agreed with Tolan that local authorities were more familiar with hardship cases than agencies like the FBI. But, as Godfrey put it, federal agencies were better equipped to execute a "plan"—by which he meant an evacuation—than were the locals. Oakland's Mayor John Slavich made the point with an indelicate metaphor, which he intended to be humorous: "We [meaning local authorities] are rationing tires. We don't want to ration anything like this." It was left to Rep. Laurence F. Arnold (D-Illinois) to sum it up for the Bay Area witnesses: "You don't want to interfere with civil defense, but you don't want hardships to be worked on people whom you feel are loyal?"

Mayor Gaines: "Correct."

A remark by C.R. Schwannenberg, Alameda's city manager, showed how otherwise sensible people could lose a sense of proportion in the midst of the hysteria: "I would rather see 50,000 people put in a camp and be sure that we were protected than to have one person stay out of an internment camp who was a danger to the protection of this coast." To a man, the witnesses agreed that the final evacuation decision rested with none other than the individual who had ultimate responsibility for coastal defense: General DeWitt.[147] This was, of course, precisely the point that army loyalist Tom Clark had made repeatedly, although his apparent insensitivity to the plight of the aliens was resented by committee members.

Thus, the Tolan Committee found itself facing exactly the same dilemma as had proved so vexing to Attorney General Biddle and his staff throughout January and February. Since they agreed that something had to be done to protect the nation's security, but had no plan, they were at a disadvantage in stopping those who did. But it is doubtful the committee realized it was following the path of the Justice Department. Nonetheless, the Tolan Committee had played a significant role in the drama.

The efforts of the Tolan Committee and so many others to reverse the government's relocation policy finally paid dividends during the summer and fall of 1942. Now Secretary of War Stimson, ever mindful of the political, economic, and morale aspects of the relocation program, gathered his civilian staff in the War Department to scheme how to reign in General DeWitt. Still, there were many anxious days ahead for the aliens. They waited, not knowing how long their discomfort would last.

SEVEN

"Hundreds of thousands of people"
The Government Retreats

It is unthinkable that we should treat this matter lightly.
—The Tolan Committee, March 1942

S HIFTING MOMENTUM GOVERNED the evolution of alien policy on the West Coast in the spring of 1942. At first, it belonged to people who were simply afraid of other people. But before the thing was completely out of hand, it switched to those whose fears were more practical—to those who could count votes and did not like the addition.

No sooner had the War Department wrested alien policy away from the Justice Department, than and civilians in Washington, including some in the War Department, decided to put an end to it before it jeopardized the war effort and left the country with a bitter postwar legacy. Rep. Tolan had warned California Attorney General Earl Warren during his committee appearance that "the problem...looming before us as to where [the aliens] are going to go as the evacuation increases [is that] it may run into hundreds of thousands of people."[148] But Tolan and the other men of caution had not counted on the tenacity of John DeWitt. Not until he stood virtually alone in the San Francisco Presidio, abandoned even by his most zealous allies, did DeWitt back down. Even then, he brazenly demanded written exoneration from the consequences of being ignored.[149]

Before the Tolan Committee embarked on its mission to rescue the aliens, there were rumors in San Francisco that the Italians and Germans would not be relocated immediately, and that certain exemptions would be granted to the two groups. Behind the rumors lay these developments: well before Pearl Harbor, Attorney General Biddle had written of the economic consequences—especially the labor shortage—"which would have been involved in attempting to [relocate] hundreds of thousands of people indiscriminately." For morale purposes, he wanted a mechanism found by which a million and a quarter enemy aliens could be examined individually.

But Biddle's top lieutenant, James H. Rowe, Jr., believing the FBI was overworked, questioned this approach. Thus, Paul V. McNutt, former governor of Indiana and the new administrator of the Federal Security Agency—which would oversee the health and welfare of the displaced aliens—received a directive from the attorney general on January 31. "It is the intent of the United States that this operation be carried out with the smallest possible loss of human resources," advised Biddle. Many of the aliens were contributing directly to the war effort, including, of course, those in the armed forces. Now, both Stimson and Biddle told the president that the army did not have enough men to guard the Japanese *as well as* the Italians and Germans. All of this gave Richard Neustadt, social security regional director in San Francisco, hope that the rumor he had heard—that the Justice Department believed there would be "some let-up" on the Italians—was true.[150]

GENERAL DEWITT WAS sensitive to the pressure from above, albeit contemptuous of it. He had assured the Tolan Committee that there would be no mass evacuation, only "necessary" and "humane" removals carried out systematically. This assurance was the first hint that the War Department had decided to scale back the expulsion program. On February 20, Stimson had instructed the general to develop plans for relocating German aliens, but to ignore the Italians for the time being because they were potentially less dangerous and there were so many of them. In a separate communication the same day, McCloy told DeWitt to give special consideration to bona fide German political refugees as well. Taking advantage of the opening presented by Stimson's orders to DeWitt, Attorney General Biddle announced that there would be no wholesale revocation of professional and vocational licenses of enemy aliens, which Governor Olson had proposed. And U.S. Attorney Frank Hennessy said his office would accept applications from enemy aliens in San Francisco who wanted to continue to work in restricted zones.[151]

As the deadline neared for the first large relocation scheduled for February 15, the pace of exemptions quickened. Enemy aliens in the armed forces were reclassified as friendly—so long as they had enlisted before December 11—and Stimson approved pending literacy amendments to the 1940 Nationality Act, favoring some aliens. The Pittsburg delegation returned from Washington confident that their request for an unrestricted area in the city for extreme hardship cases was being given "full consideration." Indeed, General DeWitt had approved a last minute reprieve for aged (over 75) and bed-ridden aliens. Eventually, there were so many requests for exemptions of this kind that a blanket authorization had to be issued.[152]

DeWitt's first Public Proclamation on March 2 divided all Italian, German, and Japanese nationals, as well as Japanese American citizens in Military Area No.1 (the western halves of the Pacific states plus southern Arizona), into five classes. The order put Japanese aliens, persons of Japanese ancestry, and "dangerous enemy aliens" in greatest jeopardy, but DeWitt hinted that most of the Italians and Germans might have to go as well.[153]

This veiled threat forced the War Department to face the implications of a mass evacuation. McCloy impressed on DeWitt that he should forget about the Italians and Germans; the Japanese problem was already a burden on the army. Stimson had come to realize that the problem of evacuating enemy aliens from the entire coast might be unmanageable. He confided in his diary—like Biddle—that confusion reigned at the cabinet meeting of February 27 because nobody realized how big the relocation job would be.[154]

DeWitt's ambiguous statements also alarmed the Tolan Committee. Told by the Los Angeles County Defense Council that the FBI could handle the Germans and that the Italians were not particularly dangerous, the committee received a contradictory report the next day of increased public pressure within California to remove German and Italian aliens. Two days later Tolan learned that twenty thousand panicky Italian and German aliens had applied for their final citizenship papers. When the committee questioned Tom Clark, Rep. Arnold warned him:

> We are reluctant to see policies created here [concerning Germans and Italians] which may stand as precedents for subsequent action in other parts of the country where the size and scope of the problem are of such enormous magnitude as to jeopardize the very war effort.... It is unthinkable that we should treat this matter lightly.[155]

Clark, evidently not yet in sync with the War Department, assured the committee that DeWitt was thinking of removing Italians and Germans only from Military Area No. 1, where approximately eighty-six thousand of them lived. If one subtracted the exemptions, he guessed, the total number of evacuees would not be that great—provided they behaved themselves. Some committee members, weary of Clark's hard-nosed attitude, were worried about the public reaction nationally to the relocation of Italians and Germans. "There isn't a day that passes," said Rep. George H. Bender (R-Ohio), "but what there aren't at least half a dozen speeches made on the floor of Congress relating to this issue."[156]

Obviously, the Tolan Committee wanted something more concrete than what it was hearing from Clark. And so, two days after Clark made his vague commitments, three members of the committee met with McCloy in San Francisco, after which a joint communique proclaimed that the conferees "were in thorough agreement on steps which have been taken and which remain to be taken."[157]

Despite this apparent top-level accord, documents that were unavailable to Tolan show that DeWitt and the provost marshal general's office remained wedded to a course of mass relocation. For example, DeWitt told the Federal Reserve Bank in San Francisco—which had responsibility for the evacuees' property—that it should definitely expect to care for the needs of Italians and Germans. The Senate Committee on Military Affairs, looking into relocation on its own in Washington, tried, with little success, to learn from the provost marshal general's office how many enemy aliens there were and how many the army wanted to remove. The committee wanted to be able to estimate the impact nationwide since, as it concluded based on what it was hearing, that, "The same thing is going to have to be done on the East Coast." The PMG's representative, Colonel B.M. Bryan, chief of the alien division, replied that about one 100,000 people would be put in concentration camps, 60 percent of them Japanese and the remainder, about 40,000, divided equally between the two European enemy alien groups.

Tom Clark continued to insist that his hands were tied. One of the lucky aliens who appealed to Clark was Father Gabriel Joseph Zavattaro. He had moved out of San Francisco's North Beach to St. Joseph's parish in Oakland. The priest managed to get Clark to agree to let him pursue his naturalization, make sick calls, and conduct funerals further than five miles from the church.[158]

Fr. Gabriel Zavattaro

When the regulations about all the aliens who would not be allowed to live in certain areas came out, I could not live where I was—even though I was a superior at the junior seminary, even though I was a priest. According to the law, there were no exceptions. Since the exclusion order was published in the newspapers, and I didn't want to get into trouble with the government, I moved from Richmond to Oakland, where we had a parish. But it was very difficult.

I approached Joe Alioto, who was a government attorney in Washington, D.C. He said, "I'll see what I can do." That's why—when, later on, there was an investigation from Washington into the case of the Italian parents with sons in the army or navy who could not stay in their homes or could not leave their homes—the situation of those who had already sworn allegiance to the United States but for technical reasons did not have citizenship papers, was presented with the other cases. And when the decree came allowing the Italian aliens with children in the army to go back to their homes and be completely free, it included those who had already sworn allegiance to the United States before the war broke out, but for technical reasons were not yet citizens. So after a couple of months I was allowed to go back to Richmond.

IN ITS PRELIMINARY findings of March 19, the Tolan Committee expressed its fear about the size of the expulsion in unambiguous terms. The government, it pointed out by way of analogy to the Italians and Germans, had not removed the Japanese from Hawaii, despite the obvious threat to American security there, because the Japanese made up 37 percent of Hawaii's population. On the other hand, the Japanese were only 1 percent of the population of the Pacific states. Italians and Germans on the mainland had built different kinds of communities than the Japanese, and where the Japanese had only one economic base, agriculture, the Italians and Germans pursued a variety of occupations. Thus, the committee concluded,

> Evacuation policies instituted for German and Italian aliens on the west coast have direct Nation-wide import because there are many thousands of these aliens in other parts of the country.... The numbers involved [in the Japanese evacuation] are large, but they are by no means as large, for the whole country, as those who will be involved if we generalize the current treatment of the Japanese to apply to all Axis aliens and their immediate families.... Any such proposal is out of the question if we intend to win this war.[159]

Exemptions, the committee scoffed, were no substitute for a "well-developed program" for removing only truly dangerous individuals and allowing the rest to stay. In particular, there needed to be a grace period for the aliens to complete their citizenship because of bureaucratic foul-ups and general rigidity of the system. And the consequences could be tragic. For example, a man who was forced out of his home in Monterey, where he had lived for forty-eight years, had died in Salinas.[160]

On March 20, President Roosevelt issued Executive Order 9106, exempting additional classes of Italian and German aliens from restrictions so they could apply for naturalization after being cleared by the attorney general.[161] If a decision to widen the exclusion program was necessary, those in Washington with their ears closest to the ground—led by the president—wanted a minimal number of Europeans involved.

During the last week of March, DeWitt issued his long-anticipated orders excluding everyone of Japanese ancestry from the West Coast. The evacuation,[162] as the army insisted on calling it, would begin in April. In the meantime, no Italians or Germans would be allowed to leave Military Area No. 1 without permission. DeWitt again called on the Federal Security Agency in San Francisco to help with the evacuation, which, he reiterated, would include Italians, Germans, and Japanese. Elderly Italians and Germans, those who were related to servicemen, those awaiting naturalization, or who were in poor health, DeWitt exempted.[163]

Still not confident in his own bureaucracy, particularly DeWitt, Stimson arranged for a private channel of information about the alien situation on the West Coast. Alfred Jaretski, Jr., a New York City corporate lawyer with recent refugee relief experience in Europe, went to work for McCloy in Washington as a special consultant. Supreme Court Justice Felix Frankfurter, an old War Department crony and close friend of Stimson's, had probably recommended Jaretski to the secretary. Frankfurter had another acquaintance in the War Department, his neighbor and evening walking partner in Georgetown, a man the justice knew well enough to call "Jack" McCloy. No doubt Frankfurter apprised Jaretski of the urgent telegram he had received from Berkeley's Monroe E. Deutsch, who thought it an "unprecedented" blow to all American principles to expel an entire group of citizens because of their ancestry—meaning the political refugees from Nazi and Fascist regimes, not the Japanese. Jaretski's appointment was interpreted by one friend of the refugees as good-faith evidence that the War Department was "not unsympathetic" to the idea of exempting aliens that had "convincingly cast their lot with the [United States]."[164]

Soon thereafter, Jaretski wrote Stimson from his Washington office that there were approximately eighty-thousand Italian and German enemy aliens on the West Coast subject to possible relocation, who should not be classified as disloyal. Not only would their removal be unjust, Jaretski emphasized, *"but of more importance in this period of national emergency would be the undoubted national repercussions of such a movement....* If public apprehension is unnecessarily aroused in respect [to] these alien groups, public clamor for protection will greatly impede the war effort." (emphasis added)[165]

McCloy, who had received a note of concern about some refugee friends on the West Coast from Mrs. William G. McAdoo (Woodrow Wilson's daughter), sent Jaretski off to the West Coast to keep an eye on DeWitt. Meanwhile, he reassured McAdoo that her friends would be safe.

With Jaretski on his way, McCloy turned to DeWitt and chastised him for ordering Italian and German aliens out, which, he said, had created "aspects to this problem [that] affect the country generally." The still-skeptical DeWitt telephoned Bendetsen the same day to say that he would employ a wait-and-see approach with Jaretski.[166]

There were other behind-the-scenes attempts in Washington to influence DeWitt's superiors. The president received a memo from Biddle, saying there was no important congressional support to remove Italians and Germans. Biddle and the War Department also worried about the possibility of reprisals against Americans in enemy hands should their nationals in the United States be mistreated. Biddle's aide, James Rowe, Jr., believing that too much attention was being paid the political refugees, cautioned that it would be unfair to exempt the anti-Nazi group but not Italians who had lived in the United States most of their lives. And finally, a conference of district attorneys informed the provost marshal general of its conclusion that "to attempt to intern all the million and a quarter alien enemies would mean serious economic disruption involving about 15 million people directly," thus handicapping war production.[167]

McCloy, exasperated by his inability to restrain DeWitt, huddled again with Tolan's group. Later he met with Earl Warren and had to be heartened by Warren's counsel that the public along the West Coast was no longer worried about either the Italians or Germans. This upbeat news somewhat matched the results of a nationwide survey issued by the Office of Facts and Figures, showing that people considered the Italian aliens much less dangerous than the Germans. There were rumors as well that some Italian fishermen might be able to go back to sea, and accurate reports that more than twenty aliens had moved back to their homes in Pittsburg due to DeWitt's exemptions.[168]

But suddenly, the possibility of more drastic action resurfaced. Biddle now wrote FDR that he feared the army planned to evacuate enemy aliens from the East Coast as well.[169] Stimson, who saw the attorney general's letter, sought to ease the president's mind: "It was a foolish matter without any foundation...and Biddle ought to have been ashamed of himself." There would be no "mass" evacuation of the East Coast; the army would do it "very carefully with very small numbers." Tallies aside, the secretary was being slightly disingenuous, providing he knew what his assistant was up to. For McCloy had written General Joseph McNarney, chief of the Army Field Forces, that, as the war progressed, it might be necessary to remove Italian and German aliens from the East and Gulf coasts. McCloy went so far as to suggest that McNarney send his eastern and southern defense commanders to the West Coast to study the evacuation methods being employed there.[170]

Stimson may have been satisfied that the problem on the East Coast had been laid to rest, but he still had to sell the idea of a limited relocation to his officers out West. DeWitt continued to oppose the suggestion that individual loyalty examinations might be a way to sort through the aliens, and Bendetsen agreed that there were "a lot of dangerous" Italians and Germans out on the coast who had to be removed. Jaretski, McCloy's new troubleshooter, patiently explained to Bendetsen that any mass expulsion of Italians and Germans would mean more relocation camps:

> If there's any sizable evacuation, from the West Coast it's going to inflame public opinion.... It's going to mean there's going to be a sizable evacuation from other areas. Therefore, we are loathe [sic] to go into any wholesale program of this kind, unless where defense is necessary.... There's a lot of difference whether you're talking about moving [twenty thousand] people, or moving two or three thousand.[171]

But Stimson's thoughts on this subject, on which his assurance to the president rested, had not yet filtered down through the War Department's chain of command. Lt. General Hugh A. Drum, commanding general of the Eastern Defense Command, publicly announced his intention to establish prohibited and restricted areas covering the entire Atlantic seaboard and inland—some sixteen states and fifty-two million people, fulfilling the Tolan Committee's worst fears. Even Bendetsen thought Drum would "run into more headaches than he's ever had in his life." Drum insisted, however, that only "such evacuations as may be considered necessary will be [done] by selective processes."[172]

Some who read this statement found it ambiguous. Tolan wrote both Biddle and McCloy that the phrase, "selective processes" created too much uncertainty and would undoubtedly lower the aliens' morale. Biddle agreed with Tolan and took the matter up with Stimson. Later he assured Tolan that the secretary of war shared the congressman's concern. McCloy, too, expressed complete sympathy: "I believe we have a common approach to this problem." Nonetheless, he took the precaution of meeting again with a Tolan Committee staff person on May 7, resulting in a committee request that the president put out a revised order precluding alien relocation in areas other than the West Coast.[173]

Although the East Coast situation had been resolved by FDR, General DeWitt still had to be dealt with. On April 27, the same day that Jaretski issued his warning to Bendetsen and General Drum announced his exclusion plans, Clark again rekindled doubts. He wrote to Rowe that, "Anyone who had the idea that General DeWitt is going to delay the evacuation of German and Italian aliens is in error. He has consistently said publicly and otherwise that he intends to evacuate these groups as soon as his program with reference to the Japanese is completed." Rowe, who passed Clark's letter along to Edward Ennis, also a member of the anti-War Department clique in the Justice Department, wrote cynically in the margin, "I think you had better talk to McCloy [?] about this. We will soon see who is the boss. I'm betting on DeWitt."[174]

Roosevelt, by now thoroughly alarmed by the repeated warnings from the Justice Department and complaints from Capitol Hill and New York, swung into action. He ordered Stimson to take no action against Italian or German aliens on the East Coast without first consulting him—period. Alien control, he said, except for the Japanese, was a civilian matter, and all this talk about evacuations was having a bad effect on morale. Ever the politician, FDR assured New York governor Herbert Lehman that no collective evacuation of Italians or Germans was contemplated. But Stimson, mindful of his responsibility to protect the country against dangerous individual aliens, thought the president was being unduly panicked by the Justice Department, and he argued successfully that the War Department's prerogative to remove dangerous *individuals* not be compromised.[175]

Meanwhile, the indefatigable DeWitt pressed on, threatening in early May to put six to ten thousand Italians and Germans in "relocation centers in a manner similar to that employed in the case of persons of Japanese ancestry." Bendetsen warned McCloy that the general was serious. DeWitt, he emphasized, believed that the probability of German retaliatory raids grew stronger as each month passed, and was proposing to justify removal of all other enemy aliens not then exempted as "an essential war measure." But Bendetsen himself stepped back from this new and dangerous precipice. Separating his views from DeWitt's, Bendetsen recommended to McCloy that there be no movement of Italians by groups, merely a continuation of the Justice Department's individual internment policy. But Bendetsen could play rough too, and he added that if the Justice Department failed to act more diligently, the War Department should exert energy under Executive Order 9066 "similar to that taken in the evacuation of the Japanese."[176]

Following two quick conferences with a more contrite Bendetsen (now in Washington to press his and DeWitt's proposals on the War Department in person), McCloy found a compromise solution. He told Stimson there was little danger from the Italians, although more so from the Germans. DeWitt and Drum needed the authority to remove, but not to detain, dangerous individuals, he urged, but this power should be used sparingly. The generals should be required to make weekly reports of the numbers involved to the assistant secretary. It would help, too, he added, if the FBI stepped up its investigations and detentions. When DeWitt learned that McCloy and Stimson did not agree with his proposed mass evacuation of Germans and Italians as an essential war measure, he demanded written instructions exonerating him from all consequences of this exception.[177]

When the War Department conducted a series of internal conferences on May 15 to prepare Stimson for a cabinet meeting later that day, it had the Tolan Committee's latest report at hand. The congressmen were continuing to hammer home the logic of their earlier paper: the size of the Italian and German communities—more diverse and ten times larger than the Japanese—presented "problems more vast and far reaching than the Japanese.... Emergency measures must not be permitted to alter permanently those fundamental principles upon which this Nation was built." It now appeared clear to the committee, as it had not in February, that the expulsion of the Japanese might "serve as an incident sufficiently disturbing to lower seriously the morale of vast groups of foreign-born among our people."[178] If the Italians and Germans were not relocated, the committee hinted that in this respect the Japanese relocation had not been in vain.

Clearly, the conclusions of the Tolan Committee, now public, were effecting attitudes in the War Department. Almost word-for-word, McCloy recommended to Stimson, and Stimson, in turn, recommended to the president what Bendetsen had written four days earlier, with one exception: there would be no evacuation of Italians and Germans similar to that of the Japanese. The resulting draft recommendation for Roosevelt was intended to reassure the president that rumors (presumably circulated by Justice Department officials) of further mass relocations were unfounded. "We intend *no* mass evacuations on the East Coast," the document stated categorically. And after explaining DeWitt's proposals to the president, Stimson concluded: "I personally think we should have no mass evacuation either on the West Coast or the East Coast other than the Japanese unless there is some outbreak of [F]ifth [C]olumn activities." If the FBI stepped up its work, that would "create much less of a dislocation than...a mass evacuation."

Stimson continued along the line proposed by DeWitt: the president should empower the commanders on both coasts to exclude individuals, both aliens and citizens, based entirely on military necessity and Executive Order 9066. Roosevelt immediately approved Stimson's recommendation, expressing relief that the secretary had, as FDR put it, "laid a ghost." Biddle believed the new policy vindicated the position taken by the Justice Department from the start. Still, movement of individual aliens and citizens was to be done in "strict secrecy."[179] DeWitt had yet to receive his final orders. McCloy wrote the general that FDR and Stimson had approved Executive Order 9066 "with the expectation that the exclusion would not reach such numbers [as proposed by DeWitt].... We want, if at all possible, to avoid the necessity of establishing additional relocation settlements." DeWitt did not get the waiver of responsibility he had insisted on. But he was granted authority to satisfy his concern about individual Italians and Germans, so long as he proceeded with "caution and discretion" and kept in mind that his job was to protect vital installations and not to persecute individuals. McCloy ordered DeWitt to end the curfew on Italians and Germans when the Japanese were gone and to clear future public announcements.[180]

BY APRIL 1942, with the Italians and Germans settled in their new residences and the Japanese on their way to Manzanar and other relocation camps as far east as Arkansas, plans were developed to extend the hearing board process to all relocated Italians and Germans. Thirteen boards would handle the forty northern California counties and their largest cities; eight others would hear cases in the seventeen remaining counties.[181]

Unaware of these plans, the Tolan Committee had urged in its final report in mid-May that local hearing boards be created to "obviate mass evacuation." The hearing board system, the committee argued, "recognizes that birth in the land of the enemy does not necessarily make for disloyalty any more than old age or infirmity...make for loyalty." In order to minimize the adjustments that the aliens had to make during and after the war, it made sense to the committee that the hearings be undertaken as soon as possible; considering their numbers and dispersion, alien morale was vital to the war effort. By July, Ennis's AECU was seriously considering the committee's recommendation.[182] But the unit never took any final action; there was no need for it.

Between May and October the wheels of government ground inexorably toward a total relaxation of restrictions. On the recommendation of his staff, Bendetsen advised DeWitt to rescind curfew and travel restrictions because they were unenforceable and were hampering the war effort. On July 11, President Roosevelt would call for the reclassification of aliens "with a view to greater utilization of their services in war production," but DeWitt vowed not to drop the curfew until the Justice Department took concrete action to support his authority to exclude individual aliens.[183]

The president had taken his cue from Jaretski and Archibald Mac-Leish, director of the Office of Facts and Figures. Both men had recommended immediately after the decision not to relocate the Europeans that Italian aliens and German expatriates should be reclassified as friendly. MacLeish's office believed that "loyal Americans" of Italian or German descent ought to be included in the war effort, and Jaretski wrote passionately of the expatriates, explaining how such a move would lift the morale of the aliens as well as anti-Nazi partisans in occupied Europe. He had to know, of course, that the latter would produce favorable "political repercussions" for the administration at home.[184]

Two weeks later McCloy began to explore with army G-2 (intelligence) the possibility of removing Italians from the enemy category. The State Department was worried about reprisals against diplomatic staff abroad, but it wondered whether such a move might adversely affect national security. The acting chief of staff of G-2, General George V. Strong said he doubted the propaganda value of any relaxation because the Italians were under the control of the Germans and it would not deter spies or dedicated Fascists.[185]

Nonetheless, on June 27, with the Japanese gone, General DeWitt bowed to the inevitable and abolished the six-months-old prohibited and restricted zones (except in certain sensitive areas) in the Western Defense Command. Only the curfew, a change-of-residence requirement, and travel restrictions remained. A month later, and in follow-up letters in September, Ennis revealed that the AECU was contemplating the establishment of loyalty hearing boards to screen individual enemy aliens, and that travel restrictions had been relaxed.[186]

Lily Boemker

How did you know you could move back? Were you notified individually?

No, we weren't notified. They put up notices at the post office. So we moved back and things started to look up. But in the meantime, my mother became sick. With the anxiety, the pressure, and the stress she became a diabetic. We couldn't understand what it was. She was going to the doctor, and he couldn't find out what the matter was. And then when we moved back to Arcata a doctor in Eureka found that she was a diabetic.

Your mother felt that this was somehow connected to your having to move?

We all felt that way, yes.

What did you think about the government's policy?

When you read about the Japanese and how they were put into concentration camps—well, look what they did to us. They should compensate us somewhat.

IN MONTEREY, THE news that relocation had been rescinded came as a godsend for those who needed the Italians and Germans to harvest fruits and vegetables. For the fisherman, however, DeWitt's June announcement promised much less; they would be allowed back in town, but not on their boats. Mike Bommarito and Frank Balesteri, a couple of easygoing Monterey fishermen, had been—as the local newspaper put it—"away for several weeks pending Uncle Sam's decision about the proper place of residence for some of his nephews." Despite the uncertainty, the mood was lighthearted. Balesteri told a reporter, "You can write in the paper that my vacation is over.'[187]

On Columbus Day, October 12, 1942, a day of special meaning for Italians, Attorney General Biddle announced that Italian aliens in the United States would no longer be considered enemies. As Biddle remembered it later, the idea of reclassifying the Italians was Ennis's and that Roosevelt, who wished he had thought of it himself, immediately gave the move his blessing, calling it "a masterly stroke of international statesmanship *and* good politics."[188]

But the aliens waited, wondering whether DeWitt would heed Biddle's initiative and issue the necessary orders to free them from the remaining restrictions. A week after the attorney general's speech, DeWitt grudgingly lifted the residue of military restrictions on the Italians. Said one Italian in San Francisco's North Beach, "I am an American again, huh?" DeWitt left the fate of the fishermen to the navy and coast guard. But it appeared that the latter (acting for the navy) intended to hold the aliens to the letter of an 1917 espionage act that prohibited enemy aliens from boarding ships in American waters. Pittsburg fishermen hoped they would at least be allowed back into shallow waters, and the chamber of commerce suggested an obvious inference: restoring fishing rights would be an economic boon.[189]

In Washington, Interior Secretary Ickes regarded these delays contemptuously. Like FDR he was a practical man, and he told the president that since meat was about to be rationed, and therefore the need for sea-food was that much greater, Roosevelt should get as many fishing boats back to sea as soon as possible. The culprit, Ickes complained during a cabinet meeting, was the army, which had confiscated over 500 boats to the navy's 150. "We can't supply the army with fish if the army has taken all the fishing boats," reasoned Ickes. According to Ickes, Stimson returned a blank stare.[190]

Appropriately enough, considering the importance of political symbolism to this story, the announcement that the fishermen would be released from their confinement came on Election Day, November 3 (signed by FDR on October 27). Of no small consequence in eventually persuading navy secretary Frank Knox to relent were the 218,000 Italians in New York, the 45,000 each in California and Massachusetts, the 62,000 in New Jersey, and the fact that most of the fishermen on both coasts were Italian. Just to be completely safe, however, the ever-cautious Knox stipulated that 50 percent of the crews had to be American citizens.[191]

Anita Maiorana Ferrante

Do you know why the boats were returned after a year and a half?

Yes, I do. The fishermen were so anxious to get their boats back. It was the means of their surviving, and my father didn't like having to rent a boat when he had his own. So they sent letters asking the navy to release these boats because they were needed for the armed forces' food supply. Fishing was the food program that was needed for overseas. The navy listened and they heard. [My father's boat] the Diana came back sooner than some of the rest of them. They did keep the others that they had equipped for more specialized missions.

It was unbelievable. I often hear about the Japanese. We also had our share of trouble, but it was just a situation where the government had to take some action. You can't be bitter about something that has already occurred. We had never really been in this type of war. We had to protect our coastline, and this was hard...harsh...mean. It had to be done. At the time, the Italians were very bitter that they had to leave their homes, of course. But I'm looking at it from today's point of view. We weren't put into concentration camps, but we were moved out, pushed away. There were just tears. My father could handle it; he could come back and fish. But my mother, to leave her home, her cousins. To think that a U.S. citizen would be moved—If my dad was a citizen, surely the family should have stayed, you know?

John Spataro

In May of 1944, they gave me citizenship papers. Anyone who was in the service more than six months got their papers. I went to Salinas for mine. They just asked me a few questions. As a matter of fact, they asked me, "You got a brother over there in Italy? If we tell you to shoot your brother, are you going to shoot him?" Well, I looked at that guy and I said, "I don't know what to say." He said, "If you want your citizenship papers you have to say, yes."

We stayed in San Jose about eight or nine months. Then we heard a rumor that we could go back to Monterey to fish. So we moved again. Put everything in the truck and back we came. When we arrived, we found out from the coast guard that we could stay, but not fish. I thought, "If I can't fish, what am I doing back here? Everybody else is fishing and I can't?" We stayed about ten days and moved again, this time to San Francisco. In those days, you could find houses. My wife's sister had a lot of apartments, so we didn't have any problem. Just went there and moved in. I worked at the Western Park shipyard for about a year. Made good money. Eleven dollars a day. You know, there were a couple of thousand people in this one place, and I could have sabotaged it right there.

BIDDLE AND ICKES earnestly took up the cause of the Germans in November. Biddle believed there were 100,000 German farmers in the United States, most of them refugees, and he wanted to free them of the stigma of enemies. Ickes thought that alien doctors from German and Austrian universities could be put to work on Indian reservations and in army camps. The two men urged the president to make a preliminary statement to get the idea rolling.[192]

Their efforts paid off. During the first week of January, despite his lingering fear that some expatriates were impostors planted by the German government, DeWitt removed most of the restrictions on Germans, although they remained technically classified as enemy aliens. But DeWitt was not the only one to believe the fake refugee story: Roosevelt did as well One refugee confronted this pervasive myth by pointing out that genuine refugees would expose an impostor in a minute.[193]

THE DISCOMFORT AND anxiety of the aliens and their families was over. They were free to resume near-normal lives. Justice Department officials, civilians in the War Department, and strategic members of congress finally realized that it was neither feasible nor necessary to remove Italian and German aliens en masse. There was little likelihood of Germany—much less Italy—attacking the Pacific Coast, DeWitt's fantasies to the contrary notwithstanding. It was believed that, because investigators had more information relative to dangerous individual Italians and Germans, they could be handled more efficiently than the Japanese. But the principal consideration in taking the decision was that relocation would create a logistical nightmare. Alfred Jaretski summed up this outlook in June 1942: "Any action with respect to the Italians and Germans on the West Coast would have serious repercussions in other parts of the country where the alien populations were much greater." He emphasized three key problems:

> The...impossibility of moving en masse approximately [one million] aliens of Italian and German nationality, or any very substantial number of them. The terrific cost involved in any such action, including the dislocation of our economy and the effect on public morale. And the fact that the vast majority of this group are believed to be loyal or harmless."[194]

So powerful—so simplistic—has the theme of racism been that the government's pragmatic response to the alien crisis, particularly in choosing to distinguish between the Italian and German influence in the country and that of the Japanese, has been almost entirely absent from historical accounts of relocation. But no one who reads Secretary Stimson's reply to a request from House Speaker John McCormack (D-Massachusetts) that he look into the Japanese threat on Hawaii can fail to notice that the secretary applied the same principle to the Italian and German situation on the mainland:

> Our greatest difficulty in dealing with [the Japanese] problem," Stimson wrote, "is the *economic aspect*. The Japanese population is so interwoven into the economic fabric of the Islands that if we attempted to evacuate all Japanese aliens and citizens all business, including that concerned with the building up of our defenses, would practically stop."[195]

It was indeed the presence of millions of Italians and Germans enmeshed in the economic, social, and political fabric of the country that made the logic of Hawaii imperative from California to New York. Retreat had been sounded; reason would prevail.

Still, there remains another, peculiar dimension to this story. In contrast to the petty bickering of the bureaucrats and General DeWitt's mean-spiritedness, the government had pursued a course at the outset of its relocation program—albeit without fanfare—that revealed its sensitivity to the aliens' plight.

EIGHT

"Italians take care of their own"
The Puzzle of Government Compensation

*Enemy aliens should not become unduly alarmed, because they will
receive every consideration. We will not just try to give it to them, we
WILL give it to them.*

—Tom Clark, February 1942

HOW DOES A government show compassion toward those victimized by its policies? Traditionally, through financial assistance, and to its credit, the United States government moved in this direction in 1942. Yet virtually none of the Italians and Germans who would have been on the receiving end—many who could have used some help—accepted it. Records of the Federal Security Agency, the parent body of the Social Security Board, which ran the assistance program, confirm that only small amounts were drawn from the $500,000 account specially earmarked for alien relief. And there is something else quite remarkable: no one interviewed for this book recalled hearing about the money.

Perhaps the former aliens simply forgot about the money after all these years. Perhaps they turned down the offer or put it out of their minds because they distrusted a government that had already inflicted so much hardship. They had their pride. But one thing is certain: no one reading about relocation in the newspapers in 1942 could have overlooked the information about the money. In nearly every announcement having to do with the relocation, the aliens were told where to go for information about financial aid. That some of the interviewees are highly educated suggests that something other than illiteracy lay behind their reticence.

The form of assistance available to Italians and Germans differed from that provided the Japanese. The sole means of aid available to Italians and Germans was a special presidential fund. The Japanese were supposed to be helped by an Alien Property Custodian, whose job it was to insure that personal belongings were identified and warehoused for the duration of their relocation. (As late as March 18 DeWitt insisted that the custodian's responsibility included Italians and Germans.) Once interned, the welfare of the Japanese—such as it was—became the responsibility of the War Relocation Authority (WRA).[196]

The mayor of New York City, Fiorello LaGuardia, wrote to Franklin Roosevelt early in 1942 on behalf of the non-Japanese aliens, whom LaGuardia believed had been left out of provisions to reimburse Americans suffering losses from enemy action. FDR did not reply until August. But the president's belated answer, which revealed the existence of a special fund for enemy aliens from his own emergency account, more than satisfied his honor. LaGuardia relished reading aloud the entire letter during one of his periodic radio broadcasts, giving him the opportunity to contrast FDR's charitable treatment of enemy aliens in the United States with Hitler's brutal oppression of his own people.[197]

Richard Neustadt, regional director of the Social Security Board in San Francisco, whose job it was to care for evacuees in northern California, first heard about the possibility of financial assistance for enemy aliens on January 28, 1942. He understood he was to quietly disburse about $5,000,000. But nobody knew where the money would come from. Apparently, Attorney General Biddle first proposed that the budget bureau release the money from the president's emergency fund.

Neustadt estimated he would need $3.5 million in assistance to care for approximately 50,000 people, of whom 15,000 would need shelter and 9,000 medical care. But an additional 72,000 required intermittent relief. As Neustadt envisioned it, the state would provide the office space and do the paperwork, and the federal government would put up the money. In time, the program did become a cooperative venture between the Social Security Board and the California Department of Public Welfare, with the federal government reimbursing the state agencies in large part. California also waived its customary welfare residence requirements. Beneath the public façade of cooperation, however, lurked a thinly veiled distrust. The director of the Social Security Board warned Neustadt not to trust the state agencies with federal money that historically had a way of being siphoned off into the black hole of state "administration" costs.[198]

When Neustadt had received no formal confirmation of funding by February 3, he panicked: "We are about to face a deluge of people!" he cried to his boss, Paul McNutt. "The most serious problem...will be housing.... There are no houses to amount to a dam [sic] and in some places there will be terrific resentment.... They can't build houses between now and the 24th."[199]

Three days later things were no clearer. A telegram informed Neustadt that the budget bureau had requested the half-million dollars from the president's fund, and the Justice Department "guessed" there would be about 8,000 alien enemies moved by the twenty-fourth. But Neustadt's superiors admitted, "We won't know until next week the size of the problem—nor is there any way of guessing" (the Justice Department estimate notwithstanding). Social security officials hoped the children and grandchildren of the aliens would shoulder most of the burden. Certain Italian societies did tell Neustadt that a large number of their people would go to families and friends "under their own steam." But they warned that some aliens would commit suicide rather than go begging to state offices. Tragically, they were right.[200]

At the Presidio, Tom Clark had first thought of adding a special note to the personal relocation mailings, telling the aliens the location of employment offices where the assistance effort would be centered. Everything was printed and ready to go the night of February 1, when the post office balked at delivering the notices and Clark's scheme unraveled. Sobered by this snafu, the demoralized Neustadt was sure that, had the plan succeeded, everyone caught in the removal would have known the facilities were there. Instead, the single sentence, "Go to the nearest public employment office for advice and assistance," was hastily added—in small print—to the eleven-by-fourteen expulsion signs posted in prohibited and restricted areas.[201] The press, however, did its best to salvage the situation by reporting the information that might have been overlooked by anyone merely glancing at Clark's placards. It is probable, too, that the papers reached more readers than the scattered posters tacked up in out-of-the-way places.

The first newspaper announcements of the impending relocation on February 4 and 5 emphasized that there would be resettlement help from the Federal Security Agency, the Social Security Board, and the U.S. Employment Service. Directions were quite specific. In Eureka, for example, the people to see were Margaret Stutsman and John Herndon in Room 206G of the post office. The aliens were to apply for work or unemployment insurance outside the prohibited zones. They could receive up to twenty dollars a week for a maximum of twenty weeks while the employment service tried to find them new jobs. They were also eligible for rent and utilities. Attorneys ready to advise the aliens of their civil rights were on call through the social security offices.[202]

Page One of the *Pittsburg Post-Dispatch* told its readers the location of the social security office in that city—Black Diamond St. Enemy alien families in Monterey who were unable to finance the necessary removal from the city or to support themselves afterwards were to contact the Federal Security Agency and, after moving, apply immediately for new jobs through the state employment office.[203]

Ample information about the money appeared in the *Los Angeles Times*. Not satisfied, however, that the federal government knew how to handle "his" aliens, Mayor Bowron decided to appoint a Committee on Alien Relations composed of citizens from all areas of the city. The committee picked up the necessary information from federal agencies and then told the aliens how to comply with the relocation order and where they could move. By February 9, only a "trickle" of aliens had shown up at Los Angeles area social security offices. But the next day and during the rest of that week, the trickle turned into a deluge. The same thing happened in San Francisco. In Monterey, over 300 aliens had come for information or aid by the thirteenth, and the FSA office was "swamped" with inquiries on the seventeenth.[204]

Don Raffaelli

Did you know about the fund to aid people who were relocated?

I've been working for the government now for thirty-odd years. I'm in the public works department for the county. The information about that fund was probably put in the legal section of the newspaper. If you don't want people to know about it you put it in small print. Was it on the front page?

Not always, but it was included with the rest of the news about the restrictions.

Very few of the Italians knew English. They probably wouldn't have known about the money unless they had somebody in the family who could read for them. When this was happening, even I didn't speak English. We lived in an Italian ghetto. We spoke only Italian. When the first non-Italian kid moved on the block, we thought he was from outer space. I don't recall seeing an English newspaper in our house until I was in high school and I started delivering papers.

To the best of my knowledge, no one lost his property, unlike the Japanese.

I also learned a work ethic at an early age. You took care of yourself, your family, and your friends. Everyone helped each other. They always worked. There was pride. If one person didn't take the government money, then nobody else would either. It was part of being in a clique. If you do something different than the clique, then you're ostracized. And I think cliques were important. There had to be that mutual support.

FOLLOWING THE PATTERN of the New Deal and the wartime civilian bureaucracies, the structure of the assistance program looked like alphabet soup. To implement its responsibilities, DeWitt's command had created the Wartime Civil Control Administration (WCCA), which utilized services and facilities available through a number of federal agencies, including the Farm Security Administration, Federal Reserve Bank, the bureaus of Public Assistance and Employment Security of the SSB, and the Public Health Service. Expenses incurred by the Federal Security Agency for WCCA operations were met initially from the presidential allocation. Administrative expenses were fully funded and assistance costs reimbursable in large part by the WCCA.[205]

The Bureau of Employment was responsible for registration and employment referral, and helped persons secure unemployment compensation. The Bureau of Public Assistance provided service and assistance for transporting people and their belongings. The aliens were told that, if no new homes were available outside the prohibited zones, Civilian Conservation Corps (CCC) camps would be made available. These camps were not to be thought of as "internment camps," cautioned the government, but as "housing facilities for homeless people." The Works Project Administration (WPA) readied itself to put the aliens to work in reclamation, reforestation, and road construction. There was even discussion of the possibility of some Italians and Germans being placed on farms in the Sacramento River Delta. But Neustadt quickly pointed out that since most Italians were vineyardists and fishermen, and the Germans primarily clerical workers and professionals, they would not make particularly good farmers. He did not think that the older Italian fishermen could be trained to work in defense plants, as had been suggested by officials higher up in the bureaucracy.[206]

Federal Security Agency rules required that families meet the relocation deadline (which left them little time to find housing) and, insofar as possible, relocate in the same county, even if that meant moving more than once to find adequate accommodations. If an alien wanted to move outside his county, the agency had to determine whether employment or other means of support was available.[207]

Aliens eligible for assistance were what the government called a "normally constituted family"—including dependents—affected by exclusion, detention, or relocation. If an employed adult citizen son, for example, opted to stay with his relocated alien family, he too was eligible. If only a portion of a family moved, assistance went to that portion. Separated family members could also benefit.[208]

But the programs did not work as intended. According to some, they were never given a chance. In Los Angeles, the Council of Social Agencies said that information about assistance was not being disseminated among the aliens. When the chairman of the council accused the metropolitan dailies of having "no interest" in the information (which was not true), Neustadt immediately alerted the Italian-language newspapers. Always sensitive to public relations, Neustadt sent a memorandum to all Western Defense Command personnel imploring them to treat the aliens with dignity and courtesy, and to avoid creating unnecessary hardships.[209]

There were also, of course, problems due to the size of DeWitt's relocation program: an employer in Santa Cruz logically wanted to know what the Social Security Board intended to do after the aliens had relocated outside the prohibited areas and were without legal access to social security offices. Similarly, curfew and travel restrictions kept the aliens away from employment offices. Two days after the first relocation deadline had passed, Neustadt still did not have the answers to these and many other vexing questions, but he promised to deal with problems, somehow. The biggest headache remained the larger evacuation scheduled for February 24, which would include many aliens who had no alternative housing or relatives to turn to. It was precisely these challenges that caused Neustadt to publicly oppose mass evacuation of aliens from California a week before the final deadline. Within a matter of days after this decision, he was to become one of the most persuasive witnesses to appear before the Tolan Committee, one of the few to combine genuine compassion with pragmatism.[210]

Some of what Neustadt told the committee ought to startle anyone today who does not recall the government's offer of assistance. Records indicate that most of the aliens affected by the relocation order did respond to the announcements. Of the 9,000-10,000 aliens who were expected to relocate, Neustadt revealed that 6,500 had visited social security offices for information but only 140 requested aid (67 in Monterey). He attributed this to their pride. By Thursday, February 19, 2,300 of the 6,500 had already moved or found new homes; 1,300 others said they could find their own housing without help from the government; and 500 admitted they would need help, with perhaps 100 of these requiring emergency aid. In Los Angeles, the director of the social security assistance program reported that Italians and Germans were about half of those (1,200) who had come in for information, advice, or assistance. The aliens clearly preferred to exhaust their own resources before asking for help. Although they qualified for the same amount given to families with dependent children, or, if single, an amount equivalent to an old-age pension, they did not ask for it.[211]

Eventually, the Tolan Committee concluded that the Italians and Germans would not present "a major resettlement problem." If they were not taking care of their own needs, they were being provided for. And unlike the Japanese, whose presence in California provoked hostility, the committee did not find any evidence that Italians and Germans were unwanted anywhere, although some employers would not accept those referred to them by the agencies.[212]

Alessandro Baccari, Jr.

Did you know that the government offered financial aid to people who were relocated and had lost their jobs?

I learned about that many, many years later, when I was doing research for books. But no one broadcast this; no one spelled it out.

It was in the newspapers.

A lot of things were in the paper. But you have to remember Italian pride. First of all, the Italians had their own kind of welfare. They don't ask or beg from anybody. They take care of their own they're independent. Pride is so important to an Italian. They're not manipulators of federal, state, or city money. That's never been their style, even today. When they could take advantage of situations, they didn't. Many Italians who knew about the government program refused to accept it because they believed they would have to go through the same kind of interrogation and problems that they faced before. "To hell with the government," they would say.

Benito Vanni

You mentioned things that various people did to help the family.

Our landlord was Italia Malerbi. She was 100 percent Italian. She helped us a lot during [my father's] internment. And, I'll never forget the sisters at the Presentation Academy. They used to give us cans of food all the time, and clothing. They were very nice about that. My sis-

ter and I both had free tuition to the parochial school. I went to St. Peter's and Paul's, and my sister went to Presentation Academy. I guess the nuns felt sorry for us. They didn't have to give us clothing or canned goods. They'd say to me, "Come up on Friday night." We lived on Union Street, and from Union we'd walk up to Mason and Broadway, about four blocks, and then we'd pack everything home in boxes. Another agency that helped us was the Italian Welfare Agency run by Mrs. Bocci. They gave my mom clothing for us, and on occasion candy and used toys.

Did anybody tell you that the government would provide financial aid to families of people who were interned?

In Italy my father would have been considered a very intelligent man, but being over here in America he didn't know what the law was. He wasn't told anything. Nobody from the government came to the family. Like I say, the ones who helped the most were those sisters; we got by on what people gave us. One time they shut off the gas and electricity in the house because we couldn't pay the bill. When my dad got out he couldn't find work right away. Malerbi had a friend who lived in Sonoma, and my father went to work up there as a ranch hand for that person. For two or three months, we lived on property that Malerbi had up there. Oh, hey, yeah, she was beautiful. If it hadn't been for her and the sisters at Presentation Academy, I don't know where we'd have been.

I don't think the Italians ever got anything for being in concentration camps. The Japanese got so much. But the Japanese were treated rotten, I'll tell you that much, 'cause Japan was at war with the United States. Right around the corner from me was a Japanese laundry, and the owner was a good friend of mine; I've forgotten his name. When you went through the front of the laundry, if you had to judge a book by its cover, you'd say, "What a dump." But when you went past the laundry into the living quarters you had to take your shoes off. I was there when they picked up him and his whole family. He was crying. I was crying, 'cause I lost a pretty good friend.

Fr. Gabriel Zavattaro

What did the Church do to aid the Italian aliens who were forced to move?

I was not here at St. Peter's and Paul's at the time; I was in Richmond. But, of course, I visited here frequently. They made some special arrangements for the aliens. Since many of the old Italians could not come out at night because of the curfew, they moved devotions to the daytime hours to give people a chance to come to church. And similarly, they assisted them in every way, helping them to get in touch with their children, letter writing, and assisting in whatever kind of help they asked for.

TECHNICALLY, ALIENS COULD return to their homes and jobs in the prohibited zones as early as the end of June and assistance continued to be available to them after that. But, based on conversations with the aliens, it is clear that many of them remained outside the zones *after* June 1942.

When the German aliens were released from their remaining restrictions in December 1942, the government continued to assist only the families of men who remained interned (Chapter 9) and Italian fishermen who had failed to find jobs as fishermen or anything else since the lifting of restrictions.[213]

Vitina and Joe Spadaro

Did you know the government planned to give money to people who were relocated to help them out?

Vitina: *We didn't know anything about that. When the government decided to take the boats it was considered something that had to be done, like when they drafted your son. It was a way of helping the government. Now that you say this about the fund, I feel they should have done something to help out all the families. Financially it was very difficult.*
Joe: *Not only that, but my father-in-law had to hire a lawyer and pay him to go to the government to get his boat back. The government should have made that easier. He also had to pay for a trip to San Francisco and back, where the boat was based.*
Vitina: *To tell these families to leave their homes and go somewhere else and rent, that meant extra expense. To charter different boats, when they already had their own fishing boats, and then the loss. We were losing money all the way around.*
We also heard what was happening to the Japanese. Then somehow the word got around that they were going to do the same thing to the Italians. My mother always lived in fear that the Italians were going to

be put away. That's why she was so nervous about being home in the evening by eight o'clock. There was talk that they had spies out in the street. She never wanted to go out. I think they lived in fear all that time.

ODDLY, THE AMERICAN government received assistance of its own from Germany during this period. Hoping to retain the loyalty of Germans in the United States, the Nazi government offered to pay for the welfare of German aliens who wanted to be repatriated after the war. Before January 1, 1943, when the money stopped coming, only eight German aliens had received funds—channeled through the Swiss legation—from the Fatherland. After that, no one expressed a desire to continue and respective county welfare departments picked up the aid without interruption. There was continued assistance, too, for the families of men who had been released from internment camps with medical problems or who needed help in rebuilding their lives. But such aid was minor, involving only five Germans.[214]

The assistance program settled into a routine and took on a fancy official name in November 1942—"Services and Assistance to Enemy Aliens and Other Persons in Need Because of Restrictive Action of the Federal Government"—which continued in use until the end of the war. A program with such a pretentious title could not avoid some accounting of its disbursements. Unfortunately, the detailed records of assistance to Italian and German aliens from February to November 1942 cannot be retrieved. Some summary data, however, does give an idea of the scope of the program.

Ten California counties distributed assistance to enemy aliens from July 1942 to June 1944: Alameda, Contra Costa, Humboldt, Lake, Los Angeles, Monterey, San Diego, San Francisco, San Mateo, and Santa Clara. A report in March 1943 indicated that San Francisco and San Mateo counties had dropped out of the program. The amount of money involved from November 1, 1942 to May 30, 1943 was negligible as such things go ($7,589.72), and the number of individual cases involved ranged from twenty-nine during the peak month of January 1943 to six the following May. The case load dropped significantly with DeWitt's order releasing the last of the aliens from restrictions in December 1942, but the demand never quite reached zero because of the government's obligation to continue aid to families of men who had been interned and the unemployed Italian fishermen.[215]

Suddenly, the Social Security Board announced that the federal spigot would be turned off on July 1, 1943. But the board soon relented and payments resumed on July 16, with the counties making up the loss.

State officials paid out an additional $14,634.61 from June 1943 to June 1944. Administrative costs for the roughly year-and-a-half period from 1942 to 1944 came to $14,436, 72 percent of the total amount of aid. It is evident, too, that some counties disbursed almost no aid, which is no doubt part of the reason why none of the aliens recalls the program today: from November 1942 to August 1943, alien assistance in Humboldt County averaged only $18.94 a month.[216]

Jennie Maffia

Did your parents know there was financial aid available through social security?

I didn't know that. The government must have thought, "Well, let's keep those things hidden." Can I go back and get it now? [laughs] *I'm sure there isn't anybody of the Italians that I knew that ever got a cent.*

Frank Buccellato

Did you know that the government was prepared to help financially?

Is that right? Nobody ever said there was any agency we could have gone to.

Was there any thought of not obeying the relocation order?

No, there wasn't, really, because we felt that, well, let's go along with it and see what they're going to do. I thought that they'd take care of us, but they didn't. Why didn't someone say, "You have so many children, we'll help you financially." Nobody said anything. Save themselves some money if they didn't.

The Italian people have a lot of pride. You'll see very few Italian people going for welfare, very, very few. Other nationalities, they'll go. I don't want to mention who they are. But the Italian people? They really have to be down and out, where they can't help themselves. With all the children, my mother never had any help from welfare, the city, or anything. Always my help.

As my brothers grew up, they worked and helped pay for the home my dad had left. It wasn't as bad as the Depression, though, because of the way we lived and the way we were brought up. We could just sit down and eat a plate of spaghetti and we'd have enough. Fry a pan of potatoes, and that's it. You didn't know what you were missing, I guess. We'd get by, see? But today you couldn't do that. The kids today, they want everything. My mother just cooked some spaghetti, maybe with some butter, or if she'd have some tomatoes, she'd make it with sauce. There was no meat, nothing else. That was the cheapest way to get by.

THE MOST PLAUSIBLE explanations for the Italians' refusal to go on the dole in February 1942 and their subsequent lapses of memory would seem to be pride and the effect of time on memory. Although many of the aliens speak of a desire for compensation today—most of them jokingly—it is the apology and redress payments to Japanese Americans that disturbs them, not unheard of or overlooked welfare opportunities in 1942.

NINE

"They've taken my husband away!"
Individual Internment and Exclusion

There appears to be no positive correlation at all between the number of exclusion cases and the number of defense facilities within the geographical limits of the service commands.
—Francis Biddle, August 1943

THE SAGA OF Italian and German aliens in World War II is about more than relocation. On December 8, 1941, President Roosevelt had authorized the arrests of potentially dangerous individual enemy aliens and Italian and German Americans of enemy ancestry. This *individual internment* program must not be confused with mass relocation. The Justice Department ran a two-tiered structure of restrictions: one for the aliens who were relocated out of prohibited zones, as we have seen; and the other for "dangerous" individual aliens and citizens arrested by the FBI throughout the war (approximately 3,500 Italians, 5,300 Japanese, and 6,000 Germans). The Justice department put them into barbed-wire camps in various parts of the country.

Simultaneously, the army carried out an *individual exclusion* program in its Western, Southern, and Eastern Defense Commands. The xenophobic DeWitt, pushed by the public's demand for scapegoats, with which he was in accord, resisted establishing hearing boards for relocated aliens, thinking it too time-consuming. Indeed, no hearing boards ever functioned in California for the relocatees. DeWitt also distrusted the Justice Department's civilian hearing board system for dangerous individual internees.[217] To DeWitt, Biddle and his men were far too sentimental about this potential threat when the country required tough-mindedness. So he used Executive Order 9066 to justify the authority of all defense commanders to exclude individuals who had escaped the Justice Department's dragnet. Only military officers staffed these hearing boards. Then DeWitt either exiled them 150 miles or more from the coast, or he ordered their incarceration at remote army facilities thousands of miles away. We turn first to the individual internees.

Alfonso Zirpoli

I'll give you [an] illustration [of our problem with the army]. There was a German farmer who had some dynamite that he used to blow up tree stumps. They wanted me to file a complaint and have him arrested. I said, no, I wasn't going to do that. Pretty soon I got word from Washington that DeWitt had complained to the secretary of war, and that he [in turn] had gone so far as to mention it to the president. Well, I explained it to the satisfaction of all concerned. But this shows you how severe he was. John McCloy was the one to whom DeWitt complained about people that I wouldn't prosecute. That's when I got the letter from the attorney general asking me to explain the situation. I wasn't going to prosecute people who hadn't done anything harmful. You know, they'd pick people up for possession of searchlights!

PREPARATIONS FOR THE individual internment program began well in advance of anticipated need. In the early summer of 1939, FDR had placed the responsibility for espionage, counterespionage, and sabotage in the hands of the FBI, the Military Intelligence Division in the War Department (G-2), and the Office of Naval Intelligence (ONI) in the Navy Department. Hoover's agency acted as the central clearinghouse. These agencies began the process of compiling lists of those who the government believed meant to harm the United States and should be arrested when war came. In deciding who was to be apprehended, the government initially resolved all doubts in its own favor. The lists were funneled to the Special Defense Unit (SDU) in the Justice Department, which prepared a master list known as the "ABC" list. Lawrence M.C. Smith, a career Justice Department lawyer, led the SDU and kept the ABC list. Biddle brought in Edward J. Ennis from the Immigration and Naturalization Service (INS) to organize detention and internment facilities. The government found itself better equipped to deal with enemy aliens in 1941 than it had been in 1917 due to the investigation of questionable individuals and organizations that began in 1939, the Alien Registration Act of 1940, and the central role of the FBI.[218]

These preparations were first put to the test in December 1939 and again in May 1941. The FBI, tipped off by the seductress "Cynthia," swooped down on Italian and German merchant crews in New York and sent them packing to the desert internment camp at Ft. Stanton, New

Mexico, and from there to Ft. Lincoln (Bismarck), North Dakota, and Ft. Missoula, Montana.[219]

The proclamations that the president issued on December 7-8, 1941—authorizing the FBI and other agencies to round up dangerous enemies—drew their legality from Section 21, Title 50 of the U.S. Code. It, in turn, derived from the Alien Enemies Act of July 6, 1798, as amended on April 16, 1918. In sum, during wartime, alien enemies were subject to apprehension without warning and detention or deportation depending on the whim of authorities. But even before President Roosevelt had a chance to sign the summary proclamations in December 1941, the FBI, under orders from Attorney General Biddle, began to arrest and detain several thousand aliens from the ABC list, including Italians and Germans. The Immigration and Naturalization Service provided detention facilities.[220]

Assistant U.S. Attorney Alfonso Zirpoli had known in advance of the existence of the ABC list. He recalls that it focused in particular on German American Bundists and Italian American veterans of World War I. But there were many others, too: American citizens sympathetic to Italy or Germany and persons of Italian or German descent of unknown citizenship status.[221]

Clerks had neatly arranged the names, addresses, and citizenship status (if known) of each person to be picked up on three-by-five cards distributed for the occasion to squads of FBI agents and local police. Federal authorities took other precautions as well. Guards suddenly appeared at Italian and German embassies and consular offices. Embassy telephone and mail service ceased; funds for embassy officials were frozen; airlines were told they could not carry passengers or express to or from Italy and Germany; and businesses with war contracts were told to be on the lookout for saboteurs. When the FBI arrested German correspondents in the United States, the Nazis ordered American newspapermen in Germany into their homes, promising that "whatever might be done [to you] as reprisal [will] be done 'in the noblest form.'"[222]

Alfonso Zirpoli

As a result of the attack on Pearl Harbor, a big part of our fleet was destroyed and the possibility existed of an attack on our coast. People got excited and panicked a little. There were headlines about people putting mines under the Golden Gate Bridge, shelling off the coast of Oregon and in the Santa Barbara area.

General DeWitt became disturbed, and the War Department finally got the president to issue an executive order that was approved eventually by Congress. Under that order, DeWitt could make a proclamation as to what should or shouldn't be done. And the first proclamation was to bar all Germans, Italians, and Japanese from certain areas, particularly all of the area north of Beach Street in San Francisco. Tom Clark, who later became attorney general and a justice of the Supreme Court, was designated as the Washington representative. I was the assistant in charge of the Enemy Alien Program in the U.S. attorney's office. The primary problem was the Japanese. There was also a question about the Italians and Germans. National security became paramount.

In anticipation of the possibility of war, the FBI had already made checks on people. They were informed well in advance. For instance, they had the names of all the Italian veterans of World War I [Ex-Combattenti. They had all the names of members of the German [American] Bund in the area, and members of a certain Japanese society, the Hokubei,[223] *who presumably owed their allegiance to the Emperor. They had to be arrested on presidential warrants. I was the one who executed the warrants. Well, I really couldn't execute individual warrants, because the first two days we picked up about 1,500 people and sent them to our immigration camp at Sharp Park. What I would do was to issue an order to pick up the "following people" who were noncitizen Italian war veterans. Or I would say, "these are all members of the Hokubei," or, "these are members of the Bund." And they were picked up accordingly.*

The Italians were sent to a camp in Montana—Fort Missoula—and the Japanese were eventually all gathered and taken down to the Tanforan racetrack here in San Francisco and then on to different camps elsewhere. I had the responsibility of enforcing these orders.

The curfew went into effect; you had to be in after sundown. In addition, you could not travel or leave without a permit. And you had to surrender all guns and lighting signals of any kind. To add to the hysteria, one of the shops that was raided was a Japanese gun shop. They confiscated God knows how many guns and some twenty thousand rounds of ammunition. The next day they made another raid and maybe they got five rounds of ammunition. But the headline would read, "Two Hundred and Five Thousand Rounds of Ammunition." This excited the population of San Francisco. The governor of California expressed great fear for the safety of the Japanese, and thought that this idea of getting them together was a good one. The Japanese were well regimented. The Italians and the Germans were not. They were more individualistic. It was pretty hard to regiment the Italians. I mention these things as indications of the different types of attitudes you had to think about.

John Molinari

I became keenly aware that our government had a list of potentially dangerous persons. On Pearl Harbor day, military and FBI agents took these persons into custody. I, as an attorney, got calls from mothers and wives—"They've taken my son away!" "They've taken my husband away!" They just moved through the community and rounded up people that they had on this list. And I knew a number of them; several were clients of mine. They were not disloyal to the United States, but they had a certain pride in the accomplishments of anything that Italy would do. Perhaps at some Italian organization meeting they had gotten up and said, "Isn't Mussolini great?" "For the first time Italy is recognized as a power." "He's doing all these wonderful things, restoring agricultural land and the swamps, making the trains run on time," and things like that. A very good friend of mine was one of those who was taken that night. He was an American citizen, born in Italy, and he was proud of things Italian. He bought a film that showed Mussolini and some of the things that he had done, and showed it at a meeting of a community organization. He bought the film on Market Street in San Francisco. "Castle Films," I think they called it. It didn't come from Rome; it was an American documentary. Our government had done a thorough job of pinpointing people who might be a threat to our national security.

I finally found out where those who had been apprehended were being kept. They were out to the Salvation Home on Silver Avenue in San Francisco. It's a school now; I forget the name, but it's on Silver Avenue. I went out there a few times after I found out where these people were. They had military tribunals to screen them. It was sort of an informal hearing. Some of the hearing officers were reserve lawyers that I knew, who were reserves in the judge advocate department of the military. The conversations would sometimes go like this:

"Johnny," meaning me, "is this guy all right?"

"Oh, yeah, he's loyal. He's not a problem."

Most of them were released within a few days. But I guess if the government—out of an abundance of caution—had any apprehension that these people would commit any sabotage or whatever, they just moved right in. I'm telling you, I had a hectic two days, people calling me at home.

Nobody ever attacked [J. Edgar] *Hoover on whether the FBI had probable cause [to arrest these people] or not. Looking back, in our climate today, you'd [sue] for most anything. In those days, you were a little hesitant about taking on the government in wartime. You might be accused of being disloyal if you took the cudgels from one of these persons. The upshot of it was that most of them were released within a few days when the government was assured that these guys were all right.*

Alessandro Baccari, Jr.

How did the government get information about individual Italians?

Informers were those who were anti-Fascist in their political thinking. Unfortunately, many innocent people became victims. However, when the government began to take the view that all Italians, like the Japanese, should be sent to relocation camps, a strange phenomenon took place. The informers realized that they, too, were subject to suspicion, so they stopped informing.

Your father thought it was important that you visit the camps where the Italians were being taken?

Yes, to see family friends. The majority of Italians [who were interned] *were sent to a camp set up at Sharp Park, located on the coast of San Mateo County. It was there that we went to visit those who were confined. There was also a place in San Francisco where Italians were sent. It was located on Silver Avenue. The building today is occupied by the Simpson Bible College. The majority of those who were* [excluded] *American citizens were sent off to Nevada. Others were sent to Chicago. One prominent Italian American attorney sent to Chicago was given a job working for the Internal Revenue Service. It was a farce. The period of internment for Italians and Germans lasted less than a year. What the Japanese went through was truly tragic.*

I remember going to Tanforan, a former racetrack located in San Bruno, to visit my childhood piano teacher. All he could do was cry. He wouldn't even take time to talk to me except to pat me on the head occasionally and tell me to "be sure to practice daily."

THE ROUNDUP PROGRESSED swiftly, though not with the breadth that Hoover desired. He had hoped to be able to arrest American citizens of Italian and German extraction right away. But without probable cause, he could not. So hee urged his superiors in the Justice Department to get specific legislation that would authorize the apprehension and detention of "persons who might fall within the category of so-called [F]ifth [C]olumnists," whether they were citizens or not. But the director said he would not assume "the responsibility for reaching the decision as to who is or is not to be arrested."[224]

By eleven o'clock on the morning of December 9, the FBI had arrested and turned over to the INS eighty-three Italian and 497 German aliens, including sixty from San Francisco. It embarrassed Biddle that Hoover's men had apprehended so few Germans, and Hoover was worried that if any of them were released by the Justice Department's hearing boards and later committed acts of sabotage, "the FBI would bear the full responsibility in the eyes of the public." He need not have been concerned: by February 4, the FBI had picked up 261 Italians and 1,361 Germans, and it continued to make arrests throughout 1942 and 1943. Yet the courts never convicted a single alien of an act of sabotage during the war. Although about 60 percent of all enemy aliens were Italians, the government arrested only 3,278 Italians during the war (10 percent of the aliens taken into custody) but interned only 112 for any length of time.[225]

Joe Cervetto,
San Rafael

I came to this country in May 1933, on the S.S. California. *When we got to Los Angeles after coming through the Panama Canal, I got a very sore throat. I couldn't talk too much. So, when we got to San Francisco, they took me to a doctor. They left me in the navy hospital on Nineteenth Avenue, where they operated on my throat. It was very infected and I couldn't talk anymore.*

I had no intention of staying. I was working on the ship as an interpreter, and someday I hoped to become an officer. Of course, I liked to travel. I had three brothers up in Oregon and a sister in San Francisco. After I got out my brother-in-law came and picked me up. I had called 'em, told 'em I was in the hospital. In the meantime, the ship left.

The fellow from the consul general's office came to see me. And he said, "You've got to find yourself a little job until we have another ship to take you back." But I had lost a hell of a good job. And by golly, they had a little party for me the second day I was out of the hospital. They invited some people there, and they said, "What the hell—you have your chance. Why don't you stay here?"

"I don't have a passport." The Consul General had it. *"I don't want to jump ship or anything like that."*

"Look, you should consider. You got a good chance to stay here."

"I'm not going to be a deserter." There was this one guy; he had a hotel. His name was Ratto. *I don't know which hotel, it's downtown* [in San Francisco], *on Post Street. He said to me, "I got an idea. How old are you?"*

"Well, I'm going to be twenty-five in June." June was right around the corner.

"Wonderful. This is your chance to stay here. Christ, you stay twenty-five years in Italy. Now you're gonna stay twenty-five years in this country, you make some money, you get married and you have a family."

You know, it hit me. I think I said, *"My golly, you're right. I could do it."* So, I stayed.

Right after Pearl Harbor I was president of a window cleaner's association, and I had a movie projector. I used to buy those "Castle Films" of the war in Europe. But I could not be out after eight o'clock. I used to show those films at our window washer's association meetings, always before eight o'clock, though. One day, John Molinari saw me. He wasn't my attorney; I didn't even know him. He saw me at some market in North Beach. And he said, "You Joe Cervetto?"

"Yes, sir." I thought he was going to give me a job or something.

"I work with the attorney general's office."

"I'm glad to meet you."

"I understand that you showed a movie of the war."

"Golly, that thing was made over here."

"Someone reported you to the FBI. Besides, it was eight-thirty before you got home. You better not do it anymore."

So I said, *"Thank you very much."*

Then one day I was having dinner with my wife and my daughter. I had a little girl by that time. And there was a knock at the door. My wife, she goes and opens it, and there was a policeman, and FBI, and everything. And she said, "Yes, what can I do for you?"

"Where's your husband?"

"He's having dinner." I was in the kitchen listening to an Italian program on the radio. And all of a sudden, a funny thing happened. This Italian program quit, and they put on music. My wife came and said, *"These people here, they want to see you."* I hadn't finished my dinner, but I went out to meet them, and they said, *"You Joe Cervetto?"* There were three of them. *"Yes, sir,"* I said.

"Come with us."

"Can I get my coat?"

"No, no, come the way you are." And I said, "God, it's cold out-side, you know?" So my wife went to get my coat, and they said to the wife, really rough, "All right, you get the coat," and they took me away. I was in the civil defense at the time, a fire marshal, and I thought, "Maybe they want to drill me for something." I never thought it had anything to do with my showing those movies or being out late. So I said, "Can I get my little civil defense sack, too?"

"Forget about that. Just get the jacket and don't talk too much. Let's go." I thought, "My golly, they kidnap me!" I didn't know anything; I couldn't say anything. And they took me to this place out on Silver Avenue, the old Salvation building. I told the guy, "I didn't have any dinner I was just starting to eat." "Well," he said, "forget it. Tomorrow you get a breakfast." They gave me nothing, just one blanket. In the morning when they picked us up I thought, "Hey, this is something serious." They used to pick up those guys and send them to Missoula [Montana]. They picked up one guy that was a window washer, but he was in the First World War in Italy. One was a very prominent attorney. I remember they picked up this guy [Francesconi] that I was listening to on the radio when they grabbed me. He was talking about cigars, then all of a sudden, music. And you never heard his name again. That was the end of his program. They snatched him when he was playing music and the goddarned thing went off.

They put about fifty of us in a big truck and loaded us onto a boat. I thought, "Oh, oh, this is not too good." They took us to Angel Island [in San Francisco Bay]. There were some other guys on the boat, some Germans that were sunk on the Graf Spee. *Some were sailors; others were officers. Later we played soccer with them on the island. There were only Italians and Germans there, no Japanese. The Germans were on one side and we were on the other. Altogether, there were fifty, sixty, maybe 100 people there. They used to have a boat come in every day, back and forth. I guess they brought water and food, too. Angel Island was very nice. We had our own kitchen, our own place to eat.*

I was lucky that I had a good man who worked with me, named Delveccio. He didn't see me at work in the morning so he told my wife. At that time, though, we used to fight all the time and she didn't give a damn where I was anyway. [laughs] Delveccio must have read about my being picked up, or heard it by way of rumor, I don't know.

No official came to your wife and said that you had been taken to Angel Island?

No, nobody showed up. So, anyway, over there on the island, they had this room with a big light at the end, and they brought us in there one at a time. Nice lighted place, and you sit there and you talk. They wanted to know how I had managed to be here: "Tell us your story." They asked me constantly, "Are you a Fascist?" I wasn't. I said, "Look, my mother always told me that if you tell the truth you don't have anything to worry about." But every day they asked me the same damned question, and I said the same thing. And this guy here, one day he said, "Listen, you. Where did you learn to tell me the same story every day?"

"My mother told me that when you tell the truth you never have to be scared of making a mistake. But you have to tell the truth. I never belonged to the Fascist system. I signed to join the party because I saw that in Italy everybody was happy, everybody was content, everybody had a job. I was in the Merchant Marine after the Royal Navy, and I was treated good. I don't have any complaint against Mussolini, 'cause he never did anything to me. I didn't have anything to do with politics." But I did make an application that I wanted to be a member of the Fascist party. What I think they thought was that I was a spy—you know, young fellow, knows the language. They thought I was sent here to blow up some bridge or something. Interrogation every day. "Were you a member of the Fascist party?" And every very day the same reply: "I told you, I signed but I never swore allegiance." The day I was supposed to swear—I remember it like it was now. They sent me a letter one year after I made the application. They said, "You got to buy yourself a black shirt and a hat." Jeez, I thought they gave it to you! You had to buy the shirt, a black shirt and a hat, and come to Genoa. "We gonna swear you into the Fascist party," like the Communist party and the Nazi party. What you gonna do? You're working there. So what the hell did I do then?

I was supposed to swear on the twenty-first of April 1933, and that's the day I left for the United States. I never swore; I never got any paper. I signed that I wanted to join, but I never got my paper that I was in. And this guy didn't believe me. He said, "Yes, you belong to the Fascist party and you came here with the idea of doing something."

Then, for some reason, my ex-wife talked to [John] Molinari. She had gone to complain one time to Molinari that I didn't treat her right or something. So Molinari, he was working with the FBI, I guess.

One day they came in and this guy said, "We found out that you told us the truth."

I said, "Well, thank God."

"We send you ashore." I went to Sharp Park before they released me. It was surrounded by barbed wire; no barbed wire on Angel Island.

I don't know how I convinced them; by being persistent and telling the truth, I guess. They couldn't believe the truth, but it was true. They knew when my ship left Genoa, the thirteenth of April 1933. And they knew I never swore for the Fascist party. I never had any use for it.

Had you thought about becoming an American citizen before the war?

I came in 1933, and after five years, I applied. See, I jumped ship; I was a deserter. But I married an American citizen. So my congressman got an act of congress to let me stay in America. He sent in the papers and my history. Then I was here legally and could make my first citizenship application. Then the war started and...good-bye application. They didn't make any citizens at that time; they stopped it right there. After the war I made another application and became a citizen in 1946.

When they released you from Angel Island, were you still restricted at home?

Oh, yeah. You had to be home by 8:00 p.m.

Judge Molinari was in charge of selling war bonds, and they had a bond rally in Washington Square. Everybody was coming from all over North Beach to hear the judge. He told them to buy bonds to help win the war. Like before, they used to tell them to sell the ring, the gold ring to help Mussolini win the war. Now the judge said, "Buy the bonds to help America win." He wanted me to help him. I said, "How can I help you? I can't stay out after eight o'clock and you're gonna have the rally at eight." He said, "I'm gonna talk to somebody, the police." He let me go to the place and they gave me permission to stay out till ten o'clock. Then I told him, "Look, now that I have this permit, I would like to have it permanently if I can, so that I can stay out two hours later and get out in the morning two hours earlier." He said that the police would have to do that, so I went to the police and they took fingerprints and everything. It was on the top floor of their building at Kearney and Washington Streets. I made out an application to get out more at night and they approved it. They said I was doing all right, helping sell the bonds, you know, so you're okay. And I never had a problem with the police, just getting some tickets [for violations] sometimes, that's all. Since I could get out a little bit earlier in the morning, my business went better.

I got divorced during the war. My wife fell in love with one of those Italian prisoners. I had invited them over to the house, and before I knew it, she fell in love with one of those guys. He had been captured in Africa, so I sued for divorce. She went back to Italy with him, but she found out he was already married.

John Molinari

Were you aware of a place called Sharp Park, in Pacifica?

I just knew it was there, that people had been put there. But I think that was sort of a temporary thing. The interesting thing was that, as the war went on, we had Italian prisoners of war in this locality, so it may have been at Sharp Park, also somewhere in the Alameda naval area, if not the base itself. Things got a little incongruous. These Italian prisoners would be released on weekends and would come over, and the Italian families would invite them for dinner, and they were beginning to consort with their daughters, and marriages resulted. I had a couple of cases there involving marriage breakups where the POW replaced the husband. Judge Zirpoli and I collaborated in the defense of an Italian grower down in Half Moon Bay who felt sorry for some of these POWs. I don't know how he did it, how they were getting off, but anyway, he employed them on weekends to work since labor was short. He was giving these POWs some work and, of course, it was against the law to do it. But he didn't go to jail. I don't remember whether there was a fine imposed or what. A lot of people were employing these POWs. They were young, able-bodied, and they wanted to make some money before they went back to Italy. So they just merged into the community and, here again, the Italians took to them. I remember them walking through the district wearing special uniforms so that you could tell who they were.

Joe Cervetto

What were your feelings about what was happening to you?

Well, I didn't have any hate or anything. At that time, my main objective was to work and make some money. I never got involved in taking sides or anything. I tell you what, though, I never showed those films again, and I still have them. I'd been a good Italian all the time. I couldn't say that Mussolini was no good, but I think he made a mistake in getting together with Germany. He should have stayed by himself. Italy was in good shape when I came over to this country. That's why I had no intention of staying here at first. I had a good thing. I had social security, unemployment insurance, medical care, compensation, too.

Do you think that if you had gotten over your illness and gone back to Italy, the government there would have made trouble for you?

Oh, absolutely. My brother came to Italy [from the United States] *for a visit in 1927. The carabinieri arrested him. They didn't put him in jail, but they said, "Why the hell didn't you go to war? You're a deserter." But he was an American citizen, just back to Italy for a visit. I went to see some people at city hall. I said, "I'm in the navy, you know. What happened to my brother?" We gave 'em a few bucks; that's all. Just like the Mexican police, they just wanted a little money under the table. I never wanted to go back there, but I did in 1950, after I became an American citizen, and many other times.*

PROBABLY NO WARTIME operation could have been carried out reasonably in the pressurized political atmosphere of the winter of 1941–42 in California. And, as with the relocated aliens, there were bizarre incidents to illuminate the problems created by condemning an entire class of people. In Los Altos, near San Francisco Bay, Dr. Fritz Hansgirg, aged fifty-two, the German-born, Austrian inventor of a new magnesium process—by which pure magnesium is extracted more cheaply from the ore—was arrested by the FBI as a dangerous enemy alien. Hansgirg had emigrated to the United States in May 1940. In these facts, there was nothing particularly unusual. But authorities wanted both to punish and to exploit Hansgirg. Following his hearing before a three-man board, and despite Attorney General Biddle's desire to free him and the War Department's urgent request that he be allowed to carry on operations at the Permanente, California, plant, Hansgirg remained in his San Jose jail cell and ran the plant from there. He phoned orders to his plant engineers on the sheriff's telephone. And he had other privileges not accorded ordinary detainees: access to a nearby hotel for bathing and permission to go to his office when really needed. His character references were also noteworthy: the sheriff described Hansgirg as a "charming old man" (at age fifty-two!), and shipping magnate Henry J. Kaiser, among others, worked to get him released. On Christmas, the whole Permanente staff descended on his cell with gifts and a tree.

Hansgirg's wife, fearing her husband would be deported, said that the inventor had been an outspoken anti-Nazi in the 1930s and fled Austria right after the assassination of Chancellor Engelbert Dollfuss (July 1934). Hansgirg had filed for American citizenship, but as in the case of many other aliens, the Japanese attacked Pearl Harbor before he completed his naturalization. That Hansgirg had left Austria for Korea to build a plant and stayed five years did not endear him to Uncle Sam; at that time Japan controlled Korea. He also did part-time consulting for the South Manchurian Railroad, also controlled by Japan. An additional difficulty was Hansgirg's wife: allegedly, she had written letters to her son by a first marriage. He was an officer in the German army.

Eventually, Hansgirg was interned at Stringtown, Oklahoma, and then paroled to teach chemistry at Black Mountain College in North Carolina, where he spent the rest of the war years.[226]

ATTORNEY GENERAL BIDDLE had put Edward J. Ennis in charge of his department's AECU on December 22, 1941. Ennis's responsibilities included the establishment of procedures for hearing and reviewing the cases of those arrested by the FBI and other civilian law enforcement agencies. Ennis also had to coordinate Justice Department activities with other interested departments, including, of course, the army.[227]

The attorney general appointed civilian hearing boards in every federal judicial district to hear cases and make recommendations. Each board consisted of three or more citizens experienced in working with the enemy alien population. A U.S. attorney also attended the hearings to present each case to the board. Informality prevailed. The FBI read its reports and, along with board members, questioned the alien. The alien might present affidavits or even call witnesses in exceptional cases. Some aliens had lawyers, but they were not permitted in the hearing room. The boards waived the usual rules of evidence. The U. S. attorney present challenged FBI agents when they substituted opinion for fact, but the press and public were excluded. Hearings normally took about twenty minutes to half an hour. The board's recommendation then went to the AECU, where Ennis reviewed it to insure uniform application. Finally, the attorney general ordered release, parole, or internment. On average, reviews took one month to complete but most of them, according to the Justice Department, one week. By October 5, 1943, 14,807 alien enemies had been taken into custody, including 3,503 Italians and 5,977 Germans. Only 5,705 of all those arrested were interned. The rest the government either released prior to a hearing, paroled, or released after a hearing, except for 470 pending cases, 40 who had died after their arrest, and 44 who were repatriated. It was these boards that Congressman Tolan saw as potential models for those he believed were essential to screen the Italian and German aliens facing mass relocation in February 1942.[228]

Alfonso Zirpoli

When these people were taken to Sharp Park, they were entitled to hearings and I conducted them. One of the questions I would ask the Japanese, Germans, and Italians—all of them—was: "Whom do you want to win the war?" Of the Japanese who were rounded up, not one of them said the United States. They either said, "Japan," or, "We hope that nobody wins." I couldn't understand this. One Japanese had a son who was a captain in the American army, and I said to him, "I don't understand."

"Well, you have to understand that I was born in Japan. My son was born here."

I also asked this same sixty-four dollar question of the Italians and Germans at their hearings. They wanted the United States to win the war.

You would think that the Japanese would have sensed what answer you wanted, and have answered that way.

No, they were very regimented. They came in with permits for curfew and everything else before they were ordered out. They were so well regimented that everything was in proper order. The Italians and Germans came in individually.

There were three members on the hearing boards. I would present the case to them for their ruling. The FBI would also testify. Once, one of the FBI agents was getting completely out of line, expressing his personal views. I called him on it, and he got sore. I said, "Well, all right. If you want all of this on the record, we'll put it on the record." He stopped right there. I had 200 cases to present in Arizona. The northern California cases were all heard in the grand jury room of the Federal Building in San Francisco.

Some of those who testified would say, "I'm a good friend of Assistant U.S. Attorney Zirpoli. We're members of the same club—Il Cenacolo." This was a club the Italians had formed back in 1929. Their headquarters were on the second floor of the Fairmont Hotel. It was a beautiful suite. When the war broke out, we gave it up because there was a shortage of space and they needed rooms for the military. We never did reopen in that suite, but the club met continuously, and still

meets. It was composed of business and professional men in San Fran-
cisco. Members included professors at the University of California, A.P.
Giannini, president of the Bank of America, his son, Mario, Guido
Musto of Musto Marble Works, the mayor, doctors, and lawyers in San
Francisco interested in Italian culture. We had the director of the opera
and people of that character. So, as I said, some of these fellows at the
hearings would say that they knew me.

IF THE ATTORNEY general decided to intern suspect individuals after a
hearing, they were sent to one of sixteen camps run by the Border Patrol.
Forts Lincoln (Bismarck, North Dakota) and Missoula (Montana) had
been prepared in April 1941. Secretary of War Stimson confirmed the
existence of the camps in a letter to Rep. Leland M. Ford (R-Santa
Monica), in which he informed the congressman that the rumors were
true: "The War Department is constructing internment camps in the interior for all classes of interned enemy aliens." The first arrivals at Ft.
Missoula were 125 Italians in May 1941. When the Japanese attacked in
December, there were already 285 internees—all blockaded Axis seamen—at Lincoln and 1,000 at Missoula.[229]

By February 16, three days before the president signed the West
Coast relocation order, 264 Italians and 1,393 Germans had been interned
at Bismarck and Missoula. In December 1942, Ft. Lincoln became ex-
clusively a German camp and remained so until 650 Japanese arrived in
1945. A pastor from Oakland, Dr. W.P. Reagor, visited Ft. Missoula for
five days and gave a glowing report of conditions and morale to the Tolan Committee. He described the management of the camps as "wise,
practical, and kindly, but still, they were surrounded by barbed wire,
guard towers, and floodlights. Forts Lincoln and Missoula, like other
Justice Department camps, were subject to the Geneva Convention of
1929 and inspection by the International Red Cross.[230]

Alfredo Cipolato

One day they sent a bunch of Germans to Ellis Island, where the immi-
gration service was keeping enemy aliens, and three other Italians and
myself were ordered to go along. From Ellis Island, we went by train to
Fort Missoula in Montana.

There were never any hearings, either in New York, Ellis Island, or
later at Fort Missoula, and we were never interrogated. Life in Mon-
tana was calm and the food excellent, even though the camp was sur-
rounded by a high wire fence and guards. There was a beautiful li-

*brary, tennis courts, and other athletic facilities. We were never both-
ered. We put on concerts and theatrical productions, and I participated
in these. Later, we had to stop because the musicians' union in
Missoula said that the city's programs were being hurt financially by
this. We called the camp [Ft. Missoula],* "Bella Vista" *[beautiful view]
as it was located in a very pretty spot. I think there must have been
about one thousand Italians there, and hundreds of Japanese.*

*After seventeen months, thirteen of the World's Fair group were re-
leased to cut sugar beets just outside the city limits.*[231] *They took us to
the fields by truck, with more guards and machine guns than prisoners.
When we said we would not work under such conditions, they agreed to
take us back and forth without heavy guard. We made thirty dollars a
month, although we never saw the money. Instead, they issued us requi-
sitions for purchases at clothing stores and so forth. Later, they sent us
to Gold Creek, Montana, about fifty miles from Butte* [115 miles from
Missoula], *also to cut sugar beets, where we lived in a huge chicken
barn. We made the place livable by first cleaning it, then hanging sheets
for curtains and making a table. On Thanksgiving that year we invited
the Italian families from Butte and we cooked a wonderful dinner.*

*After sugar beet season, we were put to work at St. Patrick's Hospi-
tal back in Missoula as orderlies and maintenance men. I was trained
as an orderly since most of the former orderlies and doctors were in the
service. We were restricted to movement of one block to the east, west,
north, and south of the hospital. Some of the Italians working at the
hospital were musicians from their merchant ships, and the rest of us
had good-to-great singing voices, and so we were allowed to join the
church choir. I was surprised when one of the choir ladies came to me
and said,* "Che Bella Voce," *what a beautiful voice. Her parents had
come from Italy to Missoula in 1908 and owned a neighborhood grocery
store there that delivered olive oil, pasta, and other Italian food for the
prisoners. She spoke enough Italian for us to communicate, so we
started seeing each other regularly and got married October 5, 1943.*

*I received greetings from Uncle Sam in January 1943 to report to the
army, but I took a job instead with the Northern Pacific Railroad,
which deferred me, as it was a vital war job. I received a deportation
notice in 1945. My wife called Mike Mansfield, our representative in
Washington, and he immediately got the deportation proceeding stopped
and advised me to apply for citizenship immediately, which I did. I had
to have two prominent Missoula citizens as my sponsors until I became
an American citizen in 1948.*

Every year I celebrate my "American" *birthday on April 25, the day I
arrived at New York. My family all come home then for a big dinner*

with birthday cake topped with an American flag. Then I have my real birthday party, my "Italian" birthday on October 5, which is another big family celebration.

Benito Vanni

My dad was taken to immigration, which was at the top of Silver Avenue.[232] It's now known as Simpson Bible College. From there, he was sent to Sharp Park detention camp, now Sharp Park golf course. Everybody who belonged to the Ex-Combattenti at that time was supposed to have been a spy. Also I think my dad's mouth got him in trouble, 'cause he always spoke about what America was doing wrong and what Italy was doing right. He was interned between six and nine months, and was home for Thanksgiving of '42. We visited him two or three times; we had no means of transportation down there. I remember wire cyclone fencing ten or twelve feet high. I'm sure it had barbed wire on top, but I can't swear to it. When you walked up you couldn't see the whole camp it was so big.

My dad was pretty tough. He definitely was picked up because he talked a lot, and nobody else knew he talked a lot except those people he hung around with. He used to go to DeMartini's Cigar Store, which was on the corner of Union and Columbus Avenue. He played cards there all the time. It was a regular hangout for Italians. Hey, he talked about the military, about the war. So, I say if anybody turned him in it was somebody from DeMartini's that had something against him. They were vindictive. If they had something against him, and to get him in trouble they'd say, "He's a spy." Maybe the government had something on somebody, and to get the heat off himself, that person would say that my father called Roosevelt an s.o.b., or that he'd like to put a bomb in the Presidio and blow up the place. "So what the hell, I'd make some points for myself with the FBI. The heat's off me 'cause I turned this guy in; I'm like a government witness." They turned the guy in, and they were a spy themselves.

IN EARLY MAY 1942, Attorney General Biddle revealed that he had decided to intern more than half the aliens arrested throughout the country to date (but only 43 percent of Italians and Germans). The rest had been paroled or released outright. Some observers have suggested, perhaps correctly, that this discrepancy between the number of Italians, Germans, and Japanese who were interned reflected the racial underpinnings of the policy.[233]

WE TURN NOW to the army's *individual exclusion* program. From August 1942 to July 1943, the Western Defense Command examined 335 cases and excluded 174 aliens and citizens from the coastal area, including several *prominenti* (elites) and forty Ex-Combattenti who it believed were pro-Fascist. The state assembly's Un-American Activities Committee (Tenney Committee) had no enforcement powers itself, but its allegations regarding domestic Fascism influenced General DeWitt's subsequent decision to expel twelve Italian Americans from California on October 19, including, Ettore Patrizi, Remo Bosia, Renzo Turco, and Sylvester Andriano.[234] Andriano, like Alfonso Zirpoli a member of Il Cenacolo, had to be relieved of his position as chairman of the Selective Service Board from which he had been working to subvert the war effort, if one accepts the truth of the accusations against him.[235]

Alfonso Zirpoli

Among those ordered out of this area was Sylvester Andriano. He had been the attorney for the Italian Consulate. He was the president of the Italian school and of the Italian Chamber of Commerce. They elected him president of the Chamber because his opponent was a known Fascist and we didn't want anybody of that character to be head of the Chamber of Commerce. So here's Andriano, who's selected with a clear understanding that this is the proper man to head the Chamber of Commerce, and he was ordered out of the area by DeWitt.

He went to Chicago. After he'd been there for a while, he returned to San Francisco to see his mother in Santa Clara County. When he returned I received a phone call from Martino, an Italian agent of the FBI, at three o'clock in the morning. He said, "Andriano's here in violation of DeWitt's order. What shall I do?" I said to the agent, "Don't do anything until nine o'clock. Come into the office then and talk to me and Mr. Hennessy, the U.S. Attorney." He came in, and Hennessy and I decided that, by golly, we weren't going to do anything. The order would have to come out of Washington.

As it turned out, that wasn't necessary. By then, the commanding general was no longer DeWitt, and the new general [Emmons] said to Andriano, "You know, Mr. Andriano, if you weren't here in violation of DeWitt's order I would vacate that order." Mr. Andriano thanked him, and he left. And the next morning the general received a phone call from Mr. Andriano. He said, "General, I don't want to make it uncomfortable for you. I'm here in Reno and I want you to know that I'm out of the area." And the General said, "I want you to know that there's a courier on his way with an order vacating General DeWitt's order."

I mention Mr. Andriano because a number of prominent lawyers—Andriano was a well-known lawyer, a former supervisor, a former chief of the San Francisco police commission—went to see him and said, "They can't do this. You're a citizen. This is in violation of your constitutional right. We want to go to court for you." And Andriano said, "No. I don't want to do anything that detracts in the slightest degree from the war effort." There was a real patriot.

Another citizen who was ordered out was Luigi Vinci of the Bank of America. He had been in the Balilla. Vinci still had his old uniform, which the FBI had learned about. So he was ordered out. They sent him up to Montana, to the fort, and he was such a great administrator that the commanding officer put him in charge of the whole camp. Eventually he was ordered released, and the commanding officer said, "My God, I was just going to take my two weeks furlough." So Vinci said, "Go ahead, take your furlough. I'll stay another two weeks." So he stayed on and then came back here. When he applied for citizenship that commander came out to testify for him.

Another man that was ordered out was Renzo Turco, a well-known lawyer. He was told he had to be out of the area by one o'clock on a given day. I've forgotten the date. The FBI came to see me and said, "What are we going to do; he's not out of the area? He won't be out until three o'clock." I said, "For God's sake, let him alone! Let him get out!" So he went to Chicago and went to work for the Internal Revenue Service as a lawyer. And of course at the proper time he returned.

Ettore Patrizi was the publisher of the Italian daily. We had two Italian dailies in San Francisco. His was L'Italia. These papers had continuous publication, in excess of 100 years; more than any American paper. And these were dailies, mind you. Well, he was ordered out of the area, and he went over to Reno. There were people who were known to have attended parties at the consulate; they were ordered out. Most of them went to Reno. Later they all returned.

In England, everybody got a hearing before they were ordered out. Now it seems kind of strange. If that was the situation in England, why wasn't it possible for us to do it? Well, of course, the answer is that you had thousands of Japanese; you couldn't do it. You didn't have the equivalent of that in England.

And you couldn't do that with the hundreds of thousands of Germans and Italians in this country?

No, you couldn't. But those would have been noncitizens. You see, this thing went so far as to include some citizens, and that's where they really went too far. They were entitled to a hearing before they were excluded.[236] *DeWitt really had a genuine fear as far as the Japanese were concerned. Whether it was justified, I don't know.*

BECAUSE OF DEWITT'S stubbornness in the relocation matter, the departments in Washington expended a lot of energy making sure the general proceeded with discretion in exercising his authority to exclude. The most important considerations communicated to DeWitt were that he act selectively and in absolute secrecy, and that he furnish support for his prisoners "as may be necessary in your judgment." Again, the Justice Department balked but then reluctantly agreed to allow DeWitt to operate independently, so long as he consulted one of the Justice Department's representatives on each occasion. Suspects did not have to have committed an overt act. Thus, FBI arrests continued, as did DeWitt's exclusion program, although the general still complained to his superiors that the Justice Department was not fully supporting him.[237]

The familiar and interminable battle between the Justice and War Departments continued into 1943. Biddle had taken a personal interest in the Andriano case, as well as that of a German woman named Julia Kraus. The attorney general wrote the president that no evidence existed to sustain Andriano's expulsion. His crime: he had been vocally pro-Mussolini before the war. As for Kraus, it was true that she had been connected with pro-German propaganda efforts before Pearl Harbor, Biddle admitted, but since then, she had turned state's evidence against truly dangerous people. Biddle simply could not believe that either of them presented a military danger, and he told FDR that DeWitt's exclusion order was so broadly drawn that he did not believe the courts would sustain it. In July, in order to dramatize his disgust with the army, the attorney general ended the system of detention lists and danger classifications that had governed his own department since Pearl Harbor, a system he now described as "impractical, unwise, and [itself] dangerous."[238]

To McCloy, Biddle said much the same thing. What he wanted from the army—or what would be more acceptable to him than present policy—was an exclusion order based on dangerous or hostile *activities*, not simply on allegations that the subject sympathized with Italy or Germany before the war. A great many Americans, the attorney general chided, more influential than the ones being excluded continued to express views harmful to the objectives of the United Nations. What about them? Either this group was also dangerous per se and should be expelled, or as a class, they were not a military threat. The government could not have it both ways. It made no sense, he concluded, to pick people at random. Fish or cut bait.[239]

In the army's view, however, Biddle was "too sympathetic" to potential enemies, and to wait for a suspect to commit an overt act would endanger the country. Moreover, the army "objected strenuously" to any arrangement that contemplated either the residence or employment of paroled internees in the WDC, because they still represented a threat to "military security." The deputy commander of the Eastern Defense Command told McCloy that exclusion was a vital military weapon that could not be sheathed just because an "uninformed public" was too squeamish to have it used. Press on, he urged. Because of Justice Department objections, the East Coast exclusion program had never been given a fair trial.[240]

Remo Bosia
San Carlos, California

Although I was born in Madera, California, I was educated in Europe in the gymnasium and lyceum. I was five years old when I was brought to Italy. I returned to the United States at the age of eighteen, landed in San Francisco with twenty dollars in my pockets, and established myself in North Beach, the Italian district. After a while I got a job as a reporter at L'Italia, the local Italian newspaper. At that time, the chief editor was Paolo Pallavicini, the novelist, who was to become my father-in-law.

When Mr. Pallavicini died of a heart attack a few years later, Mr. Ettore Patrizi, the publisher, promoted me to his position and I became editor in chief and married Marcella, the novelist's daughter. As chief editor, I was in charge of everything that was published with the exception of politics. I wrote a lot of editorials, but never about politics. Politics was the job of another man, a fellow of Swiss origin. To be truthful, the newspaper had Fascist tendencies. As for the publisher, he was a man of two loves: America and the land of his birth, Italy. But he also was an admirer of Mussolini. As for myself, I never wrote an article favoring Il Duce—articles praising Italy yes, but in praise of Mussolini no, never.

During my stay at L'Italia I wanted to learn how to fly. So I became a pilot. Bay Meadows, the racetrack, used to be an airport, Curtiss-Wright field, and that's where I learned to fly. One of the men who instructed me was Captain William Fillmore.

One Sunday morning I was the first one to arrive at the [newspaper] office. It happened to be December 7, 1941. The Teletype was clicking away as usual, then it tolled, "Cling!" which means a bulletin is coming in. I picked up the tape and read: "This is the White House, Pearl Harbor has been attacked." I was shocked. Immediately I wrote an editorial to this effect: "Now is the time for all Italian Americans to show their patriotism." From that moment on, L'Italia *became a 100 percent American patriotic newspaper.*

The next day I called Fillmore to tell him I wanted to enlist in the air corps. I said, "Bill, I want to come in as a pilot and you know I'm a good one." He agreed that I was. He talked some more, then remarked, "Come over and see me in my office." I went to the Presidio, Bill filled out the application, and I said, "Well, what do I get? Second Lieutenant?" He answered, "Oh, no, First Lieutenant for you, but you're a little old. (I was thirty-six at the time.) We need younger pilots, and we desperately need people who can speak languages. You speak Italian and French. Let's request air corps intelligence." So we did. Then he added, "OK, now go home, take a leave of absence from the newspaper, make all the necessary arrangements with your family, and be prepared to be called in a couple of weeks."

Two weeks went by, three, four, five then three months. I called Fillmore and he said, "You have no idea what's going on in Washington, in the War Department. It's a mess. This [war] happened so suddenly, it caught us unprepared. The bureaucracy takes a long time. Don't worry, you'll get your commission in due time."

Another month went by. Finally, one day [in October] I was in my office when two men came in and at the front desk they said, "We would like to speak to Mr. Remo Bosia." They were secret service agents attached to DeWitt's headquarters. They said, "We are here to serve an exclusion order on you." I was to appear at the Whitcomb Hotel downtown, room so-and-so, on such-and-such a date, at such-and-such a time, and show cause why I should not be excluded from the Pacific coast.

One can imagine how I felt. I was a native son. At any rate, I went to the meeting at the hotel, a hearing they called it. There were about eight to ten officers facing me, all in dress uniform, from captain up. They told me that I was under suspicion as a potential enemy of the country.

"If you want proof of my patriotism why don't you let me prove it? Take me in [the air corps] and send me anywhere, even to Italy, even if I have to go and kill my own cousins, nephews, and uncles." The officers were all smiling; I felt reassured. But three or four days later a notice *came in the mail: "You are to be excluded from the Pacific Coast, and the closest you can be to the coast is 150." I didn't blame those officers; they were serving under DeWitt.*

Three days after the exclusion order, I went back to the Whitcomb Hotel and asked to see the "big shot." I was referred to a Major Ashwort to whom I said, "I would like to join the army air corps. If you think I'm too old for that, then send me to Reno as an instructor. Fillmore will testify as to my qualifications."

"No," answered the Major. "Impossible. Come back tomorrow and report to me." Going back to Ashwort, I asked if he had taken a favorable decision concerning me.

"The decision is that you have to leave the Pacific Coast," he said, "at leat 150 miles east of San Francisco. You must let us know just where you go." I replied it would be Reno, but that I had no intention of being considered an enemy of my country. Rather than being excluded as an enemy, I said I would enlist in the army as a private. Taken by surprise, the major answered, "Well, if you enlist you'll be out of our hands and we'll have nothing more to do with you. Make sure you're back here at seven PM when the bus will leave for Monterey." Monterey was an induction center and I was going to be inducted there.

Three or four days after arriving at Monterey, everyone in my group was rounded up for an examination. They wanted to know each man's qualifications. I had asked for "intelligence" in the air corps. The exam was not easy but I passed it with flying colors.

Early one afternoon soon after that, a sergeant entered my barracks and yelled, "Hey, Bosia, somebody wants to see you. Come with me." I did, and we landed in the office of the classification officer, a lieutenant by the name of Riley. As I entered he smiled and said, "Congratulations, Mr. Bosia, you made it. Top man." Lt. Riley said that within two weeks I would be sent to St. Petersburg, Florida, where there was an air corps intelligence school for new officer-candidates.

Meanwhile, weeks went by. Battalions and companies were leaving the center for the train station to be shipped to their camps and assigned to training. Finally, I was told to pack my gear; orders had arrived for me to leave that day. Several hundred of us assembled on a field for instructions, ready to move at once. The roll call began, but when it was over everyone had been called but me. Instead, two MPs came over and put me under arrest.

I was put to work digging ditches on the highway between the Presidio and Monterey proper. One morning I was working in the mud when an automobile stopped nearby. My wife and daughter were in it, but there was also a guard with a rifle standing over me. My daughter called, "Daddy!" and I ran toward the car, which was only fifteen or twenty feet away. But the guard pointed the rifle at me and shouted, "Halt!"

Back to the guardhouse I went. The next day I was called to another hearing presided over by a Colonel Grier. He told me, "You're free now. Get your duffel bag. You leave for Florida tomorrow with another company." But they didn't know DeWitt. I was arrested again "on orders from the San Francisco Presidio," a sergeant told me. The officer of the day in the guardhouse told me that the next day I would be taken to Ft. Douglas, Utah, to face a general court-martial. "General court-martial for what?" No answer.

The following day two guards picked me up and took me to the station. As soon as we changed trains in San Francisco, they removed my handcuffs; they didn't want to embarrass me on a train full of passengers. We arrived at Salt Lake City in the middle of the night. It was cold and snowing. The guards didn't know where to put me. I said, "Fellows, I'll land in the guardhouse anyway, so let's go there." I was back in jail, two or three stories underground.

Weeks and months went by, during which, I must admit, they treated me well. Finally, one day two officers, Captains Bold and Campbell from the quartermaster's office came to see me to say that it was their task to defend me.

"Defend me from what?"

"You are charged with the violation of three articles of war plus specifications. If you want, you are also entitled to a civilian lawyer." I was charged with enlisting fraudulently, of being a potential enemy of the United States, and of bilking the army of room and board—stuff like that. I was puzzled. "Do you mean that you two and I are going to win the war against DeWitt?" They told me to write down my story from the beginning.

The court martial lasted two days. In the end, I was acquitted. I have the record here: "We find Private Remo Bosia not guilty of all charges and specifications," read the president of the court. The judge advocate, who was the prosecutor, really wanted to send me to Ft. Leavenworth for thirty-eight years at hard labor on each count.

But do you know what really happened? On the day following my acquittal, at roll call, I was handed a shotgun and put to work guarding a squad of prisoners. As I had been in jail most of my army life, I had had no basic training and didn't even know how to handle a rifle. Then another incredible thing happened. I was assigned to the office of Colonel Pratt, the post commander, and put in charge of Teletype machines! My duty was to register everything that came over the machines *and transcribe it. Most of those messages were classified and revealed secret information from the War Department or from other commands. I could not believe it; one day a potential enemy of my country, then an MP, and today custodian of high military secrets!*

Anyway, my two army lawyers said, "Let's call Marcella and tell her the good news. Captain Bold suggested that she visit me. She arrived a couple of days later in Salt Lake City. Captain Bold said that I had been given permission for a week's leave. Before I was to meet Marcella downtown I took a last look at the Teletype—and there it was staring at me: "General DeWitt orders Private Bosia transferred immediately to Ft. Ripley, Minnesota." Ft. Ripley, near Little Falls, is one of the coldest spots in the United States. So I asked the colonel, "What are they doing to me now? I'm supposed to meet my wife; she just got in. And now I'm to be transferred immediately to Ft. Ripley." When I told Captain Bold he said, "Good Lord, this is unbelievable. They're sending you to Hell." He phoned the colonel and told him that Marcella had just arrived: "Give him a chance."

"OK," the colonel said, "let him stay tonight, but he's got to leave tomorrow morning." We were back at the depot the next morning, Marcella to take the train back to San Francisco, and I the train to God knows where.

Finally we arrived at Ft. Ripley, this little station lost in the mountains where it was one o'clock in the morning and about fifteen or twenty below zero. When I got off the train there was a soldier sleeping in the station. I woke him up and asked for some information. He asked, "Are you Remo Bosia?"

"Yes."

"I'm waiting for you." We drove to the fort in his car, about three or four miles, and he deposited me in front of the barracks. Inside a corporal asked my name: "Remo Bosia."

"OK," he said, "we'll straighten things out with the captain in the morning. Meanwhile, take the top bunk over there, at the end of this row." But what I thought was something to step on was instead only a clothes hanger, and as I pressed down to lift myself up to the bunk, the thing broke. I fell down, the whole bunk collapsed and everybody started swearing, but not in English—in German. I was in a prisoner's camp with German and Italian Americans who had been interned.

One morning I woke up choking with an attack of bronchitis. The camp doctor decided to send me to the general hospital at Ft. Snelling where I lay for months. Finally I was called before a medical board and discharged from the army. Before leaving Ft. Snelling where I had been transferred to the hospital, the local commanding general and the head of the local office of the FBI handed me a statement declaring that I was honorably discharged from the service. I was now a free man, entitled to go back to San Carlos and stay there for the duration of the war. But the general and the FBI had underestimated General DeWitt.

I arrived in San Carlos the day before Easter. On Easter Day, we were having dinner when somebody knocked at the door. I opened it and two men came in, apologized for disturbing us, and one of them said, "We're sorry, but you have to come with us." A few seconds went by, then one of them murmured, noticing our family gathering, "We think you're a man of good word. Let's do this: Stay home for the rest of the day. But you will have to meet us at the Ferry Building in San Francisco tomorrow morning at nine o'clock. From there we'll take you to Reno." I agreed, and went to Reno with my wife and child for about eight months.

In Reno, I'd had enough, so I wrote a letter to the President of the United States. I thought he'd never get it, but I wrote it anyway. A week later a captain knocked at the door of our apartment around midnight. He handed me an envelope. It was from Roosevelt. I was a free man again. It said, "Dear So-and-So, the order of exclusion against you is hereby rescinded by direction of the President of the United States. Roosevelt." Can you imagine how busy Roosevelt was in those days? And my letter got to him. Two days later, my family and I were back in San Carlos for good.

THE ENTRY FOR Remo Bosia on the army's "Alphabetical List of [suspect] Individuals" reads: "Orig. M[ember]—BLACK SHIRTS, Rome, Italy." Could this blacklisting have been the cause of Bosia's ordeal? Were the army's "Black Shirt" Bosia and San Carlos's Remo Bosia the same man? How serious a Black Shirt could an Italian teenager have been? Bosia was eighteen when he returned to the United States. He claims not to have been to Rome until 1950 while on holiday. The list also notes Bosia's editorship of *L'Italia*, although publisher Ettore Patrizi stated in a notarized affidavit in December 1942 that Bosia had not been responsible for the paper's editorial policy. Joining Bosia on the army's alphabetical list of 335 were some familiar names: Father Charles Coughlin; Fritz Kuhn; Patrizi; Fritz Wiedemann; Bosia's deceased father-in-law, Paolo Pallavicini; and oddly, Carmelo Zito, editor of the anti-Fascist *Il Corriere Del Popolo*. In compiling the 335 dossiers, the army came up with 25,000 additional names, a number that must have intimidated even the most persistent snoops.[241]

It is impossible to say with certainty that General DeWitt carried on a personal vendetta against Remo Bosia. We have only the hearsay evidence above, plus what Bosia adds in his autobiography, *The General and I.*[242] But it was certainly possible for DeWitt to have done so; the circumstantial evidence fits, as does what we know of DeWitt's personality. From the beginning, he gave every appearance of being a man obsessed with purging the West Coast of its enemy aliens and "dangerous" citizens. Moreover, the organizational structure of the Western Defense Command was such that General DeWitt personally exercised final judgment over the cases heard by an army board of officers.

Those present at each of these individual exclusion hearings included three field-grade officers (major and above), a court reporter, the subject, and his attorney. Each board forwarded its case resume and recommendation to the commanding general, WDC. There, the Civil Affairs Division (CAD) reviewed the file and made a recommendation to the assistant chief of staff, CAD, Col. Bendetsen. Still making its tortuous way to the commanding general, the file next went to the appropriate local U.S. attorney for his recommendation, then back to CAD for presentation to DeWitt. Importantly, the power to exclude devolved to the commanding general as an individual, not an officer. He could not delegate that authority to a subordinate. By the army's own reckoning, this meant that the "entire exclusion program received an inordinate amount of personal attention from several CGs," including DeWitt. In cases that DeWitt excluded individuals, the hearing board, the U.S. attorney, and the CAD concurred 81 percent of the time; in cases that he decided against exclusion, 84 percent. A member of one board refused, as a matter of principle, to exclude any American-born suspect regardless of his record. Inevitably, DeWitt demurred, and consequently a number of cases—perhaps Bosia's—were recommended for exclusion by the CAD where the board had recommended nonexclusion.[243]

AS THE TIDE of real battle abroad turned in favor of the United States in 1943, the army began to re-examine its exclusion policy. By the end of that year, with Italy a co-belligerent, the army rescinded all exclusion orders on Italians unless the individual had an "extreme [F]ascist history and connection with espionage agents." Apparently, one did, and he was kept far away from the West Coast. In February 1944, with the threat of German invasion removed, the army reprieved all Germans who had been involved with the Bund. In September 1943, Lt. Gen. Delos C. Emmons replaced DeWitt as commanding general of the WDC. Under his tenure, from September 1943 to June 1944, 155 of the previous exclusion orders were rescinded and two suspended. Seventeen men, however, continued to languish in distant barracks. Emmons's replacement, Maj. Gen. Charles H. Bonesteel, freed all the remaining Germans in June

1944, except two who allegedly had close Japanese ties. They came home after V-J Day.[244]

After the war, many of the Italians who had been arrested wanted to know who had informed on them. FBI reports on such matters were, of course, confidential, and Alfonso Zirpoli refused to divulge anything from the files. In addition to the ethical question involved, an additional problem existed. Some of those providing information to the FBI were friends and family members of the suspects, perhaps a nephew or sister-in-law who did not get along with the person under investigation, or a wife seeking grounds for divorce.[245] The situation underlined the fundamental flaw of a policy that assigned group labels to individuals. It also brings to mind Louis Goldblatt's warning to the Tolan Committee: "One-half [of] the Nation will be standing guard over the other half. What a merry-go-'round that will be. Where is this to end?"

Remo Bosia at the old Curtiss-Wright Airport, now Bay Meadows racetrack
near San Mateo, California, 1939.

Georgia Massei, Eureka, California, 1940.

Simpson College, formerly the INS detention center on Silver Avenue, San Francisco.

Alfonso Zirpoli, San Francisco, ca. 1968.

Joe Cervetto as Christopher Columbus embarks for Aquatic Park in San Francisco in 1986, a reenactment of Columbus's landing in San Salvador in 1492. Cervetto, also a native of Genoa, Italy, portrayed the discoverer in the annual rite from 1957 to 1989, when his son took over the role.

Ermete Vanni, San Francisco, in the early 1950s.

TEN

"An experience never to be forgotten"
Reflections on a Historical Event

The fact that in a time of emergency this country is unable to distinguish between the loyalties of many thousands of its citizens, and others domiciled here, whatever their race or nationality, calls into question the adequacy of our whole outlook upon the assimilation of foreign groups.
—The Tolan Committee, May 1942

TOWARD THE END of our conversations, a few of the interviewees reflected on their experiences:

Alex Frediani

WE MOVED; THE *whole family. We had to come to Eureka to find a place to live south of Fourth Street. Dad stayed at Hammond [lumber mill]. He'd go back and forth on the little ferry. Mother had to be home by eight o'clock at night. There was a little resentment on my part because I didn't want to leave Samoa [across Humboldt Bay from Eureka]; all my friends were there. I had two brothers-in-law, one in the marines and the other in the coast guard. I couldn't really believe that my mother would do any harm to this country.*

We found a place on F Street, and we stayed there for about three months. Then we rented a place on B Street. My sister was in school down south, and she came up for the summer because my mother kept telling my dad, "Let's buy a home." But my dad, he was the type of guy who thought, "Let's hold it right here. The war will be over and then we'll go back to Samoa"—the status quo, you know. Well, my mother never did want to go back, so when my sister was here she and my mother went out and found this house on Fifth Street and bought it. My dad came home and they told him, "We're moving."

"Where are you moving?"

"Well, we bought a home." He was a little upset, but he went along with it. Later, when property values were climbing, he'd tell his friends that he bought the house. He'd take all the credit and she got none.

So, as it turned out, [relocation] was the best thing that ever happened to us. We got out of Samoa; my dad bought a home and some property. He was the type of person who would have lived in Samoa the rest of his life, and when it came to retirement, he'd have nothing. Property after the war went sky high. So the thing worked out real well.

Did your mother ever say anything about her situation?

No, but she didn't vote for Roosevelt in '44. I think it had something to do with her having to move. Definitely. She didn't say so, but she always told me that was the best thing that ever happened to her. She got out of Samoa. Otherwise she'd have lived there and never really owned her own home. Dad would never talk too much about it. If he had his family and his church, he was happy. Mother would tell it around, she'd say, "Tell General DeWitt, thank you. I got out of Samoa and got my own home."

Vince Massei

Do you think it would have made any difference to your mother and others like her if the Italians had attacked the United States the way Japan did?

I think so. If Italy had got into the war through collusion with Germany and Japan they should have been treated similarly. People, like my mother, were innocent, but you can't just go on one or two cases. San Francisco had a big Italian population. What do you do about them?

Maybe they were a little tough on the Japanese by putting 'em in camps. I've never followed it closely, although you hear a lot of comments both ways as to whether the government should pay restitution to these people. I've never thought they should compensate my mother. I listen to these talk shows quite a bit at night. I wake up in the middle of the night and turn on KGO [San Francisco radio station]. You ever listen to KGO? There's times when this Japanese situation has come up pretty strong. It's a tough situation, but the government, to my way of thinking, goes out and tries to pacify certain groups. Only the war's over, so why do that? Just because my mother had to move out of her house—I mean, how bad was she hurt? I don't think she was hurt that bad. She was living with the family. Now, if she was living in some kind of relocation camp where her life would have been. Well, that would have been different. I think maybe then I'd have thought that she should be entitled to something from the government. But how can the government make restitution to all these people?

I think a lot of people get worked up over this—this might sound a little screwball—because all this money is being spent, poured down the drain on a lot of stuff. More about this is coming out, like how these big contracts with these big outfits are making fortunes. Well, this perturbs a lot of people. If the government's got that kind of money to pour down the tubes, I want some; we're entitled to it. The only thing I've thought that I would have liked to have gotten from my government was a good medical plan so that I didn't have to go and beat my brains out against medical plans today. I think this is one thing that the government owes me. That's the only thing, and I have no other qualms. I don't think the older generation was looking for something for nothing; you always wanted to say, "It's mine because I earned it." But today, God, everybody's looking for something for nothing.

Steve Antongiovanni

My parents didn't feel that they suffered anything from the war; they kept thinking about their families back in Italy that had really gone through it. Right after the war, the first thing to do was to find out what had happened, who was still living [and] who wasn't. I remember the first letters that came over—reading the lists of those who had died during the war. We used to send CARE packages to our family because they weren't exactly flush, even though they had never suffered hunger or destruction. Everything was in disarray. There were no streets, no power. There was money but no products. It was completely demolished. Even if you sent them money, there was nothing they could buy. So we sent big packages of clothes and some money, but we didn't have that much money either. Finally, they got back on their feet and people started going over there. Mrs. Pieri was the first one to go, in 1947.

My dad's father died in 1939 and his mother passed away during the war. It wasn't until 1969 that my parents could afford to go back to Italy with me. Dad really enjoyed it. He never thought he would live to go back. I said, "Dad, tell me what you think it's going to be like."

"Oh, I know what it's like. It hasn't changed that much."

"You have to remember, they've been through a war. It's all been destroyed and there isn't the money like here."

"Here it's too much; there's too much waste," he said.

We flew from Oakland to Scotland nonstop, which my dad just marveled at. He said, "My God, it took me twenty-one days to cross the first time." My mother was real nervous on the plane, and my dad was kind of a character. He said to her, "What are you so nervous about? If it goes down it's not your plane. Let it go." You know, she had to think about that for a minute.

We landed in Milan, got off the plane, and pretty soon he says, "Why are we off the plane? When are we going to get to Italy?" We were already on the bus going from the airport in to Milan. There were freeways, cloverleaves.

"But when do we get to Italy?"

"Dad, we are in Italy. We're on the way to the Milan Hotel!"

They were greeted by a lot of people outside of Lucca, but the first thing was to go into the house. That was rather difficult because they didn't know just how my mother's brother would react. It was emotional. It had been thirty-nine years since she had seen her brother, so that was quite a thing. My dad thought Italy had just stood still, but it had changed a lot. They had paved streets, cars all over. The streets are old, the town is old, and narrow streets with little cars all over—just terrible abuse. But he really savored that trip. Then we toured. My mother had never been in any other part of Italy.

Mary Cardinalli

My feelings about all this now? It's over! It made me feel bad that they treated us like that. I don't believe the Japanese should have any compensation. If they do, everybody else should too. Why not? They think they're better than the rest of us? You know, where my mother was, there in Oakley? My God, some old woman, as old as my mother—she got so sick, the poor lady, because they got her out of her house. I thought she was gonna die. Her mouth got all full of sores. She was a mess. She was so depressed and upset that they threw her and her husband out. They were both aliens, and they were sick all the time they were out. They had no children in the service, but they did have children who were born in this country. They were horrible days, really horrible days. It was so sad and gloomy.

Do you think relocation changed your life in any way?

Sure it did. It does change your life. It's always on your mind. You think about it, that you missed a lot of your life. I missed all those months being with my husband. And my child? He was growing up. His best years—I mean months—we were spending along the highway, running here, running there. And that made me feel real bad.

It always made you feel like people were looking at you cross-eyed. My husband was afraid to go even one mile from where he was living. He took it real hard. He was really afraid. What were they going to do, sabotage?

We did come into town one night, and we had to look for a man here who was taking care of the aliens. If you wanted to come to town you had to pick him up to ride into town with you and bring him home again. He was well known in Pittsburg, an Italian fellow. Yeah, it was really something. So don't tell me the Japs suffered more than we did. Maybe they lost their property, I don't know.

Everybody was so happy to be back home. I think that [relocation] was terrible. But it makes me mad now when I hear the Japanese; they want money; they're fighting. They don't deserve any money. They're not better than the rest of the people. They started the war. I don't like to be in the same boat with them. Look what they did to us at Pearl Harbor. Killed all those beautiful boys. The Italians had no choice [in the war]. If it wasn't for Mussolini they wouldn't have fought against America.

John Molinari

Did anything in the Italian community change because of these events?

The community changed. My children, for example, don't know about any of this unless I tell them or they read about it. It's hard for them to believe some of the things. "What was it like?"—that sort of questioning. After World War II, the community began to change with the prosperity that developed; the new generation wanted better accommodations. They went to Marin County; they went to the Peninsula. North Beach began to disintegrate as an Italian community.

After World War I we used to have very active Italian organizations: Sons of Italy, Italian Catholic Federation, social organizations. They were active at a time when all fraternal organizations were active—the Druids, the Eagles, the Native Sons [of the Golden West]—which was the thing to do to get some recreation. But with the change in attitudes, television, the automobile, the airplane, some of these organizations went out of existence, some were left with just a handful of members. So the attitude of joining organizations changed drastically after World War II. And the community became diffused. North Beach, which was a solid community in the thirties when I started to practice law, has only about fifteen percent Italians now, [the rest is] mostly Chinese. So you don't have any real strong Italian memberships anymore. The young people couldn't care less about fraternal organizations. But up to World War II it was a homogeneous community where a lot of things took place and you knew what was going on. You had two daily Italian newspapers, two or three Italian radio programs daily, and morning and afternoon papers, in Italian. After the war, they merged into one and eventually it went out of existence. The only Italian paper you have now comes out of Los Angeles. It has one page dedicated to San Francisco.

Lily Boemker

My mother always told me, you should kiss the ground you walk on over here. My husband and I went over to Italy eight years ago and met all my cousins and my aunt and uncle who are still living. We saw the house and the bedroom that my dad was born in, and my mother's house and the room she was born in. They have these long stone houses, you know. My mother would bring this up. She said, "You know, when we left Italy nineteen people were living in one house." The brothers got married and just lived off the land that they could farm. This was the only thing they could live [on].

It was very, very moving to go back to Italy. The city has walls around it, and I would say it's about ten miles from Lucca. It's called Paganico. I knew all my relatives over there by name. The reason I knew was that, through the years, my mother would make packages of clothing and things like that to send. I can still remember, it was forty–four pounds; that's the limit. I was always the one to put the address on it, Paganico, Provincia de Lucca.

Our daughter went to school there for a year. And she just fell in love with our relatives.

Dominic Banducci

There is still a lot of family in Italy. I've been to Europe and I've visited my father's sisters. There's still a bond across the ocean of helping each

*other out. When I went to Italy the last time my father said to make sure
I gave some money to my aunt. I did it out of respect for him.*
*I looked at their surroundings and they're no worse off than we are.
In fact, I would say better. I mean the way of life; they don't work as
hard, and they're not as drained as we are, nor as harassed. They live
in nice homes and have beautiful appliances. People, like my father,
were forced to leave because of poverty. Somebody had to go. He never
wanted to go back, really. He never wanted to go back because he was
sort of forced to leave home to save his younger sisters who remained. I
visited his house over there an old rock house, in shambles. Nobody
lives there. Just a little building.*

BECAUSE OF THE public outcry for the mass relocation of Italians and
Germans in late January and early February 1942, why were the European
aliens spared the fate of the Japanese? The evidence presented in this
book suggests several reasons. The unpleasant memory of persecution of
German Americans during World War I, plus the lackluster enthusiasm
for democracy on the part of many aliens between the wars, persuaded authorities not to force them to choose loyalties again. The enemy alien
problem differed in 1917 and 1941, both in size and nature. When the
United States entered World War I there were twice as many aliens as in
December 1941, and most of the latter had those additional years to ab-
sorb democratic values. Yet a belief persisted in the late 1930s and early
forties—wildly exaggerated—in a Fifth Column of aliens, especially the
several thousand pro-Nazi, German American Bundists.[246] Despite this, a
few farsighted people in Washington and elsewhere worried that if such
disloyalty did exist, and if these people continued to support Nazism or
Fascism, they might persuade their millions of American-born children
to do the same. The country could not risk that while it fought for its
life. The Commission on the Wartime Relocation and Internment of Civilians concluded in 1981, therefore, that it was not because the government viewed the intentions of Italians and Germans as benign that it
decided to forego interning them.
   A second benefit to the Italians and Germans was the degree of their
assimilation into American society in contrast to that of the Japanese. By
mid-1942, the public had concluded that the European aliens were less
dangerous than their Asian counterparts. But there was more. Colonel
Bendetsen, who, as the provost marshal general's assistant and then
DeWitt's chief of staff was as responsible as anyone for the decision to
relocate the Japanese, told the Commission that most of the Japanese on
the West Coast had "concentrated themselves into readily identifiable
clusters." Thus, he implied, they were more vulnerable to relocation than

the vastly larger and more scattered Italian and German communities. In Bendetsen's view, ill-conceived federal and state policies had retarded Japanese assimilation. On the one hand, federal immigration policy and state-sponsored prejudice in California increasingly isolated the Japanese. But, ironically, the drastic treatment of German Americans during and after World War I had served, on the other, to accelerate their assimilation. And from 1932 to 1942, records of the Federal Naturalization Bureau show that Italians led all other national minorities in the number of citizenship applications. Even then, suspicion of Italian Americans, including those who were naturalized and spoke fluent English, receded at a snail's pace during World War II.[247]

Third, the German and Italian aliens were flesh-and-blood symbols of American values. Many Americans feared that under a blanket relocation policy the government might actually jail an otherwise obscure alien Italian fisherman from San Francisco named Giuseppe DiMaggio, whose most famous son was called "Joe." (In 1941 the "Yankee Clipper" had set the major league record for hits in consecutive games at fifty-six and was named the American League's Most Valuable Player.) As a Berkeley political scientist reasoned, if the army was allowed to intern Italians and Germans indiscriminately, then former presidential candidate Wendell Willkie and the mayors of New York and San Francisco, among hundreds of thousands of others, would wind up in reception centers with the Japanese.

Finally, there were simply too many of the European aliens and their extended families scattered across the nation to make a policy of relocation practically feasible. The several hundred thousand Germans and Italians living in the United States, plus their immediate descendants, represented as many as 11,000,000 potential relocatees. Policy makers in Washington who looked ahead to the postwar period were reluctant to risk alienating the loyalty of second- and third-generation Italian and German Americans.[248]

The importance of Italian and German assimilation to the relocation decision can also be demonstrated by analogy. Roger Daniels, a leading authority on Japanese relocation, recognizes that the relatively large numbers of Japanese in Hawaii, in contrast to the total population, influenced the decision not to relocate the Japanese on the islands. But he does not equate that policy—as he might have—to the decision regarding the Germans and Italians on the mainland. "It is one thing," he admits, "to incarcerate a tiny element of the population as was done on the West Coast [in the case of the Japanese], and quite another to put away a sizable fraction of the whole [in Hawaii]. Apart from the sheer size of the problem...there was the question of the disruption that such a mass evacuation [in Hawaii] would cause in the...economy."[249] Officials who sought to prevent the relocation of Italians and Germans used precisely this logic repeatedly in the spring of 1942. They believed that removal of Italians and Germans from the civilian work force would severely disrupt the economy, especially in the large urban areas on both coasts, and destroy postwar morale.

Thus economics, politics, and morale drove U.S. relocation policy during World War II, with race as a reinforcing factor. The withdrawal of perhaps millions of Italians and Germans from civilian production jobs, many in heavy industry—or even the shutdown of fishing in California—was ultimately judged too high a price to pay to thwart potential sabotage. Had there been several million Japanese in the United States, as there were Italians and Germans, the Japanese could not have been relocated simply as a practical matter. Ironically, on the other hand, had there been an unwavering policy to relocate all enemy aliens—an extreme reaction—no entire class of people, or nationality, could have been singled out for punishment. Fundamentally, the halting of Asian immigration—but not European—in 1924 and the resulting numerical implications across the country, not the attack on Pearl Harbor and its bitter emotional legacy, determined what happened to the Japanese in 1942 and why Italians and Germans did not experience the same fate. It is possible for a proud nation such as the United States, dedicated in principle to individual freedom, to come close to losing its soul during a time of crisis under poor leadership.

IN 1988, PRESIDENT Ronald Reagan signed The Civil Liberties Act, which authorized payment of $20,000 to each surviving Japanese American who came out of the relocation and internment camps, plus a lesser sum for those who had been brought to the United States from Latin America for internment. Some spokesmen for the Japanese say the money is meaningless, that it is merely a token payment for their suffering and loss. What they most want, they say, is for the government to admit that it made a mistake, to correct the constitutional error. They want their pride restored. They want to have it said that they were right and Uncle Sam was wrong.

One may agree there is no comparison in the extent of severity between what happened to the Italians and Germans and to the Japanese Americans. In most respects, this is true. But such a comparison must also take into account the principle that is at stake. Where is the principle in the government's decision not to relocate all of the Italians and Germans simply because there were too many of them? What if the situation had been reversed, if Japanese Americans had numbered in the hundreds of thousands, or even millions, and Italians and Germans only in the tens of thousands? Would the government now be offering compensation to Italians and Germans? Rep. Norman Y. Mineta (D-San Jose), a Japanese American, has said, "This [apology from the government] touches all of us because it touches the very core of our nation." And Rep. Robert T. Matsui (D-Sacramento), also a Japanese American, adds that the "specter of disloyalty that attached to Americans of Japanese ancestry during World War II is about to end. We can now look upon ourselves as proud Americans."

There is deep personal humiliation in being told you are an enemy of your country, as explained so eloquently by Japanese Americans over the years. Is it, then, so difficult to understand that what happened to Italian and German Americans during the war is a matter of their dignity and pride? It is an issue that speaks to the essential meaning of being human, as well as the core of the nation.

IT IS TOO simplistic to say that what happened in the spring of 1942 in California happened because of Pearl Harbor; too easy to say that people understandably panicked. Of course they did. But what happened also happened because there was no individual strong enough or with sufficient institutional prestige in the government to say no to the mob. Attorney General Biddle came as close as anyone to assuming this role, but he deferred consistently to Henry Stimson. It would have taken enormous courage in the face of the public tumult for Biddle to jeopardize his career by refusing to bow to the military during the first six months of the war. Moreover, the attorney general had mixed instincts: he intuitively discounted the seriousness and longevity of the emergency, but pragmatically he was inclined to give the military what it wanted. He seems not to have had a combative personality. Structurally and historically, the Justice Department was geared to deal with individual lawbreakers. The army, on the other hand, operated on a larger scale, and it had the logistic capability to handle thousands of suspects. Nevertheless, to his credit, Biddle never gave up the fight to lessen the impact of the army's policy. Rather than resign in futile protest, he bore relentlessly from within, and his fundamental common sense and regard for fair play eventually carried the day. It is testimony to Biddle's elemental decency that by the middle of 1943 the War Department had reached such a state of total exasperation with him that it conceded the game.

What happened in 1942 happened because mankind seems incapable of looking at human beings as individuals rather than as members of groups. It also happened because there are always powerful voices in an emergency to say, "Quarantine them," whether the "them" are alien enemies or AIDS victims. When society is perplexed and frustrated by drug abuse, the cry is, "Test everyone, that way we'll be sure to catch the serious offenders. The framers of the Constitution couldn't have anticipated this. It's better to be safe than sorry."

After forty-eight years, the United States finally said to the Japanese, "We made a mistake. We're sorry." But have American attitudes and reactions really changed? Is the country more likely to act now with greater prudence in a national emergency than in 1942? Have Americans acquired the courage to look at people as individuals and the patience to design remedies for society's problems, including national security, that do not assign labels?

NOTES

FOREWORD

1. The expressions, "enemy aliens" and "alien enemies," are technical and pejorative labels, implying that Italian and German aliens were truly enemies of the United States rather than simply nationals of enemy countries. I use these terms throughout the book, however, because virtually everyone in 1942 referred to the aliens as enemies.
2. *San Francisco Chronicle*, April 29, 1988; Allan M. Winkler, *Home Front USA: America during World War II* (Arlington Heights, ILL: Harlan Davidson, Inc., 1986), p. 70; John P. Diggins, *Mussolini and Fascism: The View from America* (Princeton: Princeton University Press, 1972), p. 351; James Rowe Jr., "The Alien Enemy Program—So Far," *Common Ground* (Summer 1942), p. 22.
3. "Lay off the Italians," *Colliers*, Aug. 3, 1940, p. 54.

"One does not melt souls"

4. Carlo Sforza, *The Real Italians: A Study in European Psychology* (New York: Columbia University Press, 1942), p. 116.
5. Los Angeles *Times*, Feb. 17, p. 6, *San Francisco Chronicle*, "This World," Feb. 22, 1942, pp. 4-5.
6. San Francisco *Chronicle*, Feb. 12, p. 9, Feb. 17, p. 6; *Humboldt Times*, Feb. 21, 1942, p. 1.
7. Paul Radin, *The Italians of San Francisco: Their Adjustment and Acculturation* (New York: Arno Press, Inc., 1975), p. 146; Diggins, *Mussolini and Fascism*, 143; Andrew F. Rolle, *The Immigrant Upraised: Italian Adventurers and Colonists in an Expanding America* (Norman, OK: University of Oklahoma Press, 1968), pp. 20-21, 24, and *The American Italians: Their History and Culture* (Belmont, CA: Wadsworth Publishing Co., Inc., 1972), pp. 2-3; and Luciano J. Iorizzo and Salvatore Mondello, *The Italian Americans* (Boston: Twayne Publishers, 1980), pp. 56-60.
8. Rolle, *The Immigrant Upraised*, pp. 30-31. *See also* Anna Maria Ratti, "Italian Migration Movements, 1876 to 1926," in Walter F. Wilcox, ed., *International Migrations, Volume II, Interpretations* (1931; reprint ed., New York: Gordon and Breach, Science Publications, Inc., 1969), p. 446.
9. U.S., Congress, House, *Fourth Interim Report of the Select Committee Investigating National Defense Migration*, 77th Cong., 2d sess., H.R. 2124, 19 May 1942 (Washington: U.S. Government Printing Office,

1942), p. 242; hereafter cited as Tolan Committee, "Fourth Interim Report."

10. Rolle, *The Immigrant Upraised,* pp. 26, 32; Antonio Stella, *Some Aspects of Italian Immigration to the United States* (1924; reprint ed., San Francisco: R&E Research Associates, 1970), p. 10; Tolan Committee, "Fourth Interim Report," p. 243.

11. Stella, *Aspects of Italian Immigration,* pp. 13-14, 21.

12. Tolan Committee, "Fourth Interim Report," p. 230.

13. Ibid., p. 232; U.S., Congress, House, *Hearings of the Select Committee Investigating National Defense Migration,* 77th Cong., 2d sess., pts. 29-31 (Washington, D.C.: U.S. Government Printing Office, 1942), 29: 11134; hereafter cited as "Tolan Committee Hearings"; Radin, *Italians of San Francisco,* pp. 41-42, 58-59. The commander of the 12th Naval District believed there were only 294 alien Italians and forty-one Germans living between the Mad and Eel rivers (U.S. Commission on Wartime Relocation and Internment of Civilians, *Papers,* microfilm edition, ed. by Ralph Boehm [Frederick, MD, 1983], 3: 39-48; hereafter cited as CWRIC followed by reel and frame number).

14. Radin, *Italians of San Francisco,* pp. 127-129.

15. Ibid., pp. 74-75.

16. Rolle, *The Immigrants Upraised,* pp. ix, 10; Paul Campisi, "The Adjustment of Italian-Americans to the War Crisis" (M.A. thesis, University of Chicago, 1942), pp. 161-162, and "Ethnic Family Patterns: The Italian Family in the United States," *American Journal of Sociology* 53 (May 1948), p. 443; Diggins, *Mussolini and Fascism,* pp. 78-80. See also, Jerome S. Bruner and Jeanette Sayre, "Shortwave Listening in an Italian Community," *Public Opinion Quarterly* 5 (Winter 1941), pp. 640-656; and Joseph S. Roucek, "Foreign Politics and Our Minority Groups," *Phylon* 2 (First Quarter, 1941), p. 55, both of which question Italian assimilation.

17. Morton Grodzins, *Americans Betrayed: Politics and the Japanese Evacuation* (Chicago: University of Chicago Press, 1949), pp. 152-154; La Vern J. Rippley, *The German-Americans* (Boston: Twayne Publishers, 1976), p. 198.

18. Radin, *Italians of San Francisco,* p. 113.

19. Tolan Committee, "Fourth Interim Report," p. 230.

20. Campisi, "Adjustment of Italian-Americans," pp. 177-180, 182, 184, 223.

21. Prohibition limited the Italians to bottling wines for sacrament and growing table grapes. But there were ways to get around the law, which were made possible by the Bureau of Internal Revenue of the Treasury Department when it ruled in 1920 that the Volstead Act did not prohibit home winemaking of up to 200 gallons per year (Rolle, *The Immigrant Upraised,* pp. 271-72; John R. Meers, "The California Wine and Grape Industry and Prohibition," *California Historical Society Quarterly* 46 [March 1967], pp. 19, 28-29).

"Dynamite on our shores"

22. Constantine Panunzio, "Italian Americans, Fascism, and the War," *Yale Review* 31 (June 1942), pp. 771-73.
23. Ibid., pp. 774-77; Diggins, *Mussolini and Fascism*, pp. 86-87; Max Ascoli, "On the Italian Americans," p. 46; Radin, *Italians of San Francisco*, p. 64.
24. Iorizzo and Mondello, *The Italian Americans*, p. 252; Panunzio, "Italian Americans, Fascism, and the War," p. 777; Frank C. Hanighen, "Foreign Political Movements in the United States," *Foreign Affairs* 16 (Oct. 1937), p. 16; Diggins, *Mussolini and Fascism*, p. 99.
25. Panunzio, "Italian Americans, Fascism, and the War," pp. 777-81; Diggins, *Mussolini and Fascism*, pp. 302, 306.
26. M.B. Schnapper, "Mussolini's American Agents," *Nation* 147 (15 Oct. 1938), p. 374.
27. California, *Report of the Joint Fact-Finding Committee*, p. 319.
28. Ibid., pp. 781-82; Diggins, *Mussolini and Fascism*, pp. 108, 325, 350-51; Iorizzo and Mondello, *The Italian Americans*, p. 258; "Lay Off the Italians," p. 54; Edward Corsi, "Italian Immigrants and Their Children," *The Annals of the American Academy of Political and Social Science* 223 (Sept. 1942): 105; Marino De Medici, "The Italian Language Press in the San Francisco Bay Area from 1930 to 1943" (Master of Journalism thesis, University of California, Berkeley, 1963), pp. 204, 206, 211-12; Alfonso J. Zirpoli, "Faith in Justice: Alfonso J. Zirpoli and the United States District Court for the Northern District of California," an oral history conducted 1982-83 by Sarah L. Sharp, Regional History Office, The Bancroft Library, University of California, Berkeley, 1984, pp. 19-20; Campisi, "Adjustment of Italian-Americans," p. 172.
29. Diggins, *Mussolini and Fascism*, p. 399; Alan Cassels, "Fascism for Export: Italy and the United States in the Twenties," *American Historical Review* 69 (April 1964), pp. 707-12; Iorizzo and Mondello, *The Italian Americans*, pp. 257-58.
30. Diggins, *Mussolini and Fascism*, pp. 96, 343-44.
31. Grodzins, *Americans Betrayed*, pp. 164-65.
32. Institute for Propaganda Analysis, "Axis Voices Among the Foreign-Born," *Propaganda Analysis* 4 (Aug. 1, 1941), pp. 3, 7; Alfred McClung Lee, "Subversive Individuals of Minority Status," *The Annals of the American Academy of Political and Social Science* 223 (Sept. 1942), pp. 164-65; Joseph S. Roucek, "Foreign-Language Press in World War II," *Sociology and Social Research* 27 (July-Aug. 1943), pp. 465; "The Foreign-Language Press," *Fortune* 22 (Nov. 1940), p. 92; "Steam from the Melting Pot," *Fortune* 26 (Sept. 1942), p. 132; "The Foreign-Language Press," pp. 92-93; Roucek, "Foreign-Language Press," p. 465.
33. John Norman, "Repudiation of Fascism by the Italian-American Press," *Journalism Quarterly* 21 (March 1944), p. 2; "Steam from the Melting Pot," p. 137; *New York Times*, May 26, 1942, p. 11, as cited in Lee, "Sub-

versive Individuals," p. 165. *See also*, Harold F. Gosnell, "Symbols of National Solidarity," *Annals of the American Academy of Political and Social Science* 223 (Sept. 1942), pp. 160-161.

34. Harold Ickes, *Diaries, 1933-51*, Library of Congress Manuscript Division, Oct. 15, Nov. 17, 1940, April 12, 1941, April 11, Oct. 25, Nov. 1, 1942, Feb. 20, April 3, 1943, pp. 4895-4896, 4981, 5367-5368, 6538, 7109, 7158-7159, 7462, 7589.

35. "The War of Nerves: Hitler's Helper," *Fortune* 22 (Nov. 1940), pp. 85, 112; Diggins, *Mussolini and Fascism*, pp. 107-08; Hanighen, "Foreign Political Movements," p. 16; Rowe, "The Alien Enemy Program—So Far," p. 20; Diggins, *Mussolini and Fascism*, pp. 343-44.

36. Donald S. Strong, *Organized Anti-Semitism in America: The Rise of Group Prejudice During the Decade 1930-40* (1941; reprint ed., Westport, CT: Greenwood Press, Inc., 1979), pp. 30-32; *San Francisco Chronicle*, Feb. 20, 21, 22, 1942, pp. 7, 6, and 5 respectively; Richard O'Connor, *The German-Americans: An Informal History* (Boston: Little, Brown Co., 1968), p. 437.

37. John Christgau, *"Enemies": World War II Alien Internment* (Ames: Iowa State University Press, 1985), p. 10.

38. Diggins, *Mussolini and Fascism*, pp. 262-64, 269, 276, 283, 346-47.

39. Iorizzo and Mondello, *The Italian Americans*, pp. 249-50, 259.

40. Diggins, *Mussolini and Fascism*, p. 282; Ickes, *Diary*, 15 Sept. 1940, pp. 4799-4801.

41. Diggins, *Mussolini and Fascism*, p. 325; David S. Wyman, *Paper Walls: America and the Refugee Crisis, 1938-1941* (Amherst: University of Massachusetts Press, 1968), pp. 47, 184-88.

42. Bradley Smith, *The Shadow Warriors: O.S.S. and the Origins of the C.I.A.* (New York: Basic Books, 1983), pp. 12, 15, 21, 23.

43. Ibid., pp. 38-39.

44. Ickes, *Diary*, 22 Aug. 1940, p. 4725, Nov. 6, 1941, p. 5989.

45. Wyman, *Paper Walls*, pp. 190-91.

46. Ickes, *Diary*, April 12, 1941, p. 5367; David Brinkley, *Washington Goes to War* (New York: Alfred A. Knopf, 1988), pp. 42-45.

47. Christgau, *"Enemies"*, pp. 11-19; "Nazi Eye View of San Francisco," *Time*, May 12, 1941, p. 15. Later the German government posted Wiedemann to Tokyo where he also served as consul.

48. *San Francisco Chronicle*, Nov. 10, 1988, p. B1.

49. "Aliens: Robert Jackson's Busy Week," *Time*, May 19, 1941, p. 18; "Alien Crackdown," *Newsweek*, May 19, 1941, p. 22.

50. *San Francisco Chronicle*, Jan. 6, 1942, p. 8.

"We can't fool around"

51. U.S., Congress, House, *Report of the Select Committee Investigating National Defense Migration*, 77th Cong., 2d sess., H. R. 1911, March 19,

1942, p. 2; hereafter cited as Tolan Committee, "Preliminary Report"; *San Francisco Chronicle*, Feb. 21, 1942, p. 12.

52. *San Francisco Chronicle*, Dec. 16, p. 18, Dec. 23, 1941, p. 16, Jan. 20, p. 12, Feb. 28, 1942, p. 10.

53. *San Francisco Chronicle*, Dec. 30, 1941, p. 8.

54. C.K. Schoell to John H. Tolan, "Correspondence, memos, etc., of Representative Tolan and R.K. Lamb secretary to the Tolan Committee," Jan. 19, 1942, University of California, Berkeley, Bancroft Library, file 67/14, folder A12.052.

55. Grodzins, *Americans Betrayed*, p. 276; Stetson Conn, Rose C. Engleman, and Byron Fairchild, *The United States Army in World War II, The Western Hemisphere: Guarding the United States and Its Outposts* (Washington, D.C.: Office of the Chief of Military History, Department of the Army, 1964), pp. 122-123; *San Francisco Chronicle*, Jan. 31, 1942, pp. 1, 4; *Los Angeles Times*, Jan. 29, 1942, p. 6; Eric C. Bellquist, "Tolerance Needed," *California Monthly* 43 (April 1942), p. 8.

56. Rolle, *The Immigrant Upraised*, p. 281; *San Francisco Chronicle*, Jan. 31, 1942, pp. 1, 4; Grodzins, *Americans Betrayed*, p. 277; "Conference of Sheriffs and District Attorneys called by Attorney General Warren on the subject of Alien Land Law Enforcement," Feb. 2, 1942, CWRIC 9: 610-611, 730, 745.

57. "Conference of Sheriffs," CWRIC, 9: 740-744.

58. U.S. Congress, House, *Congressional Record*, 77th Cong., 2d sess., 1942, 88, pt. 8, appendix, Jan. 5 to April 20, 1942, p. A654; *San Francisco Chronicle*, Feb. 9, 1942, p. 10.

59. Grodzins, *Americans Betrayed*, pp. 111-112; Telephone conversation between McCloy and Gullion, Feb. 17, 1942, CWRIC 28: 598.

60. He was Max Polland (or Pohland), age fifty. A seventeen-year resident of the Pacific Coast, Pohland lived on Gunther Island in Humboldt Bay, but he could not complete naturalization before being restricted. So he set fire to his home and then jumped overboard from a fishing skiff after tying an iron bar around his waist (*Humboldt Times*, 20 Jan. 1942, p. 1). The body of George M. Heckel, 73 washed ashore at Santa Cruz on February 12; it had been in the ocean three to four days. He had died of a broken neck and had numerous other injuries, which probably occurred when he was slammed against the cliffs. Neighbors who identified the body said Heckel had been despondent over having to leave his home in a prohibited area (*Sentinel-News* [Santa Cruz], Feb. 13, 1942, p. 1).

61. Grodzins, *Americans Betrayed*, p. 113; "Resolutions of county boards of supervisors in re control measures over alien enemies, Japanese, etc," 3, Feb. 20, 1942, Bancroft Library, file 67/14, folder A 15.12; "Resolutions of city governments in re control measures over enemy aliens, Japanese, etc," Feb. 9, 1942, Bancroft Library, file 67/14, folder A 15.13; "Tolan Committee Hearings," 29: 11238; *San Francisco Chronicle*, Feb. 13, 1942, p. 13. Clark, who President Harry Truman appointed Attorney General and associate justice of the Supreme Court, was ostensibly Bid-

dle's man, although he consistently supported the army's tougher approach to the alien "problem." If the army said there had to be an evacuation, Clark saw no way to stop it (CWRIC 5: 533; "Tolan Committee Hearings," 29: 11158).

62. *San Francisco Chronicle*, Feb. 6, 1942, p. 14; "Tolan Committee Hearings," 29: 11251, 11253; *Pittsburg Post-Dispatch*, Feb. 13, 1942, pp. 1, 8; Letters to Lt. General J.L. DeWitt, WDC, "Memo to Col. W.L. Magill, Jr., Provost Marshal and Director, Western Defense Command, Feb. 1942, from Galen M. Fisher, Gordon Chapman, C.A. Richardson, G. Doubleday, F. H. Smith," Bancroft Library, file 67/14, folder A16.17.

63. *San Francisco Chronicle*, Feb. 8, 1942, p. 8.

64. Pacific Coast Congressional Delegation to FDR, Feb. 13, 1942, CWRIC 2: 412-414; Letter from the Pacific Coast Congressional Delegation on Alien Enemies and Sabotage to the War Department, received in Assistant Secretary of War John J. McCloy, Jr.'s office on Feb. 15, 1942, CWRIC 1: 129; Tolan Committee, "Preliminary Report," p. 3; Conn, *et al, United States Army in World War II*, p. 133.

65. Resolution of the American Legion, Department of California, Feb. 16, 1942, "Tolan Committee Hearings," 29: 11235-11236.

66. "Historian Morton Grodzins's analysis of Warren's questionnaire to District Attorneys, Sheriffs, etc.," CWRIC 9: 757-758. The original replies may be found in the Bancroft Library, University of California, Berkeley.

67. "Tolan Committee Hearings," 29: 10988-11000.

68. Grodzins, *Americans Betrayed*, pp. 172-175.

69. Telegram from W.L. Wheeler to Philip C. Hanblet, executive officer, Office of Government Reports, Washington, D.C., CWRIC 3: 295.

70. "Joint Agreement between the Secretary of War and the Attorney General regarding Internment of Alien Enemies, July 18, 1941," CWRIC 3: 391. The government was concerned about the integrity of the labor force and that people might be harassed solely because of careless prewar statements.

71. For biographical information on DeWitt, see Maxine Block, ed., *Current Biography: Who's News and Why, 1942* (New York: The H.W. Wilson Co., 1942), pp. 196-199, and DeWitt's obituary in *The New York Times*, June 21, 1962, p. 31; Peter Irons, *Justice at War* (New York: Oxford University Press, 1983), pp. 24, 31, 38. For an example of DeWitt's leadership role, see the summary of a telephone conversation between DeWitt and Bendetsen, Feb. 1, 1942, CWRIC 5: 808.

72. Robert E. Mayer, "A New Look at General DeWitt," *San Francisco Chronicle*, May 7, 1988, p. A14; Zirpoli, "Faith in Justice," 70.

73. Literature on the Japanese internment is voluminous. Grodzins, *Americans Betrayed*; Jacobus tenBroek, Edward N. Barnhart, and Floyd W. Matson, *Prejudice, War and the Constitution: Japanese American Evacuation and Resettlement* (Berkeley: University of California Press, 1954); and Roger Daniels, *Concentration Camps USA: Japanese Ameri-*

cans and World War II (New York: Holt, Rinehart and Winston, 1972)
are three of the most important. For the view that pre-war ideology and
activity among Italians and Germans might have been a threat, see John
M. Blum, *V was for Victory: Politics and American Culture During
World War II* (New York: Harcourt Brace Jovanovich, 1976), 147-151;
Sander A. Diamond, *The Nazi Movement in the United States, 1924-1941*
(Ithaca: Cornell University Press, 1974); Gaetano Salvemini, *Italian
Fascist Activities in the United States* (1944; reprint ed., New York:
Center for Migration Studies, 1977); Bruner and Sayre, "Shortwave Lis-
tening in an Italian Community"; Hanighen, "Foreign Political Move-
ments in the United States"; Institute for Propaganda Analysis, "Axis
Voices Among the Foreign-Born"; Panunzio, "Italian Americans, Fas-
cism and the War"; "The Foreign-Language Press"; and "What to do with
Foreign Press Puzzles Officials," *Advertising Age* 22 (20 April 1942), p.
25. Commission on Wartime Relocation and Internment of Civilians,
Personal Justice Denied, Part 1 (Washington, D.C.: U.S. Government
Printing Office, 1982), p. 284.

74. 6 *Fed. Reg.* 6323, 6324; interview with James H. Rowe, Jr., Earl Warren
Oral History Project, "Japanese-American Relocation Reviewed" (Berkeley: Regents of the University of California, 1976), p. 19; Francis
Biddle, *In Brief Authority* (Garden City: Doubleday & Co., 1962), pp.
206, 210; Irons, *Justice at War*, pp. 14-15, 19, 21-22; Frederick L.
Collins, *The FBI in Peace and War* (New York: G.P. Putnam's Sons,
1943), pp. 245-247; J. Edgar Hoover, "Alien Enemy Control," *Iowa Law
Review* 29 (1944), pp. 398-399; Tolan Committee, "Fourth Interim Report," note, p. 269; *San Francisco Chronicle*, Feb. 2, 1942, p. 6.

75. Telephone conversation, Hoover and agent Nat Pieper, Dec. 17, 1941,
CWRIC 5: 502; telephone conversation, DeWitt and Gullion, Dec. 26,
1941, cited in Conn, *et al., United Sates Army*, pp. 117-118, 119; Irons,
Justice at War, pp. 27, 37.

76. Bendetsen to DeWitt, 3 Jan., Conference in DeWitt's office with Rowe,
Bendetsen, and Pieper, Jan. 4, 1942, CWRIC 2: 122-123, 124-131. Army
historian Stetson Conn states that even before the meetings between
representatives of the two departments Major Bendetsen recommended
that DeWitt insist on several measures to be taken beyond those already
ordered by Biddle. It was Bendetsen, for example, who Conn says suggested the idea of strategic areas from which all enemy aliens would be
excluded, and army authority to prescribe such zones (Conn, *et al.,
United States Army*, p. 118).

77. Western Defense Command and Fourth Army, *Final Report: Japanese
Evacuation from the West Coast, 1942* (Washington, D.C.: U.S. Government Printing Office, 1943), pp. 4-5, 19-24; Grodzins, *Americans Betrayed*, pp. 242, 274. Grodzins concludes that army control and mass
evacuation grew directly out of the disagreement between the Justice
and War Departments over the latter's recommendation that large areas

be designated as prohibited rather than restricted, and that American citizens be removed along with alien enemies.

78. Tolan Committee, "Preliminary Report," p. 2; Stimson to Rep. Leland Ford, Jan. 20, 1942, CWRIC 16: 926; Tolan Committee, "Fourth Interim Report," p. 6; Roger Daniels, *The Decision to Relocate the Japanese Americans* (Philadelphia: J.B. Lippincott Co., 1975), p. 23; Grodzins, *Americans Betrayed*, p. 240; Conn, *et al., United States Army*, pp. 120-121; Western Defense Command, *Final Report*, p. 6.

79. Tolan Committee, "Fourth Interim Report," pp. 302-303, 306, 310, 312; 7 *Fed. Reg.* 1474, 1476; Western Defense Command, *Final Report*, p. 6; Tom Clark to Dr. Harold R. Smithies, re status of Dr. Michael Wachtel, Alameda, Feb. 6, Clark to E. Clemens Horst, Jr., Feb. 7, Clark to Lawton D. Harris, Oakland, Feb. 12, 1942, CWRIC 11: 45-47, 52-53; Conn, *et al., United States Army*, pp. 122-123; Daniels, *Concentration Camps USA*, pp. 53-54; DeWitt, internal WDC memo, Jan. 31, 1942, CWRIC 2: 182-185; "Tolan Committee Hearings," 29: 11042; Clark to Ennis, Jan. 31, 1942, Biddle to Stimson, n.d., CWRIC 34: 641-643, 5: 533. The early deadline affected only about 300 people statewide, but by February 24, approximately 10,000 had to be out. The new curfew regulation limited the activities—including work shifts—of 100,000 more (*San Francisco Chronicle*, Feb. 11, 1942, p. 10).

80. Telephone conversation, DeWitt, Gullion, and Bendetsen, Feb. 1, 1942, CWRIC 4: 138-142, 261-265.

81. Hoover to Biddle, Feb. 2, 1942, CWRIC 5: 465-474; personal interview with John Molinari, San Francisco, Feb. 6, 1987. Molinari attended the meeting at DeWitt's headquarters.

82. Telephone conversation, McCloy and DeWitt, Feb. 3, 1942, CWRIC 5: 809-818, 1: 139.

83. Bendetsen to Gullion, Feb. 4, 1942, CWRIC 5: 588-592; Grodzins, *Americans Betrayed*, p. 96; memo of luncheon meeting, Biddle and Roosevelt, Feb. 7, Biddle to Stimson, Feb. 9, 1942, CWRIC 5: 419, 12: 264-265; Conn, *et al., United States Army*, pp. 130-131; Benjamin V. Cohen, Oscar Cox, and Joseph L. Rauh to Biddle, undated, but written approximately Feb. 10, 1942, CWRIC 11: 587-588.

84. Brinkley, *Washington Goes to War*, p. 54.

85. Stimson Diary, Feb. 11, 1942, Memo from Bendetsen to DeWitt, Feb. 10, 1942, CWRIC 17: 320-321, 10: 905-907; Conn, *et al., United States Army*, pp. 130-132.

86. Testimony of Edward J. Ennis, Director, Alien Enemy Control Unit, Justice Department, before the Senate Committee on Immigration, March 23-24, 1942, cited in Western Defense Command, *Final Report*, pp. 166-167. *See also*, Rowe, "Japanese-American Relocation Reviewed," pp. 6, 10-11, 29-30; Grodzins, *Americans Betrayed*, pp. 270-271; Western Defense Command, *Final Report*, p. 25; McCloy, Diary/Log, Feb. 17-18, Stimson Diary, Feb. 17-18, 1942, CWRIC 28: 598-599, 17: 238-239; Tom C. Clark, "Japanese-American Relocation Reviewed," pp. 12-13.

Clark thought Biddle caved in because he was persuaded that the army
had to maintain its rule on the West Coast and elsewhere to win the war.
87. Western Defense Command, *Final Report*, pp. 33-38; Conn, *et al., United
States Army*, note, p. 130; telephone conversation, McCloy and Gullion,
Feb. 17, 1942, CWRIC 28: 598.
88. Biddle to Roosevelt, Feb. 17, 1942, CWRIC 5: 423-424; Rowe, "Japanese-American Relocation Reviewed," p. 31; Irons, *Justice at War*, p. 62;
Grodzins, *Americans Betrayed*, pp. 271-272; Edward J. Ennis, "Govern-
ment Control of Alien Enemies," *State Government* 15 (May 1942), p.
112; Stimson Diary, Feb. 18, 1942, CWRIC 17: 238-239; Biddle to
Roosevelt, April 17, 1943, "Supplemental Report on Civilian Controls
Exercised by the WDC," Jan. 1947, ibid., 1: 349, 24: 120-122; Memo,
Bendetsen to McCloy, May 11, 1942, CWRIC 1: 287-289; CWRIC, *Per-
sonal Justice Denied*, pt. 1, p. 285; McCloy diary/log, Feb. 16, 1942,
Oral History with McCloy re his wartime diaries, CWRIC 4: 268; George
C. Warren, "The Refugee and the War," *Annals of the American Academy
of Political and Social Science* 223 (Sept. 1942), p. 95.

"What'll happen to our Papa?"

89. Daniels, *Decision to Relocate the Japanese Americans*, p. 5; Wyman, *Paper Walls*, pp. 187-188; Harold Ickes believed the transfer occurred because Frances Perkins, the labor secretary, was not up to the job (Ickes,
Diary, May 26, 1940, p. 4413); Vito Marcantonio, *The Registration of
Aliens* (New York: American Committee for the Protection of the Foreign
Born, 1940), pp. 7-9. The Smith Act is otherwise remembered for its attempt to outlaw subversive activities and advocacy of the forceful overthrow of the government. Earl G. Harrison, "Axis Aliens in an Emergency," *Survey Graphic* 30 (Sept. 1941), p. 468; Donald R. Perry, "Aliens in the United States," *Annals of the American Academy of Political
and Social Science* 223 (Sept. 1942), pp. 6-7; Beulah Amidon, "Aliens
in America," *Survey Graphic* 30 (Feb. 1941), p. 61.
90. 6 *Fed. Reg.* 6323, 6324; James H. Rowe, Jr., "Keeping Our Heads on the
Enemy Alien Problem," *American City* (Feb. 1942), pp. 56-57; Tolan
Committee, "Fourth Interim Report," p. 269.
91. *San Francisco Chronicle*, Dec. 13, p. 3; Dec. 28, 1941, p. 1; Ennis, "Government Control of Alien Enemies," p. 112.
92. *San Francisco Chronicle*, Dec. 29, p. 1; Dec. 30, 1941, p. 8; Jan. 1, p. 8;
Jan. 7, 1942, p. 10.
93. *Monterey Peninsula Herald*, Dec. 12, p. 10, Dec. 29, 1941, pp. 1-2. State
Attorney General Earl Warren determined later that the federal statute
known as, "Trading with the Enemy Act," did not prohibit the professional licensing of alien enemies (State of California, Attorney General's Office, "Opinion No. NS4108," February 17, 1942); Edward J. Ennis, "Federal Control Measures for Alien Enemies," *The Police Year-*

book, 1943, pp. 31-34; *San Francisco Chronicle*, Dec. 12, 1941, p. 8; Jan. 13, 1942, p. 6; Rowe, "The Alien Enemy Program—So Far," p. 16.

94. *Monterey Peninsula Herald*, Dec. 12, 1941, pp. 1-2,10.
95. *San Francisco Chronicle*, Jan. 3, p. 9; Jan. 6, p. 8; *Monterey Peninsula Herald*, Jan. 13, 1942, p. 5; 7 *Fed. Reg.* 844; Rowe, "The Alien Enemy Program—So Far," p. 15; Zirpoli, "Faith in Justice," p. 72.
96. *San Francisco Chronicle*, Dec. 18, 1941, p. 2; Jan. 15, p. 9; Jan. 16, p. 6; Jan. 29, 1942, p. 1; 7 *Fed. Reg.* 1474.
97. Tolan Committee, "Fourth Interim Report," pp. 302, 310, "Preliminary Report," p. 2; 7 *Fed. Reg.* 1474, 1476, 1477; Campisi, "Adjustment of Italian-Americans," p. 165; *Los Angeles Times*, Feb. 15, 1942, pp. 1, 13. The designation of restricted areas during wartime was not unprecedented. In Eureka, California, in 1918, Germans (probably aliens) were not permitted to work in "forbidden zones" or to cross designated "dead lines" during the final year of the First World War ("City of Eureka Arrest Records, 1918," Eureka Police Station).
98. This happened only to those who were interned, and certainly not to "thousands and thousands."
99. *Pittsburg Post–Dispatch*, Feb. 2, pp. 1-6, Feb. 3, pp. 1, 3, Feb. 7, p. 4, Feb. 12, 1942, p. 1; *San Francisco Chronicle*, Feb. 4, 1942, p. 1.
100. *Pittsburg Post–Dispatch*, Feb. 9, 1942, pp. 1, 6; *San Francisco Chronicle*, Feb. 5, 1942, p. 11.
101. *San Francisco Chronicle*, Feb. 5, p. 1, Feb. 27, p. 3, Mar. 2, 1942, p. 1.
102. DeMedici, "The Italian Language Press in California," pp. 4-5; *San Francisco Chronicle*, Jan. 30, pp. 1-4, Jan. 31, p. 9; *Pittsburg Post-Dispatch*, Feb. 12, p. 1, April 16, 1942, p. 1; Tolan Committee, "Fourth Interim Report," pp. 302-303.
103. *San Francisco Chronicle*, Feb. 4, pp. 1, 6, Feb. 5, 1942, pp. 1, 4.
104. *Monterey Peninsula Herald*, Feb. 7, p. 1, Feb. 16, p. 1, Feb. 21, p. 3, Feb. 23, p. 2, Feb. 24, 1942.
105. *Pittsburg Post-Dispatch*, Feb. 9, p. 1, Feb. 10, pp. 1, 3; *Monterey Peninsula Herald*, Feb. 10, p. 1, Feb. 11, pp. 1-2; *The Humboldt Standard*, Feb. 10, p. 3; *Los Angeles Times*, Feb. 7, p. 1, Feb. 11, 1942, p. 6.
106. *Monterey Peninsula Herald*, Feb. 27, p.15; *San Francisco Chronicle*, Feb. 27, 1942, p. 6.
107. 7 *Fed. Reg.* 2320, 2405, 2543, 2581; Tolan Committee, "Fourth Interim Report," pp. 163, 318, 321, 331-332; *San Francisco Chronicle*, Mar. 4, p. 1, Mar. 15, 1942, p. 1; Warren, "The Refugee and the War," p. 95.
108. Tolan Committee, "Fourth Interim Report," pp. 4, 164-165, 334-338, 340, 342; 7 *Fed. Reg.* 3964-3967; *San Francisco Chronicle*, Mar. 5, p. 6, April 12, 1942, p. 12; *Pittsburg Post-Dispatch*, Mar. 24, 1942, p. 3.

"He was a stool pigeon"

109. *San Francisco Chronicle*, Feb. 5, pp. 1, 4, Feb. 24, p. 13, April 18, 1942, p. 5; Tolan Committee, "Fourth Interim Report," pp. 330-331; 7 *Fed. Reg.* 2543.

"Absolutely going to be discretion"

110. Blum, V *was for Victory*, p. 150; "Tolan Committee Hearings," 31: 11759-11760.
111. Alan Cranston, "The Alien—and National Policy," *Common Ground* (Summer 1941), p. 98.
112. *San Francisco Chronicle*, Dec. 9, p. 16, Dec. 12, p. 8, Dec. 13, p. 3, Dec. 15, 1941, p. 7, Feb. 6, 1942, p. 21; *Pittsburg Post-Dispatch*, Feb. 13, 1942, p. 3; *Monterey Peninsula Herald*, Dec. 14, p. 3, Dec. 23, p. 7, Dec. 26, 1941, pp. 1-2.
113. *Los Angeles Times*, Dec. 9, 1941, as cited in Grodzins, *Americans Betrayed*, p. 107; *San Francisco Chronicle*, Feb. 25, 1942, p. 8; "Tolan Committee Hearings," 29: 11255.
114. *San Francisco Chronicle*, Jan. 3, p. 9, Jan. 10, p. 11, Jan. 11, 1942, p. 16; "Tolan Committee Hearings," 29: 11043-1104.
115. Roosevelt to Rear Admiral Emory S. Land, Chairman, U.S. Maritime Commission, Feb. 18, 1942, CWRIC 3: 676.
116. *Pittsburg Post-Dispatch*, Feb. 3, pp. 1, 3, Feb. 4, 1942, pp. 1, 3; Tolan Committee, "Fourth Interim Report," p. 310; *San Francisco Chronicle*, Feb. 4, 1942, pp. 1, 6; Zirpoli, "Faith in Justice," p. 65.
117. Radin, *The Italians of San Francisco*, p. 59; Letter from Right Rev. Msgr. Michael J. Ready, General Secretary, National Catholic Welfare Conference, Washington, D.C., to Biddle; Letter to Msgr. Ready from Archb. John J. Mitty, San Francisco, CWRIC 12: 243-245; *San Francisco Chronicle*, Feb. 8, 1942, "This World," pp. 4-5.
118. Memo, "Luncheon conversation with the President," Feb. 7, 1942, CWRIC 5: 419; Letter from Ruth Benedict, Los Angeles Branch of the Women's International League for Peace and Freedom, to Rep. John Tolan, Bancroft Library, file 67/14, folder A12.052.
119. *San Francisco Chronicle*, Feb. 11, 1942, p. 10; *Pittsburg Post-Dispatch*, Feb. 10, pp. 1, 3, Feb. 11, 1942, p. 1.
120. Telephone conversation, McCloy and Sen. Sheridan Downey (R–Claremont), Feb. 16, 1942, CWRIC 28: 597; Telephone Conversation between Gullion and DeWitt, Feb. 17, 1942, CWRIC 1: 126-127.
121. *San Francisco Chronicle*, Feb. 7, p. 12, Feb. 10, 1942, p. 12.
122. Telegram, Tolan to his son, San Francisco, Feb. 18, 1942, Bancroft Library, file 67/14, folder A12.052.
123. "Tolan Committee Hearings," 29: 10966-10967, 11101-11102; Tolan Committee, "Preliminary Report," pp. 15-16; Corsi, "Italian Immigrants

and Their Children," p. 105; *San Francisco Chronicle*, Feb. 21, 1942, pp. 1, 6.

124. Letter from Scavenger's Protective Association, Inc., San Francisco (John B. Molinari, attorney for the association) to Mr. Chauncey Tramutolo, San Francisco, "Tolan Committee Hearings," 29: 11288-11289, 11125.
125. Ricks to Tolan, Feb. 20, 1942, CWRIC 10: 523-524.
126. "Tolan Committee Hearings," 29: 11053,11057-11058.
127. Ibid., 29: 11133-11134. This and additional detailed testimony about hardship cases provided by Ronchi, Tramutolo, Rispoli, Neustadt, and mayor Angelo Rossi of San Francisco, as well as numerous individual letters from Italians and Germans may be found in the committee's "Fourth Interim Report," pp. 253-263.
128. "Tolan Committee Hearings," 29: 11117-11120.
129. Ibid., 29: 10967-10968; *San Francisco Chronicle*, Feb. 25, 1942, p. 8; Grodzins, *Americans Betrayed*, p. 110.
130. "Tolan Committee Hearings," 29: 10971, 11021.
131. Ibid., 11094, 11102-11103.
132. Ibid.,11168-11169, 11171; *San Francisco Chronicle*, Feb. 24, 1942, p. 13.
133. "Tolan Committee Hearings," 29: 11114-11115, 11171-11172.
134. Ibid., 11198-11200; 31: 11725-11727; Tolan to MacLeish, Mar. 7, 1942, Bancroft Library, file 67/14, folder A12.052.
135. "Tolan Committee Hearings," 31: 11631, 11634-11636.
136. *San Francisco Chronicle*, Feb. 22, 1942, p. 5.
137. "Tolan Committee Hearings," 29: 11178-11185, 11189.
138. Ibid., 11197.
139. Report by San Francisco Committee for Service to Emigrés (Federation of Jewish Charities), ibid., 11270-11272; 31: 11795-11796.
140. Ibid., 31: 11736-11737, 11807, 11879-11880; Clark to Mr. Sandor Maibaum, Mar. 5, 1942, CWRIC 10: 961.
141. "Tolan Committee Hearings," 29: 11274; Telegram from Deutsch to Frankfurter, Mar. 28, 1942, CWRIC 1: 57.
142. "Tolan Committee Hearings," 31: 11734-11736, 11762, 11861-11865.
143. *Pittsburg Post-Dispatch*, April 13, 1942.
144. "Tolan Committee Hearings," 31: 11894-11895, 11897, 11899-11902, 11919-11920.
145. Ibid., 11885-11886.
146. From a notarized affidavit, May 5, 1942, courtesy of Mrs. Susie Banducci, personal interview, Eureka, California, July 8, 1987.
147. "Tolan Committee Hearings," 29: 11095-11096, 11103, 11106-11107, 11115-11117.

"Hundreds of thousands of people"

148. "Tolan Committee Hearings," 29: 11020.

149. During the summer of 1943 DeWitt directed the operations that cleared the Aleutians of Japanese invaders, and in September was ap-pointed commandant of the Army and Navy Staff Colleges in Washington (*New York Times*, June 21, 1962, p. 31).

150. Statement of the Japanese Church Federation of Northern California, submitted by Richard M. Neustadt, Regional Director, Social Security Board, Federal Security Agency, San Francisco, Feb. 6, 1942, "Tolan Committee Hearings," 29: 11294-11295; Earl G. Harrison, "Axis Aliens in an Emergency," *Survey Graphic* 30 (Sept. 1941), p. 466; Biddle to Max Ascoli, New York, Feb. 16, 1942, CWRIC 34: 632; Rowe, "The Alien Program—So Far," p. 24; "Tolan Committee Hearings," 31: 11663-11664; Biddle papers, "Notes on Cabinet meeting of 27 February," CWRIC 3: 764; Federal Security Agency, Neustadt File: "Journal: Files of 'Alien Evacuation Folder,'" II, Feb. 20, 1942, Bancroft Library, file 67/14, folder A11.02.

151. Stimson to DeWitt, Feb. 20, Stimson Diary, Feb. 20, 1942, CWRIC 4: 381-382, 17: 243; Western Defense Command, *Final Report*, pp. 25-29; Telephone conversation, DeWitt and Bendetsen, Feb. 20, 1942, CWRIC 16: 934-936; *San Francisco Chronicle*, Feb. 20, pp. 1, 7, Feb. 22, 1942, p. 5.

152. CWRIC 4: 888-889; letter from Stimson to Harold D. Smith, Director, Bureau of the Budget, Feb. 24, 1942, ibid., 3: 39; *Pittsburg Post-Dispatch*, Feb. 24, p. 1; *Monterey Peninsula Herald*, Feb. 24, 1942; Tom Clark to Contra Costa Hospital, Martinez, CWRIC 11: 59; CWRIC 11: 58-59.

153. 7 *Fed. Reg.* 2320; Tolan Committee, "Preliminary Report," p. 9, "Fourth Interim Report," p. 163; *San Francisco Chronicle*, Mar. 4, 1942, pp. 1, 10. Officials in Los Angeles told a Tolan Committee staffer that they did not fear either the Germans or Italians as a group (Interview of Robert K. Lamb with Los Angeles County Defense Council, Mar. 2, 1942, CWRIC 10: 644).

154. Stimson, diary, Feb. 26-27, 1942; Biddle, "Notes on Cabinet Meeting of 27 Feb.," CWRIC 17: 262, 311, 3: 764.

155. "Tolan Committee Hearings," 31: 11629, 11784.

156. CWRIC 10: 644; "Tolan Committee Hearings," 31: 1781-82, 11784. The Los Angeles Council of California Women's Clubs demanded that General DeWitt immediately place all enemy aliens in concentration camps, and the Young Democratic Club of Los Angeles insisted that American-born Germans and Italians be removed (W.L. Wheeler to Philip C. Hanblet, Executive Officer, Office of Government Reports, Washington, D.C., Mar. 3, 1942, CWRIC 3: 295; "Tolan Committee Hearings," 31: 11784-11785).

157. Tolan Committee, "Preliminary Report," p. 4; *San Francisco Chronicle*, Mar. 9, p. 1, Mar. 10, 1942, p. 9.

158. Western Defense Command, *Final Report*, pp. 58-59; Tolan Committee, "Fourth Interim Report," p. 3; U.S., Congress, Senate, Committee on

Military Affairs, *Report of Proceedings*, 77th Cong., 2d sess., S. 2352, Mar. 13, 1942, not printed, CWRIC 10: 283-285, 291; Clark to George R. Keith, Los Altos, Mar. 9, Clark to Francis P. Healey, District Attorney, Contra Costa County, Mar. 13, and Clark to Zavattaro, Mar. 13, 1942, CWRIC 11: 1, 7, 66-67.

159. Tolan Committee, "Preliminary Report," note, p. 2, pp. 21-22, 24.

160. Ibid., pp. 25-26; "Tolan Committee Hearings," 29: 11131-1132; *Monterey Peninsula Herald*, Mar. 19, p. 2, *Pittsburg Post-Dispatch*, Mar. 19, 1942, p. 1.

161. 7 *Fed. Reg.* 2199.

162. By referring to relocation as an "evacuation," the army gave the impression that the aliens were being removed from danger, as though an earthquake or some other natural disaster threatened them.

163. Ibid., 2543, 2581; Tolan Committee, "Fourth Interim Report," pp. 6, 248, 331-332, 346-347; Western Defense Command, *Final Report*, p. 60; *Pittsburg Post-Dispatch*, Mar. 26, 1942, p. 1.

164. "Status of Alfred Jaretski, Jr.," Office of Assistant Secretary of War, Mar. 26, 1943, CWRIC 2: 83. Jaretski served as advisor to the U.S. delegation at the International Refugee Conference at Evian, France, in 1938, and made four trips that year to Vienna to help Jewish and other refugees after the *Anschluss* (*New York Times*, Aug. 24, 1976, p. 32); Bruce Allen Murphy, *The Brandeis/Frankfurter Connection: The Secret Political Activities of Two Supreme Court Justices* (New York: Oxford University Press, 1982), pp. 202-204, 206, 217, 240, 298, 302; Deutsch to Frankfurter, Mar. 28, 1942, CWRIC 1: 57; Lasker, "Friends or Enemies?" pp. 301-302.

165. Jaretski to Stimson, Mar. 31, 1942, CWRIC 1: 58-69. On the refugees' anxiety, see Warren, "The Refugee and the War," pp. 92-99.

166. McCloy, diary/telephone log, April 1, McCloy to DeWitt, April 8, telephone conversation, DeWitt and Bendetsen, April 8, 1942, CWRIC 28: 611, 2: 109, 4: 903.

167. Biddle to Roosevelt, April 9, 1942, cited in Conn *et al., United States Army*, p. 145; Memo of conversation on alien removal between John Burling, Edward Ennis, and Bernard Gufler, State Department, Feb. 20, memo of conversation between Bendetsen and Gufler, Feb. 21, 1942, CWRIC 3: 31-21, 36-37. The War Department's fear of reprisals was overshadowed by its conviction that if it favored the Italians over the Germans and the Japanese, there would be reprisals against Americans at the hands of Germany and Japan; Rowe, "The Alien Program—So Far," pp. 23-24; "Notes taken in Conference of U. S. District Attorneys," Washington, D.C., April 9, 1942, CWRIC 12: 572-574.

168. McCloy, diary/telephone log., 10 April; McCloy, conversation with Earl Warren, April 13; "The Japanese Problem," April 21, Bureau of Intelligence, Office of Facts and Figures in collaboration with the National Opinion Research Center of the University of Denver, ibid., 28: 612, 4:

191, 42-77; *San Francisco Chronicle*, April 18, p. 5, April 21, p. 9, *Pittsburg Post-Dispatch*, April 17, 1942, p. 1.

169. James Rowe, Jr., one of Biddle's chief lieutenants in the Justice Department, went so far as to write in *Common Ground* that Executive Order 9066 was to be extended to the East Coast ("The Alien Enemy Program—So Far," p. 23).

170. Stimson, diary, April 15, Dwight Eisenhower, assistant chief of staff, to the adjutant general, April 24, 1942, CWRIC 17: 330-331, 5: 561; McCloy to McNarney, cited in Daniels, *Concentration Camps USA*, pp. 81-82.

171. Telephone conversation, Bendetsen and Jaretski, April 27, 1942, CWRIC 4: 907-913. Bendetsen told Jaretski that the Army was very quietly exempting hardship cases.

172. Tolan Committee, "Fourth Interim Report," pp. 2, 21-22, 36; telephone conversation, Bendetsen and Jaretski, April 27, 1942, CWRIC 4: 907-913.

173. Tolan Committee, "Fourth Interim Report," pp. 22-24; McCloy, diary/log, May 7, 1942, CWRIC 28: 618. *See also* Tolan to Biddle, July 7, 1942, CWRIC 22: 850.

174. Clark to Rowe, April 27, 1942, CWRIC 25: 573.

175. This was the army's individual *exclusion* program (see chapter 9). FDR to Stimson, May 5, McCloy, diary/log, May 7, 1942, CWRIC 1: 193, 28: 618; FDR to Gov. Herbert Lehman, June 3, 1942, cited in James MacGregor Burns, *Roosevelt: The Soldier of Freedom* (New York: Harcourt Brace Jovanovich, 1970), pp. 268, 653; *San Francisco Chronicle*, May 10, 1942, p. 8; McCloy, diary/log, May 7, Jaretski to McCloy, May 2, 1942, CWRIC 28: 618, 1: 215-217.

176. Bendetsen to McCloy, May 10-12, 1942, CWRIC 12: 104-108, 1: 286-289. From April 1942 until after the war, the War Department branded certain officials at Justice as "obstructionists" because of their efforts to limit detention and internment of individual aliens and citizens.

177. McCloy, diary/log, May 11-12, McCloy to Stimson, May 14, 1942, ibid., 28: 619, 1: 195-201; Conn *et al., United States Army*, p. 146.

178. Tolan Committee, "Fourth Interim Report," pp. 11, 25.

179. McCloy, diary/log, May 15, telephone conversation, McCloy and DeWitt, May 15; Stimson to Roosevelt, May 14; McCloy to Stimson, May 15; Stimson, diary, May 15; Bendetsen to McCloy, May 15; from Biddle papers, "Notes on Cabinet Meeting of May 15"; McCloy to Drum, July 15; McCloy to Major Gen. A.D. Surles, director, Bureau of Public Relations, July 24; Surles to Byron Price, director, Office of Censorship, July 25, 1942, CWRIC 28: 620, 25: 445, 1: 194, 190-192, 285, 366-367, 17: 335, 3: 763, 5: 354.

180. McCloy to DeWitt, May 20, 1942, CWRIC 24: 816-817; Major General J.A. Ulio to DeWitt, May 22, 1942, ibid., 4: 885; TenBroek *et al., Prejudice, War and the Constitution*, p. 113. In August, McCloy would defend DeWitt's handling of the evacuation ambiguously: "I know of no

Army officer," wrote McCloy, "in whom I would place greater confidence. He has thought of more dangers that might threaten the West Coast than even you with your alert mind can conceive of" (Block, *Current Biography, 1942*, p. 198).

181. "Proposed Grouping of Counties for Organization of Loyalty Boards to Pass on Alien Enemies," CWRIC 12: 139-151.

182. Tolan Committee, "Fourth Interim Report," pp. 2, 21-22, 29-31, 33; Ennis to David Dubinsky, president, International Ladies Garment Workers Union, 22 July, and Ennis to Joseph Donald Craven, 17 Sept. 1942, CWRIC 22: 849, 883.

183. Internal WDC memo from "JA [Ulio]" to Bendetsen, July 7, Bendetsen to DeWitt, July 14, and DeWitt to McCloy, Aug. 14, 1942, CWRIC 1: 271, 273, 267.

184. Jaretski to McCloy, May 21, 1942, ibid., 1: 169-172; Bureau of Intelligence, Office of Facts and Figures to MacLeish, May 25; Office of Facts and Figures, "The Problem of Enemy Aliens along the East Coast," June 13, 1942, CWRIC 1:169-172, 301-309, 258-276. *See also* Bureau of Intelligence, Office of Facts and Figures, "Enemy Alien Minorities in Eastern Cities," June 22, and cover letter by R. Keith Lane, June 16, 1942, ibid., 6: 231-276.

185. Telephone conversation, McCloy and Col. Kroner, June 4; Strong to McCloy, June 8; McCloy, diary/log, June 11, 1942, CWRIC 28: 622, 624, 1:149-150.

186. *New York Times*, June 29, 1942, p. 4; Ennis to David Dubinsky, July 22; Ennis to Clyde C. Eastus, Sept. 7; Ennis to Joseph Craven, Sept. 17, 1942, CWRIC 22: 883, 872, 849.

187. *Monterey Peninsula Herald*, July 8, p. 7, Oct. 13, 1942, p. 2.

188. McCloy, diary/log, Oct. 15, 1942, CWRIC 28: 641; 7*Fed. Reg.* 8455. The Justice Department found only 228 Italian aliens out of 600,000 nationwide who deserved internment. Biddle hoped that Congress would eliminate the literacy test quickly, and free the aliens "to participate in the war effort without handicaps" (*San Francisco Chronicle*, Oct. 13, 1942, p. 1). By this time, too, the government had begun to look ahead to an Allied invasion of the Italian mainland. Lifting restrictions on Italians in the United States was viewed as a way to soften Italian resistance; Biddle, *In Brief Authority*, p. 229.

189. *San Francisco Chronicle*, Oct. 19, pp. 1, 8; *Monterey Peninsula Herald*, Oct. 13, pp. 1-2, Oct. 19, p. 3; *Pittsburg Post–Dispatch*, Oct. 14, 1942, p. 1.

190. Ickes Diary, Oct. 25, 1942, p. 7127.

191. *Monterey Peninsula Herald*, Nov. 3, pp. 1-2, Nov. 4, 1942, p. 1.

192. Ickes Diary, Nov. 22, 1942, pp. 7228-7229.

193. 7 *Fed. Reg.* 8455; 8 *Fed. Reg.* 282; DeWitt to McCloy, Nov. 3, 1942, CWRIC 1: 264-265; Hans Lamm, "I am an 'Enemy Alien,'" *Common Ground* 2 (Summer 1942), p. 16.

194. "Supplemental Report," Jan. 1947; Jaretski to Col. Ralph H. Tate, June 4, 1942, CWRIC 24: 120-122, 6: 292-294.
195. Charles F. Ayer to McCormack, June 6, Stimson to McCormack, July 8, 1942, CWRIC 1: 533-534, 529.

"Take care of their own"

196. 7 *Fed. Reg.* 1971, 2165; Tolan Committee, "Fourth Interim Report." The documentation of WRA activities is an archive in itself.
197. LaGuardia Archives, Radio broadcast, Aug. 23, 1942, pp. 280-281.
198. WRA: "Other Agencies Part in Exclusion, 90.4," Social Security Board Program for Exclusion, Sept. 28, 1943; Telegram from Oscar Powell to Neustadt, Federal Security Agency, Neustadt File: "Journal;" File of 'Alien Evacuation Folder,' II, Feb. 17, 1942, Bancroft Library, University of California, Berkeley, *Japanese American Evacuation and Resettlement Records*, file 67/14, folder A11.02.
199. Ibid., I, Jan. to Feb. 9.
200. Ibid.
201. Ibid., "Journal," Spring 1942.
202. *San Francisco Chronicle*, Feb. 4, pp. 1, 6, Feb. 5, pp. 1, 4, Feb. 6, p. 1; *Pittsburg Post-Dispatch*, Feb. 16, p. 1; *Humboldt Times*, Feb. 20, 1942, p. 16.
203. *Pittsburg Post-Dispatch*, Feb. 5, 1942; *Monterey Peninsula Herald*, Feb. 5, 1942.
204. *Los Angeles Times*, Feb. 5, p. 5, Feb. 10, p. 1, Feb. 11, p. 6, Feb. 18, p. 5; *San Francisco Chronicle*, Feb. 11, p. 10; *Monterey Peninsula Herald*, Feb. 14, p. 1, Feb. 18, 1942, p. 1.
205. Federal Security Agency, *8th Annual Report*, Social Security Board, 1943, p. 9.
206. Neustadt File: "Journal," Feb. 19, 1942; "Tolan Committee Hearings," 29: 11027; *San Francisco Chronicle*, Feb. 7, 1942, pp. 1, 4; Letter from V.W. DeTor, county agent, Cooperative Extension Work in Agriculture and Home Economics, University of California, Fairfield, to Roscoe E. Bell, Bureau of Agriculture Economics, Berkeley, Feb. 18, 1942, "Tolan Committee Hearings," 29: 11003-11004, 11050-11052.
207. "Tolan Committee Hearings," 29: 11031.
208. Ibid., 29: 11033, 31: 11669; "Social Security Board Program for Exclusion."
209. Robert C. Newton to Neustadt, Neustadt File: "Journal," II, Feb. 13-14, 1942; "Tolan Committee Hearings," 29: 11041-11042.
210. Letter from Samuel Leash of Samuel Leash & co., Santa Cruz, to Neustadt, Feb. 16, journal entry Feb. 18, 1942, Neustadt File: "Journal," II, 11-Feb. 17, 1942, Neustadt to Paul V. McNutt, Director, Office of Defense Health and Welfare Services, "Report on Alien Enemy Evacuation," Feb. 18, 1942, 15pp., Bancroft Library, file 67/14, folders A11.02, A11.01; testimony of John E. Cooter, regional farm placement supervisor, Social

Security Board, San Francisco, Feb. 26, 1942, "Tolan Committee Hearings," 30: 11358

211. "Tolan Committee Hearings," 29: 11024-11026, 11056-11057, 31: 11661-11662; *Monterey Peninsula Herald*, Feb. 23, 1942, p. 2.

212. Tolan Committee, "Preliminary Report," p. 23; "Tolan Committee Hearings," 29: 11026.

213. *Monterey Peninsula Herald*, June 29, 1942; State of California, Department of Social Welfare—War Services—Enemy Alien Assistance—Activity Reports to Social Security Board, 1942-48, California State Archives, F3729:101, p. 2.

214. State of California, Department of Social Welfare, *Biennial Report, July 1, 1942-June 30, 1944* (Sacramento: California State Printing Office, 1945), p. 38; Activity Reports to Social Security Board, 1942-48, p. 2; State of California, Department of Social Welfare, *Biennial Report, July 1, 1944-June 30, 1946* (Sacramento: California State Printing Office, n.d.), p. 46.

215. *Biennial Report, July 1, 1942-June 30, 1944*, pp. 38-39; Activity Reports to Social Security Board, 1942-48, p. 2; State of California, Social Welfare—Enemy Alien Assistance, Report of Expenditures, 1943-46, California State Archives, F3739:103; *Biennial Report, July 1, 1942-June 30, 1944*, p. 39; Activity Reports to Social Security Board, 1942-48, p. 2.

216. Activity Reports to Social Security Board, 1942-48, p. 2; Enemy Alien Assistance, Report of Expenditures, 1943-46, F3729:103.

"Taken my husband away!"

217. For example, see Col. Joel F. Watson, Office of the Judge Advocate to DeWitt, April 23, 1942, CWRIC 2: 101-102; "Tolan Committee Hearings," 31: 11784.

218. Hoover, "Alien Enemy Control," pp. 396-397; Irons, *Justice at War*, pp. 14-15, 21-22; Ennis, "Government Control of Alien Enemies," p. 100; Harrison, "Axis Aliens in an Emergency," p. 465.

219. Telegram from "Adams," headquarters 4th army to commanding general, WDC, Dec. 14, 1941, CWRIC 3: 302.

220. Hoover, "Alien Enemy Control," p. 398; Irons, *Justice at War*, p. 19; Hoover to all special agents in charge, Dec. 8, 1941, CWRIC 5: 454-455.

221. Zirpoli, "Faith in Justice," pp. 58-59; Memo from FBI to INS, Dec. 8, 1941, CWRIC 9: 474.

222. Collins, *The FBI in Peace and War*, pp. 245-246; *San Francisco Chronicle*, Dec. 10, 1941, p. 1.

223. Either the Hokubei Zaigo Shoke Dan (North American Reserve Officers Assoc.) or the Hokubei Butoku Kai (North American Military Virtue Society), "Supplemental Report, etc.," Jan. 1947, CWRIC 24: 365, 369.

224. Memo from Hoover to Justice Department, Dec. 9, Memo from Francis M. Shea, assistant attorney general to Hoover, Dec. 10, Hoover to Shea, Dec. 17, 1941, CWRIC 5: 446-448, 450, 452-453.
225. Internal memo from the files of the chief supervisor of the Border Patrol, Dec. 9, 1941, CWRIC 9: 475; *San Francisco Chronicle*, 9 Dec. 1941, p. 8, Feb. 5, 1942, pp. 1, 4; Memo from Hoover to Justice Department, Dec. 9, 1941, CWRIC 5: 452-453; Corsi, "Italian Immigrants and Their Children," p. 105. *See also* Joseph S. Roucek, "Italo-Americans and World War II," *Sociology and Social Research* 29 (July-Aug. 1945), pp. 470-471.
226. *San Francisco Chronicle*, Dec. 18, p. 7, Dec. 20, p. 4, Dec. 24, 1941, p. 3, Jan. 8, p. 5, Mar. 3, 1942, p. 7, *Monterey Peninsula Herald*, Feb. 7, 1942, p. 3; McCloy diary/log, 31 Mar., 16 June 1942, CWRIC 28: 610, 625. I report in detail on Hansgirg's case in *America's Invisible Gulag: A Biography of German American Internment and Exclusion in World War II—History & Memory* (New York, 2000).
227. Ennis, "Government Control of Alien Enemies," p. 99.
228. Ibid., p. 100; Lasker, "Friends or Enemies?" pp. 279, 300; Zirpoli, "Faith in Justice," pp. 60-62, 67; Hoover, "Alien Enemy Control," p. 403; Tolan to Biddle, CWRIC 1: 92; Tolan to FDR, Feb. 28, 1942, "Tolan Committee Hearings," 31: 11635; Tolan Committee, "Preliminary Report," p. 8. The INS reported after the war that it had "detained" a total of 3,278 Italians, including voluntary internees and those brought up from Latin America for internment in the United States (W.F. Kelly, Asst. Commissioner, INS to A. Vulliet, World Alliance of YMCA, New York, Aug. 9, 1948 [author copy]).
229. Christgau, *"Enemies,"* pp. vii, 20; Stimson to Ford, CWRIC 16: 926; Peter Clark, "Those Other Camps: Japanese Alien Internment During World War II," mimeographed, CWRIC 4: 199-200.
230. Clark, "Those Other Camps," CWRIC 4: 200, 218-219; "Tolan Committee Hearings," 29: 11196, 30: 11376-11377; Lasker, "Friends or Enemies?" p.300.
231. It was the Western Montana Beet Growers Association that wanted to use the approximately 1,850 Italians and Japanese at Missoula to work the sugar beet fields (Letter from Missoula County Farm Labor Committee to Montana Governor Sam C. Ford, Mar. 16, 1942, "Tolan Committee Hearings," 29: 1286-1288; Loula D. Lasker, "Friends or Enemies?" *Survey Graphic* 31 (June 1942), p. 300.
232. Detainees described the building as a huge ward with beds—with only mattresses—in orderly rows. Italians and Germans occupied the outer rows, and the Japanese, who cleaned the entire ward, the middle beds. Most detainees were handcuffed, and unarmed guards sometimes patrolled the entrance to each ward (Christgau, *"Enemies,"* p. 59).
233. *San Francisco Chronicle*, May 4, 1942, p. 5; *see also*, Irons, *Justice at War*, p. 24.

234. CWRIC, *Justice Denied*, p. 288; *Humboldt Times*, Aug. 18, 1942, p. 1; John P. Diggins, "The Italo-American Anti-Fascist Opposition," *Journal of American History* 54 (Dec. 1967), p. 591; De Medici, "The Italian Language Press," pp. 224-225.

235. Some of the expulsion orders were issued between Aug. 13 and Oct. 3, although they were not announced publicly until mid-October. *San Francisco Chronicle*, Oct. 12, pp. 1, 11, Oct. 13, p. 6, Oct. 14, p. 5, Oct. 15, p. 6, Oct. 18, 1942, p. 8.

236. The army did hold pre-exclusion hearings for each individual.

237. Memo from Jaretski to Col. Tate, June 5, Stimson to DeWitt, July 2, McCloy to Gen. Drum, Eastern Defense Command, July 15, McCloy to Gen. A.D. Surles, Director, Bureau of Public Relations, July 24, Surles to Byron Price, Director, Office of Censorship, July 25, 1942, CWRIC 1: 161-162, 366-367, 5: 354, 12: 109; DeWitt to McCloy, Aug. 14, 1942, ibid., 1: 267

238. Michi Weglyn, *Years of Infamy: The Untold Story of America's Concentration Camps* (New York: William Morrow & Co., 1976), pp. 200-201; Christgau, *"Enemies,"* pp. 82-83.

239. Biddle to McCloy, Aug. 18, 1943, CWRIC 12: 165-171.

240. Memo from Myron C. Cramer, major general, the judge advocate general to McCloy, Sept. 17, 1943, CWRIC 1: 319-321; Memo from Lt. Col. Claude B. Washburne, G.S.C. acting assistant chief of staff to Lt. Gen. Delos C. Emmons, commander, WDC, Sept. 21, 1943, ibid., 1: 797; Maj. Gen. George Grunert, deputy commander, EDC to McCloy, Sept. 23, 1943, ibid., 1: 316-318.

241. Letter from Bosia to the author, Oct. 3, 1988; "Supplemental Report," CWRIC 24: 142, 658-674; Ettore Patrizi, notarized affidavit, Reno, Nevada, Dec. 14, 1942, courtesy of Remo Bosia.

242. Remo Bosia, *The General and I* (New York: Phaedra Inc., Publishers, 1971).

243. "Supplemental Report on Civilian Controls Exercised by Western Defense Command," January 1947, CWRIC 24: 123-127, 131.

244. Ibid., CWRIC 24: 126-127, 131, 136-137, 142. In December 1941 Emmons, an air corps officer, had assumed command of the Hawaiian Department of the army from the disgraced Lt. Gen. Walter C. Short with orders to "hold the islands" (Block, *Current Biography, 1942*, pp. 246-248).

245. Zirpoli, "Faith in Justice," pp. 67-68.

"Never to be forgotten"

246. CWRIC, *Justice Denied,* pp. 288-289; Earl G. Harrison, "Civilian Internment—American Way," *Survey Graphic* 33 (May 1944), p. 229. Harrison headed the INS; O'Connor, *The German-Americans*, pp. 437, 453; Rippley, *The German-Americans*, p. 209; Daniels, *Concentration Camps USA*, p. 27.

247. Bendetsen to the Commission, June 22, 1981, CWRIC 4: 167-168; Corsi, "Italian Immigrants and Their Children," p. 103; Blum, *V was for Victory*, p. 147.
248. "Tolan Committee Hearings," 29: 11248; Carl Wittke, "German Immigrants and Their Children," *Annals of the American Academy of Political and Social Science* 223 (1942), p. 85; Corsi, "Italian Immigrants," note p. 100; Harrop A. Freeman, "Genesis, Exodus, and Leviticus; Genealogy, Evacuation, and Law," *Cornell Law Quarterly* 28 (1943), note p. 417. The Western Defense Command estimated there were 108,089 enemy aliens on the West Coast: 43% of them Italian, 19% German. An overwhelming majority of the Germans and Italians (89% and 82% respectively) lived in California (March 17, 1942, CWRIC 2: 899-900).
249. Daniels, *Concentration Camps*, pp.72-73. In his *Decision to Relocate the Japanese Americans* Daniels writes that the government dropped its plan to relocate the Italians and Germans because of its impracticability (15). Eugene V. Rostow, "The Japanese-American Cases—A Disaster," *Yale Law Journal* 54 (1945), pp. 497, 508, also believes that numbers were the key to the decision not to relocate the Germans and Italians.

SELECT BIBLIOGRAPHY

PRIMARY SOURCES

Personal Interviews

Antongiovanni, Steve. Eureka, CA. 15 June 1987.
Baccari, Alessandro. San Francisco, CA. 12 May 1987.
Banducci, Dominic. Eureka, CA. 25 July 1986.
_____, Gino. Eureka, CA. 8 June 1987.
_____, Susie. Eureka, CA. 8 July 1987.
Boemker, Lily. McKinleyville, CA. 8 June 1987.
Bosia, Remo. San Carlos, CA. 5 Feb. 1987.
Buccellato, Frank. Pittsburg, CA. 3 Feb. 1987.
_____, Rocco. Magalia, CA. 6 Feb. 1987.
Cardinalli, Mary. Pittsburg, CA. 3 Feb. 1987.
Casagrande, Gino. Eureka, CA. 24 Jan. 1987.
Cervetto, Joe. San Rafael, CA. 10 May 1987.
Cipolato, Alfredo. Missoula, MT. 17 April 1989.
Dal Porto, Lena and Nelo. Arcata, CA. 20 Aug. 1986.
Dunn, Ernesta Ghera. Eureka, CA. 15 Aug. 1986.
Ferrante, Anita Maiorana. Monterey, CA. 14 May 1987.
Ferrante, Salvatore. Monterey, CA. 14 May 1987.
Frediani, Alex. Eureka, CA. 26 Sept. 1986.
Giuntini, Ugo. Arcata, CA. 30 Sept. 1986.
Maffia, Jennie. Eureka, CA. 11 June 1987.
Mangiapane, Albert and Nancy. Monterey, CA. 9 Jan. 1988.
Maniscalco, Joseph. San Francisco, CA. 11 May 1987.
Massagli, Gino. Eureka, CA. 30 July 1986.
_____, Harry. Eureka, CA. 13 July 1987.
Massei, Albert. Eureka, CA. 23 Sept. 1986, 8 July 1987.
Massei, Vince. Eureka, CA. 8 July 1985.
Molinari, John. San Francisco, CA. 6 Feb. 1987.
Moore, Fred J., Jr., Mayor, Eureka, CA. Eureka, CA. 7 Feb. 1985.
Mori, George. Eureka, CA. 10 June 1987.
Nieri, Joe. Arcata, CA. 22 July 1986.
Pera, Anita. Eureka, CA. 14 June 1987.
Raffaelli, Don and Betty. Eureka, CA. 3 Nov. 1987.

Sichi, Marino. Arcata, CA. 15 Oct. 1986.
Spadaro, Giuseppe. Monterey, CA. 9 Jan. 1988.
_____, Vitina and Joe. Monterey, CA. 8 Jan. 1988.
Spataro, John. Monterey, CA. 13 May 1987.
Tolomei, Mary. Eureka, CA. 4 Aug. 1986.
Trezza, Ratzi. Antioch, CA. 3 Feb. 1987.
Vanni, Angelo and Nida. Arcata, CA. 7 July 1986.
_____, Benito. Daly City, CA. 24 June 1987.
Williams, Howard (pseudonym). Arcata, CA. 6 Feb. 1986.
Zavattaro, Gabriel. San Francisco, CA. 5 Feb. 1987.
Zirpoli, Alfonso J. San Francisco, CA. 13 May 1987.

Oral Collections, Memoirs, and Documents

Earl Warren History Oral History Project. "Japanese-American Relocation Reviewed." Berkeley: Regents of the University of California, 1976.
Ickes, Harold. *Diaries, 1933-51*. Library of Congress. Manuscript Division.
Japanese American Evacuation and Resettlement Records. The Bancroft Library. University of California, Berkeley.
State of California. Senate. *Report of the Joint Fact-Finding Commission on Un-American Activities in California*. 55th Sess., 1943. Part IV, Nazi Activities, pp. 218-81; Part V, Fascist Activities, pp. 282-321.
United States. *Papers of the U.S. Commission on Wartime Relocation and Internment of Civilians*, part 1, numerical file archive. Edited by Randolph Boehm. Frederick, MD: University Publications of America, Inc., 1983.
_____. Congress. House. *Fourth Interim Report of the Select Committee Investigating National Defense Migration*. 77th Cong., 2d sess., H.R. 2124, May 1942. Washington, D.C.: U.S. Government Printing Office, 1942.
_____. *Report of the Select Committee Investigating National Defense Migration*. 77th Cong., 2d sess., H.R. 1911., March 19, 1942. Washington, D.C.: U.S. Government Printing Office, 1942.
_____. *Hearings of the Select Committee Investigating National Defense Migration* . 77th Cong., 2d sess., Pts. 29, 30, 31. Washington, D.C.: U.S. Government Printing Office, 1942.
Western Defense Command and Fourth Army. *Final Report: Japanese Evacuation from the West Coast, 1942*. Washington, D.C.: U.S. Government Printing Office, 1943.

Zirpoli, Alfonso J. "Faith in Justice: Alfonso J. Zirpoli and the United States District Court for the Northern District of California," an oral history conducted 1982-83 by Sarah L. Sharp, Regional Oral History Office, The Bancroft Library, University of California, Berkeley, 1984.

SECONDARY SOURCES

Books

Blum, John M. *V was for Victory: Politics and American Culture During World War II*. New York: Harcourt Brace Jovanovich, 1976.

Christgau, John. *"Enemies": World War II Alien Internment*. Ames: Iowa State University Press, 1985.

Collins, Frederick L. *The FBI in Peace and War*. New York: G.P. Putnam's Sons., 1943.

Conn, Stetson, Engleman , Rose C., and Fairchild, Byron. *The United States Army in World War II, The Western Hemisphere: Guarding the United States and Its Outposts*. Washington, D.C.: Office of the Chief of Military History, Department of the Army, 1964.

Daniels, Roger. *Concentration Camps USA: Japanese Americans and World War II*. New York: Holt, Rinehart and Winston, 1972.

Diggins, John P. *Mussolini and Fascism: The View from America*. Princeton: Princeton University Press, 1972.

Grodzins, Morton. *Americans Betrayed: Politics and the Japanese Evacuation*. Chicago: University of Chicago Press, 1949. Midway reprint, 1974.

Iorizzo, Luciano J., and Salvatore, Mondello. *The Italian Americans*. Boston: Twayne Publishers, 1980.

Irons, Peter. *Justice at War*. New York: Oxford University Press, 1983.

Radin, Paul. *The Italians of San Francisco: Their Adjustment and Acculturation*. New York: Arno Press, 1975.

Rolle, Andrew F. *The American Italians, Their History and Culture*. Belmont, CA: Wadsworth Publishing Co., Inc., 1972.

_____. *The Immigrant Upraised: Italian Adventurers and Colonists in an Expanding America*. Norman, OK: University of Oklahoma Press, 1968.

Salvemini, Gaetano. *Italian Fascist Activities in the United States*. Washington, D.C.: American Council on Public Affairs, 1944. Reprint. Ed. with an Intro. by Philip V. Cannistraro. New York: Center for Migration Studies, 1977.

TenBroek, Jacobus, Barnhart, Edward N., and Matson, Floyd W. *Prejudice, War and the Constitution: Japanese American Evacuation and
Resettlement.* Berkeley: University of California Press, 1954.

Wyman, David S. *Paper Walls: America and the Refugee Crisis, 1938-
1941.* Amherst: University of Massachusetts Press, 1968; New York,
1985.

Journal Articles, Magazines, and Unpublished Manuscripts

Ascoli, Max. "On the Italian–Americans." *Common Ground* 3 (Autumn
1942): 45-49.

Bellquist, Eric C. "Tolerance Needed." *California Monthly* 43 (April
1942): 8, 42-45.

Bruner, Jerome, S., and Sayre, Jeanette. "Shortwave Listening in an Italian Community." *Public Opinion Quarterly* 5 (Winter 1941): 640-56.

Campisi, Paul. "The Adjustment of Italian-Americans to the War Crisis." M.A. Thesis. University of Chicago, 1942.

_____. "Ethnic Family Patterns: The Italian Family in the United
States." *American Journal of Sociology* 53 (May 1948): 443-49.

Corsi, Edward. "Italian Immigrants and Their Children." *The Annals of
The American Academy of Political and Social Science* 223 (Sept.
1942): 100-06.

De Medici, Marino. "The Italian Language Press in the San Francisco
Bay Area from 1930 to 1943." Master of Journalism Thesis. University of California, Berkeley, 1963.

Diggins, John P. "The Italo-American Anti-Fascist Opposition." *Journal
of American History* 54 (Dec. 1967): 579-98.

Ennis, Edward J. "Federal Control Measures for Alien Enemies." *The
Police Yearbook, 1943*, pp. 31-37.

_____. "Government Control of Alien Enemies." *State Government* 15
(May 1942): 99-100, 112-113.

Friedrich, Carl J. "Foreign Language Radio and the War." *Common
Ground* 3 (Autumn 1942): 65-72.

Hanighen, Frank C. "Foreign Political Movements in the United States."
Foreign Affairs 16 (Oct. 1937): 1-20.

Harrison, Earl G. "Axis Aliens in an Emergency." *Survey Graphic* 30
(Sept. 1941): 465-68.

_____. "Civilian Internment—American Way." *Survey Graphic* 33 (May
1944): 229-33, 270.

Hoover, J. Edgar. "Alien Enemy Control." *Iowa Law Review* 29 (March
1944): 396-408.

Institute for Propaganda Analysis. "Axis Voices Among the Foreign-Born." *Propaganda Analysis* 4 (1 Aug. 1941): 1-10.

Lamm, Hans. "I am an Enemy Alien." *Common Ground* 2 (Summer 1942): 15-18.

Lasker, Loula D. "Friends or Enemies?" *Survey Graphic* 31 (June 1942): 277-79, 300-02.

Panunzio, Constantine. "Italian Americans, Fascism, and the War." *Yale Review* 31 (June 1942): 771-82.

Perry, Donald R. "Aliens in the United States." *Annals of the American Academy of Political and Social Science* 223 (Sept. 1942): 1-9.

Ratti, Anna Maria. "Italian Migration Movements, 1876 to 1926." In Walter F. Wilcox, ed. *International Migrations, Vol. II, Interpretations.* 1931. Reprint ed., New York: Gordon and Breach, Science Publications, Inc., 1969.

Rostow, Eugene V. "The Japanese American Cases—A Disaster." *The Yale Law Journal* 54 (June 1945): 489-533.

Roucek, Joseph S. "Foreign-Language Press in World War II." *Sociology and Social Research* 27 (July-Aug. 1943): 462-71.

_____. "Italo-Americans and World War II." *Sociology and Social Research* 29 (July-Aug. 1945): 465-71.

Rowe, James, Jr. "The Alien Enemy Program—So Far." *Common Ground* 2 (Summer 1942): 19-24.

INDEX

Stephen ("Steve") Fox taught and wrote on American history for thirty years at a northern California university. He is the author of a previous book on Jacksonian America, as well as articles and reviews in professional journals. His most recent monograph, *America's Invisible Gulag: A Biography of German American Internment and Exclusion in World War II—Memory & History*, was published in 2000. When not writing, Steve can probably be found bicycle touring.

Printed in the United States
31961LVS00001B/244-270

9 781581 127546